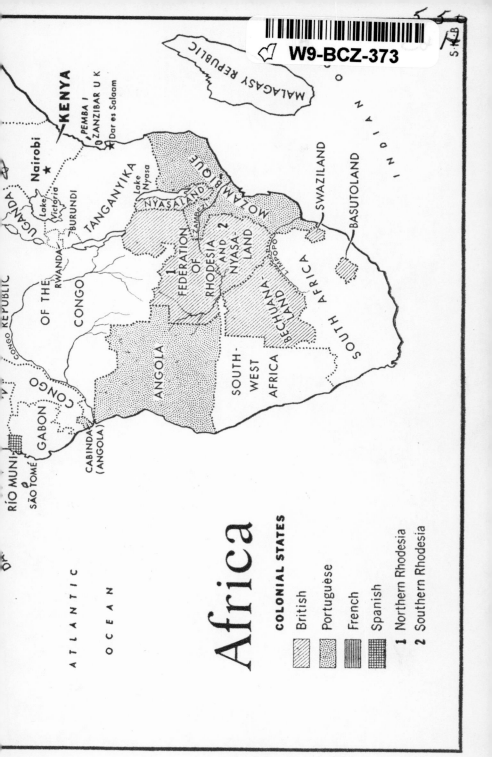

Africa

COLONIAL STATES

British

Portuguése

French

Spanish

1 Northern Rhodesia
2 Southern Rhodesia

Freedom and After

Freedom and After

by TOM MBOYA

with illustrations

LITTLE, BROWN AND COMPANY · BOSTON · TORONTO

*Published simultaneously in Canada
by Little, Brown & Company (Canada) Limited*

PRINTED IN THE UNITED STATES OF AMERICA

Acknowledgments

M Y first acknowledgment must be to the speed of change in Africa. This speed is, of course, heartening to a nationalist and a Pan-Africanist, but it is sometimes also daunting and awkward for an author. A glance at the end of this book will show you that I finished writing it in March 1963. I have been given a chance to revise it in June, and this opportunity brings home to me how much has been done in three months. Kenya has come triumphantly through an election campaign and KANU has formed a strong government. Thirty heads of African states have met in Addis Ababa, have buried the old Casablanca and Monrovia groups and raised up in their place the Organization of African Unity, with far-reaching commitments to economic cooperation. The leaders of Tanganyika and Uganda have signed a defense agreement and then, when Mr. Kenyatta had become Kenya's Prime Minister, signed a historic declaration pledging themselves to form the East African Federation before the end of 1963. Several other steps toward complete continental unity and liberation were taken: a nine-nation Liberation Coordinating Committee was set up in Dar es Salaam, and all the finance ministers met in Khartoum to set up the African Development Bank. Finally a date has been set for Kenya's independence — December 12, 1963 — and

Britain has agreed to remove its military base within a year of independence.

I expect — indeed I hope — that by the time another few months have passed and this book is published, just as many other changes will have taken place. It will mean certain passages in the book will be outdated, but that will be an error I have no wish to avoid.

I would like to thank the following friends and publications, from whom I have quoted: Gordon Hagberg, of the Institute of International Education, for his description of the airlift; *Harper's Magazine* and the *Atlantic* for comment on the airlift; President Nyerere for an extract from his booklet *Ujamaa;* the *Economist* for its description of the Ivory Coast; and the *Observer* for quotation of an article by the Earl of Sandwich.

Lawrence Sagini, Joan Wicken Odero-Jowi and Bill Scheinman gave me most helpful advice during the writing of this book, and Clyde Sanger, Africa correspondent of the *Guardian*, was of the greatest help at every stage of its preparation. And most importantly I must mention the constant encouragement and inspiration always given me by my wife Pamela.

The last and largest acknowledgment should be to the men and women of Africa, whose enthusiasm and good humor have been the chief inspiration of politicians and the main root of our conviction that this continent will set the rest of the world an example in good human relations. To these men and women of Africa, and to Pan-Africanism, I dedicate this book.

T.J.M.

Contents

Illustrations are between pages 148 and 149.

Freedom and After

ONE

Early Days

PERHAPS you will think me immodest if I begin by re-
calling the proudest day of my life. But I will begin this
way, nevertheless, because that day — December 6, 1958 —
was also a date of the greatest historical importance for
every one of the two hundred million people of Africa.

I had been to an international trade union conference in
Brussels and had flown to London to see the British Colonial
Secretary, Alan Lennox-Boyd, on behalf of the fourteen
African elected members of the Kenya Legislative Council.
I complained to him that the colonial administration was
deliberately making it impossible for African politicians to
hold public meetings around Kenya. I asked that the Emergency, which had lasted ever since the arrest of Jomo Kenyatta in October 1952, be ended at once. And I gave him
papers connected with the Kapenguria trial of Mr. Kenyatta
which added fresh doubts to the verdict, for they included
an affidavit from Rawson Macharia, one of the principal
witnesses, that he had perjured himself. So I was eighteen
hours late arriving in Ghana for the opening of the first All-
African Peoples Conference. At Accra airport I was greeted
with the news that I had been chosen chairman of the conference.

Eight months earlier, there had been (also in Accra) the first Conference of Independent African States. At that time there were only eight free states in Africa. These two conferences marked the rediscovery of Africa by Africans. As I told the Africa Freedom Day rally in New York in April 1959, this rediscovery of Africa by Africans was "in complete contrast to the discovery of Africa by Europeans in the nineteenth century." The Conference of Independent African States had marked the birth of the African personality, and the delegates had all agreed on the need for Africa to rise and be heard at all the councils of world affairs. The first All-African Peoples Conference gave birth to the African community. Unanimously the five hundred delegates from political parties, trade unions and other groups resolved to work together in full cooperation for the total liberation of all Africa.

The speeches were militant, to suit such an inspiring occasion. I recalled how, seventy-four years before, the European powers had met in Berlin to partition the "dark continent," already in the grip of what history records as the "scramble for Africa." And I went on: "We meet here in Africa to announce African unity and solidarity, to tell these colonial nations — your time is past, Africa must be free, scram from Africa."

But we were determined not to commit the same sins as the colonialists. In a discussion on the Pan-Africanist slogan "Africa for the Africans," Kwame Nkrumah said: "This should be interpreted in the light of my emphatic declaration that I do not believe in racialism and colonialism. The concept does not mean that other races are excluded from Africa. It only means that Africans shall and must govern themselves in their own countries." And I supported him: "Once the principle of 'One man, one vote' is established, we will not practice racialism in reverse." From the platform you could see that promise already being fulfilled, for the Reverend Michael Scott, Patrick Duncan and other whites were sitting in the hall as fully accredited delegates.

The eight-day conference inspired many people in many lands. Among the delegates were nationalist leaders whose names were soon to become world-famous but who were not then widely known. Patrice Lumumba went back from Accra to the Congo to address in Leopoldville a mass meeting which was a landmark on his country's way to independence. Roberto Holden started preparing his forces for the liberation battles which began two years later in Angola. Dr. Kamuzu Banda flew back to Nyasaland, fortified for what was already the inevitable clash with Roy Welensky and his federal troops in the Malawi struggle to break away from the Rhodesias and the settler-run Federation. And our seven delegates returned to Kenya more determined than ever to help take our country swiftly to the target of "undiluted democracy" and secure the immediate release of Jomo Kenyatta.

The conference was inspiring to me because the vision it offered of a continent totally free was in great contrast to the situation in Kenya at that time, which I had just been arguing about with Lennox-Boyd — the Emergency lingering on, with all the social evils it created and with the continued detention of Kenyatta and more than two thousand others.

And the inspiration went deeper than that. To be chosen, at the age of twenty-eight, as chairman of a conference which represented the passionate hopes of two hundred million people made me both proud and humble. In an attempt to explain the depths of my feelings that week in Accra, I should go back now to describe the earliest days of my life.

I was born on August 15, 1930, on a sisal estate called Kilima Mbogo, a few miles east of Thika and about forty miles out of Nairobi, in what was then Kenya's "white highlands," where only European farmers could own land. Both my parents were illiterate, but, like many other workers on that estate, they had been converted to the Roman Catholic Church by missionaries living on the estate. Most of the estate workers were Luo who had come from my own home country, which is Rusinga Island in Lake Victoria, part of the South Nyanza district in the west of Kenya.

Because my parents were ardent Roman Catholics, I was baptized Thomas in that church, and was later given the name Joseph at the time of my confirmation. According to Luo tradition, my mother added the name Odhiambo to signify the time of my birth — in the evening. And I also received the second clan name of Mboya, a traditional name in my mother's family. It is the name of an uncle who is supposed to have been a great warrior and a wise man. Today I am usually known as Tom Mboya, although my mother of course still insists on calling me Thomas.

For fifteen years my father worked as an ordinary laborer on that estate, for a wage of about one pound a month. Then he was promoted to overseer, earning £2.10s a month. Although he was illiterate, he was also wise and hard-working and determined. He was enlightened in that he knew his own mind and was clear about what he wanted for his children as well as for himself. I was the firstborn of five brothers and three sisters. There was not enough money to give the elder sister much of an education, although she can read and write. But two of my brothers are now studying in the United States.

My father saved from his meager earnings for a long time to pay for my school fees, which were about three pounds a year when I first went to elementary school at the age of seven. He was determined to give me, and as many as possible of his other children, a good education; this was not only because he wanted us to have a better standard of life, but also because education constituted a safe investment against old age. This is a general African conception of life, since no country in Africa has an old age pension scheme covering everyone.

I first went to a local mission school, where we were mainly taught to recite prayers and the Catechism. It was four miles away from the estate village and we walked the eight miles daily. The teacher had almost complete power over us, and once, when we had orders from the older boys not to go to school and my mother had agreed, the teachers came and hunted all round the village, in the huts and under the beds. They found us and took us off to school and punished us severely. Before we could enter the school, the missionaries insisted our parents must be known to be good Christians. This was determined by whether they went to the Sacrament regularly and bought their Catholic mission cards at Easter and Christmas.

After I had been two years at this local school, my father decided I should go to a school where I might learn to read and write. So I was sent to Kabaa in the Ukamba district of Kenya, southwest of Nairobi. The Akamba people make up about one-tenth of the country's population and provide a large proportion of Kenya's police and soldiers. For three years I lived with the family of a Catechism teacher who taught religion at my school. He lived very simply in a tribal manner with his wife and children in a mud-and-wattle hut with no sanitary facilities and no piped water. I remember we went many times over the weekends to help his wife draw water from the Athi River. He took me sometimes to his other home in the reserve, and I still remember how dry the land was, just scrub and thorn trees, and how the children were obviously lacking in vitamins and suffering from yaws and eyesores. Thick flies spread infections.

But the Akamba people, I found, were most humane and generous and understanding. Tribal differences did not seem to arise at any time during my three years there, and I was fully accepted in the family as one of them, especially when I came to know the language and the tribal customs, and behaved very much like one of the children in the home. My father paid about fifteen shillings a month toward my food, but it was not intended as payment for my upkeep and lodging. The teacher was very particular about our going to church every Sunday and being at school on time, and stern with any of us if we were late. There was no opportunity in the house for us to read at night — in fact, there were virtually no lighting facilities at all — and so most of the evenings we merely ate and slept and waited for the next day.

In 1942 I went to a boarding school in the Luo tribal area — St. Mary's School, Yala, in Central Nyanza. It was three hundred miles from the sisal estate, and the wartime trains did not provide normal carriages for civilian passengers. So we had to travel in some very old bogies, which had little ventilation and nothing to sit on; during the day they were as hot as ovens and at night as cold as ice. It took three days to go from the estate to the school, and if I went to visit relatives on Rusinga Island we had to walk over seventy miles. In these early years, I remember, I got great excitement from traveling. It helped me a great deal, too; not only was I able to mix with people of other tribal groups, to eat their foods and learn their customs and languages, but I also got to see places. Every time I went through Nairobi, I stayed with an uncle in the railway quarters, where each employee had one small cubicle. But I was very proud to come back to the estate and say I was one of the few children who had seen Nairobi and its many cars and buses.

At Kabaa we had learned our lessons sitting under a tree; and since we had no books or slates on which to learn writing, we used to write with our fingers or a stick in the sand. The primary school at Yala was more advanced, and the four years I spent there were at times eventful as well. Just as I entered the school there was a big strike by all the boys. They had been maddened by the way the Father Principal had locked up one of the boys and punished him so severely that his classmates thought he had actually been hanged. In their anger the boys broke practically every window in the school except the church windows, and by that afternoon the school was almost deserted. We new boys took no part in the strike — we were merely spectators; but at the age of twelve this was very exciting.

My sister and next brother were by now going to school and my father was finding the burden of school fees for us all rather heavy. Mine had risen to eight pounds a year at Yala, and so to supplement his efforts I began working during the holidays in the kitchen of the school's Catholic priests. In my first year at Yala I entered my name as a candidate for the seminary, to train as a priest; at the age of twelve, when I stayed a long time in the priests' homes working for them in the holidays, I felt very much attracted to the idea. I had also become a very keen altar boy and an enthusiastic member of the church choir at Yala. All this, and the fact that my cousin Peter Otieno was also at this time thinking of entering the seminary, influenced my thinking.

Later I decided against the priesthood. Since my schooldays I have had cause to ponder the church's position in

Africa. Every African politician will recognize that missionaries have done a lot in Africa and left an impact all over the countryside, with churches in the wildest parts of the jungle, mission hospitals and schools; in some places they have even introduced trade. But Africans have doubts about the work of missionaries when they see in many parts of Africa how the missionaries have in the past conformed very easily to the type of colonial regime in which they found themselves. Nationalists have been very critical of the missionaries who condone segregated schools and hospitals, segregated social facilities and even residential areas. Missionary social life has often reflected the behavior of European settlers and colonial administrators, and disenchantment has come when nationalists see in the missionary world itself the same system and attitudes which prevail among the settlers. On the West Coast, where there is a homogeneous African society, missionaries readily promoted African participation in all walks of life, and some of the great Africans there have sprung from a mission background. But in so-called multiracial societies, they invariably accepted the system of segregation.

There has been a change in missionaries' attitudes, but only recently. Before the Emergency was declared in 1952, most missionaries in Kenya were very much part of the colonial and white settler mentality. They were among those who constantly told the African he was not ready for various advances, that he must be patient and believe in God and wait for the day when he might advance sufficiently. They were among those who spread fear and feelings of inferiority among Africans, through the schoolchildren and through the Christians in their parishes. In no case can I recall a missionary — Catholic, Protestant or any other — fighting back and denouncing the colonial regime and

the social setup, or trying to create among Africans a new
spirit of pride and confidence in themselves. Rather, they
undermined this confidence by a negative attitude.

One reason was, perhaps, that in Kenya there had been a
long struggle between the church and the people over several matters. In early mission days the church objected to
African dances as primitive and uncivilized, and for years
there was complete conflict between the church and those
Africans who wanted to continue African traditions and
customs and stood for African culture. The church came
almost to preach to us a blueprint of the British social and
cultural system, which it regarded as indicating civilization
and Christianity. To us this was entirely a contradiction in
terms, a confusing of the European way of life with Christianity. There was as well the church's hostility to those
tribes which practiced female circumcision. Even among
those Africans who agreed the practice should be aban-
doned, the church presented its views in a high-handed
manner and tried to change the custom overnight and dealt
ruthlessly with any African who practiced it, instead of educating the people to understand why it should be stopped.
In some cases they even threatened to excommunicate Africans who practiced female circumcision.

There were, also, some churches — for instance, the
Seventh-day Adventists — which thought it immoral to give
Africans any academic education, and believed all we should
learn was the Bible from the first page to the last, and perhaps
how to do some woodwork and manual labor. Until a few
years ago the Seventh-day Adventists thought it un-
Christian for an African to want to go to high school and
college. I know of many Africans who were openly condemned in church for trying to get further academic education. In some cases Africans who defied the church on

these matters lost their teaching jobs or other employment. As a result, there are today very few highly educated Africans among the Seventh-day Adventists.

When the Mau Mau Emergency began, most of the churches at first sided with the colonial power and condemned the Africans outright. They concentrated on the atrocities which had been committed and the terrorism, and overlooked the background to these problems and the reason for the eruption. I recall missionaries of all denominations standing in their pulpits and condemning African leaders as "agitators" who had misled their people and exploited the ignorance of the masses. They referred to Africans as little children incapable of deciding what was good for themselves. One Sunday at a Nairobi service it was even suggested that any African who was suspected of Mau Mau activity should be excommunicated from the church — despite the fact that the church had no means of proving the African guilty of the suspected offense and could only judge by the government's having arrested the man and sent him to a screening camp or a detention camp. Here, clearly, morality was being confused with politics, and religious matters were being linked with the British government's measures of expediency. It created in me such a deep resentment that I was quite unable to understand what the church thought the African was. I was convinced the church had failed, as much as everybody else, to understand the sense of pride and nationalism among the African people.

About 1954, one began to see a change and to hear reactions from church leaders against the atrocities committed by government forces in Kenya. The Christian Council of Churches became more interested, and even fought the cause of the Africans in Britain and elsewhere.

The Catholic Church also began to take a real interest in politics at this time, and other churches grew concerned about the country's economic and social problems. Today the social organizations of the various churches are well established and have increased interest in many aspects of the country's life, but this was a situation unheard-of before the Emergency.

I think in the future we will see growing resentment among Africans of any further white missionaries. Many people want to see the churches Africanized as rapidly as possible, in pace with the civil service. In East Africa the process has gone some way, with a number of African bishops in Kenya and an African cardinal in Tanganyika. But Africans want to see more progress made, and one wonders what would have happened in Ghana in 1962 if the Anglican bishop had been Ghanaian rather than British.

The Right Reverend Reginald Roseveare, Anglican Lord Bishop of Accra, was deported after he told the diocesan synod that the Ghana Young Pioneer Movement had aspects "which are the cause of sorrow and fear to very many thoughtful people, Christian and non-Christian alike. Not only myself, but all heads of churches in Ghana, are shocked by the godlessness of this movement and by some of its phrases and songs prescribed for the children to repeat or to sing." He was allowed to return to Ghana a few months later, and the London *Observer* suggested that his deportation should not be taken as a general declaration of war on religious institutions so much as a Ghanaian protest at the way the Anglicans had lagged behind all other churches in "coming to terms with the Ghanaian revolution." The *Observer*'s correspondent pointed out there were Ghanaian heads of both the Presbyterian and Methodist Churches, as well as a Ghanaian Roman Catholic arch-

bishop, but "apparently all the Africanization the Anglican church had achieved was a change of name." It is very
likely, a Ghanaian would have understood the position and
spirit of the Young Pioneers better than Bishop Roseveare
did, and would have worded his criticism differently or gone
privately to President Nkrumah, rather than publicly condemning the Pioneer movement as "godless." A foreign
bishop is more open to accusation of being an instrument of
imperialism when he speaks against the state. And the result
is that both sides may misunderstand each other, leading to
deportation and unnecessary international misunderstandings.

Even with "localized" church leaders, African politicians
will want to see the church remain separate from the state
and occupy itself entirely with religious matters. Denomina-
tional schools will have to continue for some time, because
there is not enough money to support entirely state schools.
But the evolution in Nyasaland, where the government has
taken over control of administration and syllabus in mission schools, is a welcome step toward nondenominational
education. Most mission schools in Kenya are state-aided
and state-controlled to the same extent. Even less should
the church take an active part in politics. There was unnecessary ill-will and friction among the Uganda people when
the Catholic Church was under constant suspicion of having sponsored the Democratic Party and having supported it actively right up to the time when it lost the April
1962 elections, after having formed the government for a
year. Church newspapers have also been criticized for appearing partisan and backing one party or one particular
politician because he was of that church's given faith.

All this needs to end; whatever advice churchmen give
politicians should be given privately and regardless of faith.

The new states would prefer that political parties, trade
unions and civic organizations be the ones to speak publicly
on political matters. The multiplicity of churches in Africa
has puzzled many uneducated Africans, who wonder why
there should be so many except perhaps for a business interest. It has helped to create doubts, and especially since the
war has led many Africans to set up their own churches to
interpret church teachings and the Bible in a manner consistent with African tribal customs and culture. Some of
these independent churches have been established to emphasize a particular aspect of the Bible. All this — combined
with the missionaries' apparent hostility to these African
churches — has increased the demand for Africanizing the
church.

Although the situation has improved in Kenya and the
rest of East Africa, farther south there has been little
change. I remember being troubled, when I attended a labor
relations conference in Beira in 1955, by the casual attitude
of the church there to the atrocities being committed
against the people of Mozambique. The Portuguese were
using the church as an instrument to limit the scope of the
people's education, and no church attempted to fight against
this. Again, when I visited the Victoria Falls, I read the fine
and high-minded inscription on the monument to David
Livingstone there. A few yards away was a hotel built for
the pleasure of people who visit the falls and see the Livingstone statue with its inspiring words — where no citizen
of Northern Rhodesia or any visiting African was allowed
in. I was amused when I read these words again:

> On the occasion of the centenary of the discovery by
> David Livingstone of the Victoria Falls, men and women
> of all races, and from all parts of the Federation of Rho-

desia and Nyasaland, assembled solemnly to dedicate themselves and their country to carry out the high Christian aims and ideals which inspired David Livingstone in his mission here.

There have been individuals like Bishop Trevor Huddleston, who conducted an almost one-man crusade in South Africa, but it is to be regretted that there have not been enough Huddlestons in Africa. One is shocked to find a man like Huddleston criticized by some of his own colleagues in the church who thought he was provoking government hostility against the church by his actions.

All these points did not occur to me in full while at Yala, but it is possible some aspect of them influenced me as a young boy at school. When I had successfully completed my primary education in 1945, with high points in the Kenya African Preliminary Examination, the principal recommended that I go to a Catholic high school in Central Province, the Holy Ghost College at Mangu, near the Aberdare Mountains in Kikuyuland. The fees there were ten pounds a year, but a two-year scholarship from my African District Council meant I had to find only £3.15s a year. After a few months, I was asked to train as the "timekeeper" for the next year: this meant a position as a prefect. Toward the end of that first year, I was also told to train as a medical prefect, with the job of giving first aid and certain medicines to the students. When I took over the two jobs, I became one of the few boys with any responsibility at school. That year there was a strike at the school arising out of complaints over food. Nearly all the boys decided not to eat one evening as a protest. When the principal came to find out the reason, some boys were afraid and made the excuse that they had stomach trouble. As medical prefect, I was called upon to verify their stories, and I had what I then thought was the unpleasant duty of telling the truth.

At the end of 1947, I passed my African Secondary School Certificate with enough points to go on for the Cambridge School Certificate. But by that time my father's burden of school fees was so heavy that he could not afford to pay for me any longer. Also, he was beginning to tire of his job. When I had been at home, I used to go once in a while to see him at the factory, and I watched the estate workers carrying heavy burdens of sisal, dripping with water, which affected their skins. I saw them wake up for work early in the morning and come back late in the evening. I witnessed some accidents at the factory, for there was little if any protection against accidents. My family and other workers lived in villages of mud-and-wattle huts with no sanitation but the bush. We drew our water from the Athi River. The employer was brutal, sometimes to the point of beating up the workers. It was a hard life; no wonder that after twenty-five years on the estate my father was looking forward to retiring to our home on Rusinga Island. And so he left his work.

I went to visit him on the island and told him I was leaving school. I knew then merely that I had passed the examination, and only when I reached my uncle in Nairobi a few weeks later did I learn that I had enough marks to go on through high school. By that time it was too late to do anything about it. The principal had said we would have to bring our school fees with us, and I could not raise the money in Nairobi and my father had no more for me. So I had to give up hope of returning to Mangu, and toyed instead with the idea of becoming a teacher. I applied for a place at the Kagumu teacher training college, but was not particularly serious about it. I was not keen to become a teacher — I was just trying to get whatever job was available.

What influenced me most to train as a sanitary inspector was finding out that I would be earning some pocket money as soon as I joined the Royal Sanitary Institute's medical school. This meant I would not only not need to write home to my parents for money but could even help with school fees for one of my younger brothers. I started as a compounder in the chemistry section, being told this was a step on the way to pharmacy. A few weeks later, the principal said there was a vacancy for training as a sanitary inspector, and I accepted when I found out I could take an examination which allowed me to work anywhere in East and Central Africa, and that the certificate was of a standard to let me compete with Europeans and Asians who had qualified abroad. And, as well, the conditions I had seen on the sisal estate made me want to train to be able to do something about the bad health conditions in many parts of Kenya.

The medical school moved eight miles out of Nairobi to Jeanes School, where a great number of community development and other courses were run. The school has now been transformed into the Kenya Institute of Administration, where the new generation of African administrative and executive officers is being trained. After a few months at Jeanes School, I was elected president of the Student Council, a powerful body which made decisions on the use of school funds and other administrative matters for the thousand students then there. I had to draft letters, preside over meetings, discuss student matters with the principal and staff, and make sure all the school societies were running properly. I took particular interest in the debating society and the football club, and played for the school eleven. During my two years there, the Jeanes School changed

from a semimilitary to a civilian administration, and the new
principal, Tom Askwith, proved to have views very similar
to the local white settlers. I could not accept a number of
his proposed changes, and especially disagreed when he began whittling down the powers of the Student Council.
Finally I resigned as president of the council in protest.

All the same, the experience in administration I got at
Jeanes School was very useful when, within a year of join-
ing the Nairobi City Council as a sanitary inspector in 1951,
I was elected secretary of the African Staff Association and
began my interest in the trade union movement. And while
at Jeanes School I had become determined to work for my
people. I had felt sore, at the start, that there was not enough
money for me to finish high school and achieve my ambition of going to Makerere College in Uganda and probably
overseas after that. I had not known what academic degrees
I would take if I went overseas; I only felt I should go away
and come back a learned man. Each time I had gone back to
the sisal estate, things had looked strange, and I had been
discouraged when some missionaries said publicly they did
not like educated boys like us because we did not seem to
respect tradition and be subservient to the white man.
Sometimes they made us ruffle our hair and take off our
shoes before we went into church, because they said smart
appearance was evil and showing off simply to attract the attention of girls. I did not know exactly what I was going to
do for my people, but I felt something was wrong and someone should do something about it. I rebelled inside myself at
this sort of treatment.

It was in this frame of mind that I began work with the
Nairobi City Council in 1951, just one year before the State
of Emergency was declared and Kenya was thrown into
social chaos, with the British government fighting one large

section of the Kikuyu, the country's biggest tribe, and encouraging the rest of the Kikuyu and other tribes to join their side in this civil war. From my travels as a schoolboy among the Akamba, Luo and Kikuyu tribes and my years at Jeanes School, where students of all tribes were learning together, I had unusual advantages in looking at this vexed question of tribalism. I had experienced widely the positive virtues of tribalism in many parts of Kenya, and saw that it was a stabilizing factor in a society which was otherwise changing with overwhelming speed. I could also see the dangers of negative tribalism, and learned clearly how harmful to Kenya was the man who saw only good in his own people and only evil in those of other tribes. I will go into this large subject at greater length in Chapter 4, on mobilizing a national political movement. At this point I should simply record how fortunate I believe I was to have had a childhood of such widespread travel.

~~~~~~~~~~~~

TWO

Trade Unions and the Emergency

W ORKING as a sanitary inspector for the Nairobi
City Council brought me face to face with racial
prejudice in a way I had not known before.

One day in 1951, when one of my European colleagues
was away on leave, I was working alone in the food section
of the Health Department, testing milk samples. European
dairy farmers had to come to us for licenses to bring their
milk into Nairobi for sale, and our job was to see that the
milk was free of disease and conformed to certain standards.
I was in the laboratory busy with some tests when a European woman came in with a sample bottle of milk. She
looked around for a few moments and did not say anything.

"Good morning, madam," I said.

When I spoke, she turned round and asked, "Is there anybody here?"

I was a bit shocked and angry, but decided her question
was amusing. So I asked, "Is there something wrong with
your eyes?"

She was furious and rushed away to find the mayor and
the chief sanitary inspector. I had been cheeky and disre-
spectful, she complained, and the next day she brought a
petition she had persuaded other farmers to sign saying they

did not want to deal with an African and wanted a European inspector instead. The chief sanitary inspector told the woman she would have to deal with an African if she wanted her license, and the mayor took no action on the petition. He came to me later and said I should not mind these reactions, which were to be expected.

But there were a good many other racial incidents. I was put under a European inspector to gain experience, and the two of us went around Nairobi together several times in the course of our work. I was surprised to find that from time to time he expected me to sit in the car when he went to inspect premises. I refused to do this and we had some heated words. He drove back to City Hall and said we could never work together again.

A number of times I was thrown out of premises I had gone to inspect by Europeans who insisted they wanted a European, not an African, to do the job. The City Council had to prosecute some of them for obstructing African inspectors in the course of their duties. But even inside the department there was discrimination. African inspectors were paid only one-fifth of the salary which a European inspector received for doing the same job. African inspectors were told to do their work in khaki uniforms, while the Europeans wore lounge suits. I objected and said either we should all wear uniforms or should all be free to wear what we liked.

I found there were many grievances of this sort among the lower-paid workers in the City Council, the sweepers and the workers in the cleansing section in particular. Most of the members of the Staff Association belonged to this group. When I joined the City Council, the secretary of the Staff Association was just about to resign and I was immediately asked to take his place. From that point I began to interest myself in the problems of the workers and my years as a trade union leader started.

There were only 450 members of the Staff Association when I took over the secretaryship, and in eight months we were able to raise the membership to more than 1300. We spent a lot of time dealing with heads of departments over the grievances of the workers. People complained that they had not received their correct wages, or they had not been paid when they were sick, or their house allowance was wrongly calculated, or they had not got a house yet although they had worked for the Council for many years. Many grievances grew out of the bad relationships between workers and supervisors, who were all European and who expected everyone to accept their every word as law.

No machinery existed for negotiation or consultation between the City Council and the workers, so from time to time it was necessary to take matters to the government's Labor Department. In this way I got to know James Patrick and to learn from him about trade unionism. As part of the policy of the British Labour Party government to encourage trade unions in the colonies, James Patrick had been sent out as trade union adviser to the Kenya government. He was a very liberal Scotsman who was keen to see trade unionism develop in Kenya, but at the same time often puzzled about how this aim could be achieved. Soon after his arrival, he spoke to a meeting of Europeans in Thika about his job. Almost unanimously his audience told him the time had not yet arrived for the establishment of trade unions in Kenya, and he should come back in twenty years or so. When he reported this to the Labor Commissioner, to his surprise the commissioner agreed with the resolution passed at Thika. Patrick wondered why he had ever been sent to Kenya in the first place, if that was the attitude of the Kenya government. However, he decided he was going to do his best to help in advising trade unionists how to organize, employers how to deal with trade unions, and the government how to create machinery to recognize trade unions.

Through meetings with him, I became more and more interested in the trade union movement, and also in the labor laws of Kenya. I borrowed books and had long discussions on our problems. These talks resulted in my resolve to organize a more effective movement than the Staff Association to help the City Council workers.

Government hostility to trade unions was based on the belief that they meant riots and communism. The first real trade union movement in Kenya had started in Mombasa when Chege Kebacha tried to organize a union of general workers. It had by 1947 become strong in numbers, but it was an omnibus union without real sense of direction in terms of collective bargaining and joint consultation. Matters came to a head that year when the workers demanded increased wages and better conditions. The demands could not be put to any particular employer, and so they were presented as though they were political demands to the government. There were riots and looting throughout Mombasa in the general strike which followed, and Kebacha was deported to Baringo in the Northern Province.

There followed a commission of inquiry under the chairmanship of Judge R. S. Thacker, who six years later became a controversial figure at the Kapenguria trial of Jomo Kenyatta. He found that living costs around the port had risen sharply without a corresponding rise in wages, and that there was no machinery for consultation or negotiation. He recommended increases in wages and said immediate steps should be taken to create the necessary industrial relations machinery. This was the beginning of what became the formal trade union machinery in Kenya. But because of the riots and because the only person who had been able to end the rioting had been an African — Eliud Mathu, then a nominated member of the Legislative Council — many Europeans were angry. There were riots also in Nairobi in 1950 when the Transport and Allied Workers Union called a strike. Again, there was no machinery for negotiation and consultation, and the demands were couched as though directed to the government. Makhan Singh, who had been connected with the Nairobi strike as a trade unionist, told a meeting at Kaloleni about this time that he was a communist. So trade unionism was connected in the minds of many people either with riots or communism.

As a result of this background and attitude, government officers advised us to form staff associations rather than trade unions. It was easier, they knew, to deal with staff associations, which had no legal backing and virtually no right to strike. But we could not accept this negative attitude to trade unionism. We traveled around Kenya's main towns — Mombasa, Nakuru, Kisumu, Eldoret — to solicit support of other staff associations for a country-wide Kenya Local Government Workers Union. It was interesting to find that most of the men playing a leading role in the formation of local government staff associations were sanitary inspectors who had been at Jeanes School with me. This made it easy to establish close relations between our different associations.

Our big difficulty in forming the KLGWU was restriction of movement, which began when the Emergency was declared in October 1952. Like most unions at that time, we had women collectors who went round collecting members' dues, but with decrees restricting movement — particularly of Kikuyu — we could get money only from work-

ers who came directly to the office headquarters. This in
turn was very difficult because of the security forces who
used to raid the union offices, arrest many of the union officers, and search people on the roadside or raid their houses
in the African locations in the middle of the night. Normally they took away for questioning and maybe detention
anyone who was found with a union card in his pocket.
Such a person was regarded as part of the hard core of the
subversive element among the Africans. Many union members sent back their cards to the office to be kept there
rather than run the risk of being caught with them in their
pockets.

Nevertheless, the KLGWU soon became the strongest
union in Kenya. In those days unions were very poorly administered: office routine never existed; there was virtually
no filing system or any system at all. Within a year we had
created proper office routine and administration, an efficient
filing system and a large bank balance, with proper financial
administration. My experience at Jeanes School, presiding
over the Student Council and helping to administer the
finances of all the college clubs, had given me some idea
about office routine and management. My colleagues Ben
Gituiku and James Karebe could not tour the country because of movement restrictions imposed on members of the
Kikuyu, Embu and Meru tribes, but I was able to visit our
branches regularly, while they built the office system.

It is, perhaps, not surprising that the Medical Officer of
Health was annoyed about my activities. I had by then entered active politics. I was not a member of the Kenya African Union before Jomo Kenyatta and the other leaders were
arrested, although I had heard him speak at several meetings.
But I became a member just after the arrests in October
1952, because I was incensed at the manner in which this

was done and, like many young people, I felt excited at the thought that this was an opportunity for us to play some part in ensuring that the nationalist movement did not collapse. Quite a few of my friends thought I was mad when I came out at that time to take part, and especially when I accepted first the role of director of information and later on the office of acting treasurer of KAU. It was difficult to organize the party or raise funds in those days. We were always being followed by police, and expected that KAU might be banned any time. As a precaution against the party's funds being seized by the police when banning KAU, the officials sometimes carried them round in a large wicker basket and at night slept with the basket in a hut guarding it.

The Medical Officer of Health told me the City Council was concerned about my political and trade union activities, and since I knew it would not be long before I got a notice of dismissal, I handed in my resignation. Even before I had served my three months' notice, the City Council asked me to leave. For in the meantime the KLGWU had been registered as a trade union and at its first conference I had been elected National General Secretary. So I became a full-time — but unpaid — trade union official. Until the union finances increased after months of hard work, I lived on donations from some executive members and branch officials.

Our union immediately affiliated with the Kenya Federation of Registered Trade Unions. The KFRTU had been formed only in 1950 with five main unions — the Transport and Allied Workers Union, the Domestic and Hotel Workers Union, the Tailors Union, the Building Workers Union, and the Night Watchmen and Clerical Workers Union. The same week we affiliated, the secretary, Aggrey Minya, was suspended. There was a misunderstanding about his activities after he had returned from a world congress of the International Confederation of Free Trade Unions in Stockholm. So I was asked to act as temporary secretary. This dispute ended in Mr. Minya's being dismissed from his post, and in September 1953 I was elected General Secretary of the KFRTU, which was later renamed the Kenya Federation of Labor.

My interest in labor problems had led to my being appointed a member of the Labor Advisory Board in 1952 and the Wages Advisory Board in 1953. But after the banning of KAU, the work of the KFL, and of me as its Secretary-General, was as much political as trade unionist. For the KFL became the voice of the African people, in the absence of any other African organization remaining to speak for them.

There were plenty of occasions when we had to speak out. There was the mass eviction from the Rift Valley Province of farm workers of the Kikuyu, Embu and Meru tribes. An army of fifteen hundred white settlers descended on Government House one morning and demanded tougher measures against these tribes, which they suspected of being oathed by Mau Mau. The result was the eviction of thousands of farm workers from the only livelihood and home they knew. At the same time the government ignored our warnings that these evictions could only create more frustration and bitterness. There was also one November morning in 1953 when seven hundred families were thrown out of their homes into the streets in the Eastleigh suburb of Nairobi. There were many children who were left without any care when their parents were taken away to detention camps during the night. There were wives whose husbands disappeared during the course of the day, having been arrested on their way to work. There were collective punishments, with confiscation of cattle and other property. There were the "green books" which Kikuyu had to carry about Nairobi — later followed by the famous "pass books." We condemned these pass books strongly, and suggested we might have positive action in the form of civil disobedience in protest against them. We were threatened with detention if we persisted. When a boycott of buses, beer and cigarettes began, the District Commissioner of Nairobi, Arthur Small, summoned me to his office and asked me to condemn the boycott. I told him I would not do so: I had not called the boycott and I was not responsible for the conditions which created the boycott.

The only encouragement we had in our battles at that time came from the International Confederation of Free Trade Unions. They sent David Newman as their first representative in 1953 and the following year a Canadian called Jim Bury, and together we worked day and night on many of these cases. The ICFTU sent money to help feed evicted families, they pleaded our case with the International Labor Organization, they made strong representations at the Colonial Office, and briefed MPs in Britain. I wrote several articles in their publication *Free Labor World* and in other papers to help get our case to the world — the side of the unhappy story which was not receiving any publicity otherwise. At that time the only publicity from Kenya was of Mau Mau oaths and terrorist activities. Nothing was written of how some members of the security forces were given a present of money if they "shot straight and shot an African," until the ICFTU and affiliates like the American Federation of Labor gave us the use of their publications. A Nairobi lawyer, Peter Evans, who had asked for an inquiry into the behavior of the security forces, was promptly deported. Jim Bury himself was several times threatened with expulsion, and the KFL too was several times threatened with being banned. In 1956 it needed a visit by Sir Vincent Tewson of the British Trades Union Congress to prevent the Kenya government's taking that step.

Operation Anvil, the biggest sweep of the whole Emergency, began in the middle of a Saturday morning — April 24, 1954 — when Africans had already started work in the offices, shops and factories of Nairobi. The streets were suddenly full of lorry-loads of soldiers with machine guns. Cordons were thrown around the whole area. Leaving several colleagues in my office, I went down into the street. Within a few seconds I was challenged by a soldier pointing a gun at me. I raised my hands above my head as ordered and walked up to him. He gave me a shove with the butt of his gun and ordered me to walk on. I was taken to a street island where other Africans were already sitting, and ordered to squat down. I noticed that some of the people in the group were marked with paint all over their faces. Later I learned these people were either hesitant when called upon to stop or were found in what the soldiers regarded as suspicious circumstances.

For hours we waited until we were ordered into a lorry and driven to a reception camp which was surrounded by barbed wire. Here we again squatted for hours. Then we were lined up and European police officers asked each one of us his tribe and separated us accordingly. Those of us who were non-Kikuyu were led out of the camp by a European officer, who told us we were free to go home but warned us not to come back into the cordoned area. No questions were asked, no names given. Such were the methods used in Operation Anvil, in which thirty-five thousand men and women were detained.

Back at the KFL office, two European police officers had been searching the building. There was a shot through the cardboard partition and Jonathan Njenga, one of the trade unionists in my office, collapsed in his chair with a bullet in his hip. When he was taken to hospital he was classified as a terrorist, and would have gone straight from his bed to detention but for strong protests from the KFL. Again, no questions were asked. Jonathan was lucky, perhaps. A long time later and through ICFTU pressure, he received some compensation. He fully recovered and is now studying in the United States. But the KFL suffered heavily that day. Thirty-nine union leaders were arrested and most of them were detained. Only after two months of constant pressure did the Minister of Labor act. The Governor gave orders for the union leaders to be rescreened and all previous decisions on them to be disregarded. This was a plain admission by government that something was wrong with the screening methods. After the rescreening, seventeen union leaders were released. But the membership of the KLGWU was reduced from thirteen hundred to five hundred by that one day's operation. Some union offices had simply to close down, as there was no one left to run them.

That April day was only an outstanding example of the hazards we continually faced while trying to build up a trade union organization and to use that organization to right grievances and wrongs during the Emergency. There were many other incidents; many times we were whisked off from our offices and sent to screening camps. We were asked whether we knew Mau Mau agents or where oathing was taking place. For many of our members who were

Kikuyu, Embu or Meru, arrest virtually meant a one-way ticket to the detention camp. The rest of us were only saved because we did not belong to those tribes. But many times our houses were raided during the night and turned upside down in a police search. When Nairobi was partitioned off into tribal areas, I was very surprised that I was put into the Kikuyu area — Bahati — instead of being left to live in the Luo area of Kaloleni. I suppose this was because some people in the administration thought I was a bad influence, since I had been outspoken on some of the Emergency problems.

But outspokenness had its effect. We made a strong statement against the screening methods. Hooded men (or were they women?) were brought into a camp; they merely pointed at a person without confronting him with any evidence or witnesses, and on those grounds alone the person pointed at was sent off to a detention camp. There was no knowing who was under the hood — an African or a European. As a result of the KFL statement, and an appeal to the Colonial Office made through the British TUC and the ICFTU, the screening methods were changed. It was agreed that a person could be screened only by people from his own district, and an appeals tribunal was set up. But in the end, this tribunal was little use, for the onus was placed upon the detainee to prove his innocence without the help of counsel and without a chance to confront hostile witnesses.

Perhaps the biggest test we faced in that period came with the Mombasa dock strike in March 1955. The workers were demanding increased wages and the expulsion of some supervisors. I could see the strike was following the pattern of strikes since 1947 — with rioting soon starting because of the ineffectiveness of consultation and negotiating machinery. When Jim Bury and I arrived in Mombasa, the workers had just thrown out the leaders of the Dock Workers Union (which had been formed in 1954). The police were moving in the tough General Service Unit, and the army was being brought down the next day. We asked the provincial commissioner not to bring down the army, but to let us try to reason with the strikers.

There were about ten thousand people assembled on the Tononoka football ground. It was one of the ugliest scenes I have ever faced in my life. It was the first really big meeting I had ever addressed, and the atmosphere was extremely tense. There had just been some rioting, and at first it was very difficult to reason with the crowd. We hoped to get them to agree to go back to work while a tribunal was set up to look into their grievances.

One of the strikers' conditions was that there should be no policemen or Europeans at the meeting, and there was nearly a nasty incident when a European reporter came in without knowing about this. The crowd almost tore him to pieces, and I had to rush to his aid and get him into a car and off the football field as fast as possible. Then, just as we were about to reach an agreement, the employers sent in leaflets containing an ultimatum that the strikers would be dismissed if they did not return to work. That broke up the meeting.

We went to the employers and to government and said we were not prepared to take any further part unless the ultimatum was withdrawn. The next day it was withdrawn, and I talked to the strikers again quietly. On the third day they agreed to go back to work, and hearings before the tribunal started. It was the first tribunal ever appointed under the Trade Disputes Arbitration Ordinance, and the first time a trade union leader had personally represented the workers in the settlement of a strike. The employers be-

gan to realize they were dealing with a new type of trade
union. Until then they had always talked in terms of their
"prerogative" and said flatly, "We will not move an inch."
Through the tribunal we won an all-around wage increase
of 33 percent, which raised the minimum monthly wage
from five pounds to nearly seven — quite large compared
with the wages then prevailing. The whole dispute was one
of our biggest tests, and Jim Bury was very useful to us. He
gave a great deal of technical help in framing our memoran-
dum and presenting the case to the tribunal. Mrs. Meta Peel,
too, who is now the Mombasa reporter for the *Daily Nation*
and was then a Labor Office secretary, was extremely helpful.

The Mombasa strike underlined a lesson I had already
learned: that calling a strike is easy, but stopping it and
getting things back to normal and then negotiating and winning something out of the dispute is the biggest test. Later,
as General Secretary of the KFL, I would tell my colleagues
that our job was not to promote strikes but to try to achieve
for the workers their demands. In every strike I have always taken the view that my first job was to see how it could
be resolved, and try for negotiation. In the end you are going
to negotiate anyhow, and the less suffering inflicted on the
workers themselves and on the country the better. It is only
when employers are deliberately provocative and will not
agree to negotiate that I think a strike is justified and should
be supported.

A month later, in April 1955, came another union battle,
though of a different sort. For two years the City Council
of Nairobi had refused to recognize the KLGWU, and
there was therefore no negotiating machinery for settling
disputes. At length the government set up a board of inquiry
under Mr. Justice Windham, who had been arbitrator in the

Mombasa strike tribunal. The mayor of Nairobi was then Reggie Alexander — later an ally of Michael Blundell in the Legislative Council — who was adamant against recognizing the union and was trying to revive the Staff Association. The union case took me four hours to present before the board of inquiry, and Mr. Justice Windham had no hesitation in recommending recognition. He wrote in his report:

Our inquiries have impressed us with the responsible and patient attitude adopted by the Nairobi branch of the KLGWU over the question of its recognition since it was founded, with the efficiency of its organization (including the keeping of books) and with the reasonable and co-operative manner in which it presented its case to us.

In this struggle for recognition we came hard up against the difference in the British approach to trade union problems from that in other countries, particularly the United States and Canada. Jim Bury brought out the differences from the Canadian side. For a long time the British TUC had wanted our trade unions to follow the pattern set by the British trade union movement, and to reflect the same attitudes and approach to solving problems. They had to fight for recognition, and it was all a question of whether they had enough power to force the hand of the employer. The Canadian approach at first depended on a trial of strength, but over the years they had reached a point where unions were recognized by law once they had a certain percentage of membership. Also, the union structure was built on the basis of an industry rather than a craft or a general union, as was the case in the early days in Britain. This Canadian approach fitted in more easily with Kenya, as we were developing on an industrial basis also.

In later chapters I shall go into details about the other departures we found we needed to make from the British trade union model. We shall also come to discuss how Kenya's experience helped the growth of trade unions elsewhere in East Africa, and how trade unionism may best fit into the Pan-African setting (see Chapters 10 and 12). But in this chapter I have said enough to show how, despite much hostility from government and despite all the obstacles which came because of the Mau Mau Emergency, the trade union movement in Kenya grew into a vigorous body, so vigorous in fact that it was able to play, during that Emergency, a political role rarely demanded of trade unions and their leaders.

THREE

Mau Mau: Is Violence Avoidable?

IN the Kenya Legislative Council in June 1960 Sir Charles
Markham moved a resolution "that this House records its
appreciation to Mr. F. D. Corfield for his Report entitled
'Historical Survey of the Origins and Growth of Mau
Mau.'" He said he hoped the Kenya government would
learn "the valuable lessons contained in this Report." Major
Day, slightly farther to the right in his thinking than Sir
Charles, was full of praise of "such a comprehensive, de-
tailed and excellent study."

The Corfield Report in fact did a great deal of harm.
Pressure for the release of Jomo Kenyatta had been building up through 1959 and 1960, and Corfield, relying heavily
on police and administration reports, gave a totally one-
sided picture of Mau Mau and of the position of Kenyatta
in the years before his arrest. Yet the Corfield Report had
its effect on influential people. The new Governor, Sir Patrick Renison, had steeped himself in it and in background
files of police records before he made the ill-advised statement on May 10 which will always be associated with his
name:

Jomo Kenyatta was the recognized leader of the non-coopera-
tion movement which organized Mau Mau. . . . Here was an

African leader to darkness and death. . . . With the assistance of the researches carried out by Mr. F. D. Corfield, I have very carefully studied his life and modes of thought and speech and action. He planned for Kikuyu domination; he was an implacable opponent of any cooperation with other people, tribes or races, who live in Kenya. . . . From the security viewpoint I think that Jomo Kenyatta's return to political life in Kenya at the present time would be a disaster. We are not yet far enough away from all the tragedies, the hatreds and the passions of Mau Mau. . . . I ask those who have been leading the campaign for Jomo Kenyatta's release to ponder deeply what I have said about light and darkness.

Corfield had apparently made such a deep impression on Sir Patrick that it had not worn off by March 1961, when the Kenya African National Union, campaigning primarily on the issue of Kenyatta's release, had won the elections with nearly two-thirds of the popular vote. The Governor refused to respect people's wish and said in a radio broadcast: "I care for Kenya too much to contemplate his stepping from restriction to a position of authority. I ask you to read again my statement of last May. Nothing has happened since to make me wish I had worded the statement or any part of it differently."

As a result, he made it impossible for KANU to honor its election pledge and at the same time help form a government. After six weeks of constitutional crisis, he managed to form a minority government of Ronald Ngala's Kenya African Democratic Union and Michael Blundell's New Kenya Party of Europeans. When, four months later, Kenyatta was released, there were talks aimed at bringing KANU into government in coalition with KADU. These talks broke down in October and Sir Patrick again spoke on the radio. He said the failure was due to "the fear of domination" held by some minority groups and he went on: "This is no new problem; indeed, we have already faced and overcome one major attempt to enforce domination over those who did not accept such domination, in what was called Mau Mau . . ."

There are plenty of other examples of the effect of the Corfield type of thinking on the actions of British officials both in Kenya and in Britain itself. But I have chosen to quote these three statements of Sir Patrick Renison because his action, based on these attitudes about Mau Mau and Kenyatta, in refusing to release him earlier than August 1961 has had such a dire effect on Kenya's advance to independence.

When I spoke, towards the end of the debate on the Markham resolution, I said:

"The Corfield Report qualifies either for the wastepaper basket or just being burned. It has not helped in any sense at all, nor has it attempted to bring out clearly the root causes of the difficulties through which this country has passed for the last seven years.

"Some people assume, as indeed has been assumed all along — and this has formed the basis of the Corfield Report — that whenever anything goes wrong, it must be the African who has done it because he is the only black person in this country. There are many black people among the Europeans in this country. It is not a one-way traffic, this whole question of peace, harmony and friendship."

Two questions about the Emergency continue to be asked of Kenya leaders, wherever we travel abroad and even sometimes at home; so I shall try to answer them at this point. The questions are: "What was the cause of Mau Mau?" and "Do you believe in the use of violence?"

Many times during the Emergency we said categorically that Mau Mau was the child of economic and social problems which had accumulated over the years and which had not found any solution through constitutional channels. They were nearly all problems of discrimination against Africans in different forms: discrimination in employment and in salaries; refusal by government to let Africans grow cash crops like coffee, tea, sisal and pyrethrum (the lawsuit over Senior Chief Koinange's coffee trees is the most quoted case); discrimination in post offices, hotels and restaurants supported by a government which had made liquor laws laying down as an offense the selling or serving of an African with European liquor; discrimination by government in giving aid to schools and hospitals established on a racial basis; the absence of African representation in the Legislature or of any voice at all in the government; the indirect rule of the African people through chiefs and administrative officers who did not reflect any local African opinion. All these irritations together created frustrations which accumulated over the years.

There was also the sensitive problem of land. The question of land helps to explain why the Mau Mau revolution was largely contained in one area of the country — Central Province and the Rift Valley — rather than covering Kenya. The policy of white settlement had been clearly stated as far back as 1905 by Sir Charles Eliot, the British Commissioner for the East Africa Protectorate from 1901 to 1904, in his book *East Africa Protectorate:*

In other words, the interior of the Protectorate is a White Man's country. This being so, I think it is mere hypocrisy not to admit that white interests must be paramount, and that the main object of our policy and legislation should be to found a white colony.

It was the intention from then on that the highlands would become "White Man's country," and that the policy of developing Kenya should be based on that approach. In 1912 on the demand of the European Land Holders Association, a Native Labor Commission was appointed to inquire into the reasons for the shortage of African labor, and it heard Lord Delamere, the then leader of the settlers, say:

"If the policy was to be continued that every native was to be a landholder of a sufficient area on which to establish himself, then the question of obtaining a satisfactory labor supply would never be settled. . . . The soundest policy would be to curtail the Reserves, and although it might take a few years before the effect on the labor supply was apparent, the results would be permanent."

As a result, a Crown Lands Ordinance was passed in 1915, and in 1917 the Chief Native Commissioner, John Ainsworth, instructed his district commissioners that all chiefs and headmen who were not "helpful" in providing easy labor for the white farmers should be reported to the Governor — which meant removal from office. By the Emergency, as the Royal Commission on Land in East Africa showed, of the 20,000 square miles of land in Kenya with a rainfall of more than 20 inches, 5900 square miles had been reserved for Europeans, who formed less than one percent of the country's population.

An atmosphere was created over the land question in which it was no longer possible to reason, the matter became so emotional. Many families were removed from their land to give way to white settlement, and Africans never accepted the settler argument that the land had been found empty and uninhabited. Most Africans argued that although it was not our system to fence land, each piece of land was claimed by some tribe, even if at the time they were not actively using that land. This particularly applied to the pastoral tribes who moved from one area to another, and to the Kikuyu who were not cultivating some areas into which the first white settlers moved because they had at that time suffered a series of catastrophes including rinderpest.

For a long time the sensitive land question was more an issue for the Kikuyu than for the rest of Kenya. Most of the other tribes were unaffected by white settlement, for there was hardly any settlement in Nyanza Province or at the Coast or in other areas. The irritations of the color bar and race discrimination were felt almost equally throughout Kenya, although they were more intense in the settled areas and the towns than they were in Nyanza Province of the reserves at the Coast.

We have never accepted that Mau Mau was the result of any revolt by the Africans against civilization or Christianity, as has been suggested by some people. These are people who just do not understand the Africans' feelings and sensitivity. Of course it is true that Africans, more than anyone else, suffered from Mau Mau and many more Africans died. But this is true of many revolutions and anticolonial uprisings. It is normally the indigenous people who suffer most, and the Kenya situation does not appear to be unique historically. The trouble in the Kenya situation was that Mau Mau violence was met by even greater violence from the British government and its security forces. If we must condemn the violence of the Mau Mau, we must equally condemn British violence against it. During the Emergency most publicity was centered around what the Mau Mau did and very little was concerned with what the security forces did. The many Africans who disappeared never to be seen again, the many people arrested in the night who never came back, the fact that some security forces were reportedly paid so many shillings for each person they shot — these were atrocities that came out only in part during court hearings at the time. It is unlikely that the full story will ever come out, because at most district headquarters there have been bonfires of documents relating to the Emergency period, but there are many facts which cannot be burned into oblivion.

In 1958 the All-African Peoples Conference debated the question of whether or not African nationalism should commit itself to the use of violence or to the Gandhian philosophy of nonviolent positive action. As conference chairman, I supported the large majority of the delegates who felt strongly that violence as a policy could not work. These delegates, however, thought that violence had never really been the policy of any nationalist party until it was driven to it. Where constitutional channels do not exist, then nationalists will resort to the only other means — which is force. In Algeria, Kenya, and Angola, the frustrations which precipitated violence were clearly there, and the colonial powers of France and Britain cannot escape responsibility for having precipitated this violence. The long history in both countries of demands being made in a nonviolent manner, asking for constitutional changes, by men like Ben Bella, Roberto Holden, Ferhat Abbas and Jomo Kenyatta, shows that violence was never the policy of the nationalists until driven to it in the last resort. Another violent situation which is even now building up is that of South Africa. Unless constitutional methods can bring the results needed, an eruption is inevitable — and nobody can ever argue that violence was the policy of Chief Luthuli and his African National Congress or the Pan-Africanist Party. The question, then, is not whether it is wrong to use violence, but whether nationalism can be expected to remain silent when provoked to the extent it has been in these countries, and when there is no constitutional channel through which nationalism can achieve its objectives.

If one can draw a general rule, it is that in any colony where there has been considerable white settlement, violence has become inevitable, although it was not the original policy of the nationalist party. Uganda and Tanganyika escaped this form of violence on their paths to independence, but Nyasaland and Northern Rhodesia had to pass through it in 1959 and 1961. The reason is that where there has been white settlement, there has been resistance to constitutional change, and this has created more obstacles to nationalism.

It is also true that it was not until Mau Mau had erupted that logical changes began to take place towards improving African conditions in Kenya. The color bar began to disappear, racial discrimination in the civil service was ruled out by the Lidbury Report in 1955, wages improved, and in many other ways Africans were given fuller recognition. The Lyttelton Constitution in 1954 brought the first six African elected members into Legislative Council, and the Lennox-Boyd Plan in 1957 increased this to fourteen: both these constitutional changes came during the Emergency. There was also the Royal Commission on Land in East Africa of 1953-1955, and the Swynnerton Plan, which was aimed at accelerating the development of African agriculture.

This spate of changes must lead anyone to believe that had it not been for Mau Mau, perhaps these changes would never have taken place; at any rate, they would never have come as quickly as they did. Again, it is sad but true that until the eruption of violence in Algeria and Angola, the world had been content to remain silent about the sufferings of those people under colonial rule. It appears the world's

newspapers are more interested in areas where there is violence than in areas where nationalists are working quietly
and slowly towards their ends. And this poses the question
of who is really to blame for violence and of whether or
not it is the only method by which nationalists can awaken
the world to the plight of their people. One cannot expect
African nationalists to wait until the world comes to their
aid, because by experience they have got the world to help
them only when they have become active, and never before.

It is not possible, I believe, to use in Africa the same
Gandhian methods which were successful in India. The circumstances are entirely different, and the spiritual approach
does not seem to be easily transplantable to African soil.
Even those African leaders who accept Gandhi's philosophy
find there are limitations to its use in Africa. The most one
can do in the spirit of Gandhi is to follow a course of positive nonviolent action — but always with the understanding
that it could lead to violence. It would be futile to think
otherwise, because you are dealing with a hardened local
situation in which there are desperate settlers ready to pro-
voke the people into violence and ready themselves to use
violent methods against a positive nonviolent nationalist.

I cannot do better at this stage than recall the wise words
of the great English reformer John Bright, who in 1866
declared:

I have never said a word in favor of force. All I have said has
been against it — but I am at liberty to warn those in authority
that justice long delayed, or long continued injustice, provokes
the employment of force to obtain redress. It is in the ordering
of nature and therefore of the Supreme that this is so, and all
preaching to the contrary is of no avail.

If men build houses on the slopes of a Vesuvius, I may tell
them of their folly and insecurity, but I am not in any way pro-

voking, or responsible for, the eruption which sweeps them all away. I may say too that Force, to prevent freedom and to deny rights, is not more moral than Force to gain freedom and secure rights.

In the Corfield Report it is argued that the Kenya African Union never gained a following beyond the Kikuyu, and in the passages I quoted at the beginning of this chapter Sir Patrick Renison obviously backed up this view when he said Kenyatta "planned for Kikuyu domination." Corfield has some difficulty in explaining why seven of the nine office-bearers of KAU were non-Kikuyu, but he insists on saying of Kenyatta, who became its president a year after its formation in 1947:

There is no doubt that the ideal for which he aimed was first and foremost the growth of KAU as a strong political organization covering the whole of Kenya and, once this had been achieved, he would emerge as the African leader of an all-African Kenya, in which the Kikuyu would be the dominant influence. . . . He however failed to build up KAU as an all-African union — by a combination of circumstances and his own personal failings. His twin Achilles heels were the stand made by those loyal and pre-dominantly Christian Kikuyu who foresaw the ultimate disaster of domination by the atavistic Mau Mau, and his autocratic bear-ing which antagonized the leaders of the other tribes. . . . In July 1947 attempts were made to form branches of KAU throughout Nyanza, but they never took root as KAU was al-ready suspect in that area as a purely Kikuyu organization.

Corfield, I suppose, wrote in this vein because this was the reflection of universal views in the administration of that period. He took little or no trouble to ask African views. In the original (and unpublished) version of his report he had an appendix of names of people who had given evidence to him, and there are only four Africans on the list. When he was later challenged on this point, he claimed he had interviewed "more than a score" of Africans. The fact is that KAU, in demanding for Africans more land, better wages, better housing and better social services, was popular with all Kenya Africans; it was voicing African opinion.

After Kenyatta's return from Britain in September 1946 and his assumption of the KAU presidency, the moves to make KAU a mass movement covering the country began. It penetrated non-Kikuyu areas later, both because the frustrations were fiercer among the Kikuyu and because they had already been organized before the war in the Kikuyu Central Association. But KAU branches were established in Mombasa, Kilifi and other places in Coast Province, in Machakos and Kitui among the Kamba people, in all districts of Nyanza, even in Masailand, and in the Rift Valley several prominent Kalenjin people were associated with it. It was able to hold big public meetings all over Kenya — in Kisumu, Kakamega, Mumias, Kisili — and collections were taken throughout the country to pay the air fares of Peter Mbiyu Koinange and Achieng Oneko when they presented KAU's case to the United Nations Assembly in Paris in 1951. The way in which Luo and Baluhya leaders like Fanuel Odede and W. W. W. Awori took over the leadership of KAU after Kenyatta's arrest, determined to keep the party going, shows that this was hardly an organization devoted to dominating Kenya with Kikuyu.

Perhaps it is appropriate at this stage to say a word about Jomo Kenyatta, the father of our nationalism. In a speech in New York on African Freedom Day, April 17, 1961, I said:

"Speaking of the father of your country, let me speak for a while about the father of my own country Kenya, the man who perhaps more than any other represents the African personality: Jomo Kenyatta. He has been imprisoned for the past nine years, most of that time not only deprived of his liberty, but deliberately made to suffer — confined in areas which are unhealthy, extremely hot, mosquito-ridden and deserted. Jomo Kenyatta is still imprisoned in this year of 1961, despite that wind of change we have heard so much about. How can his continued imprisonment do anything but poison relations between Britain and ourselves, between black and white?

"Denial of freedom to Jomo Kenyatta and the other detained people of Kenya is a mockery of justice. It is a sheer injustice and a contravention of the United Nations Declaration of Human Rights to restrict anyone without a trial or after he has completed a prison sentence. The demand that the Governor of Kenya must know what Kenyatta thinks before he can release him conflicts with his assertion that Kenyatta is a security risk — since he confesses ignorance of Kenyatta's views — and in the minds of our people smacks of blackmail. If the Governor wants to know Kenyatta's views why doesn't he visit him? He has consistently refused to do so.

"Reactionary groups and newspapers, particularly your own press, have painted Kenyatta as the leader of Mau Mau. These efforts to bring back the horrors of the past, including reproduction of alleged Mau Mau oaths and atrocities, attempt to connect Kenyatta with these activities. Yet no African believes in the verdict at Kapenguria in 1953. The judge, a retired white settler, was brought back and given special powers and jurisdiction to try Kenyatta. He was promptly retired after the trial! The witnesses were handpicked and especially sheltered — if not trained. Three years ago, the chief witness against Kenyatta confessed that he had committed perjury, and had been bribed by the Kenya government to do so. The atrocities referred to in the press were committed long after Kenyatta's arrest and imprisonment. He could not have committed them.

"The present crisis in Kenya will not be resolved, cannot be resolved, until Jomo Kenyatta is given his unconditional freedom. Our people love him and are determined to make this undisputed leader of the African people the head of our first independent government. Our people respect him, not only for himself, but for his character, for his integrity and judgment and iron will. But they love him most for the enemies he has made."

What I said then lived to be true, and Kenyatta is not only free now, but Prime Minister of our first African government. His broadmindedness and concern for Kenya since his return have given the lie to the Renisons and the Western press which campaigned against him in an effort to destroy his image in the eyes of our people.

The basis of what I have said in this chapter about Mau Mau, I originally wrote in a pamphlet called *The Kenya Question: An African Answer*, which the Fabian Bureau published in September 1956. This was toward the end of the year I spent at Ruskin College, Oxford, studying political science and economics and specializing in industrial relations.

Through the connections I had made as a trade unionist, with men like Walter Hood of the British TUC and Edgar Parry, who was then Labor Adviser to the Colonial Secretary, I had been recommended for a scholarship to Ruskin, which was offered me by the Workers' Travel Association. I had spent some months abroad in 1954, in Switzerland, Belgium and Britain, and later at a workers' education seminar at the ICFTU Calcutta Labor College in India. It had been difficult to get a passport at that stage of the Emergency, and (though it may seem strange now) I had to align myself with Moral Re-Armament to get out of Kenya. I stayed a few days at the MRA headquarters at Caux before going on to the ICFTU in Brussels. Before I left Caux I made a statement saying I did not believe Moral Re-Armament was the right approach to Kenya's problems and was anyway in conflict with my trade union thinking. I never saw Dr. Frank Buchman of MRA again after making this statement, although while I was in Caux he had wanted to talk for a long time about Kenya. On that first visit to Britain in 1954 I made representations to the Colonial Office against conditions in the detention camps and the screening methods used in the arrests of Mau Mau suspects.

Since my own education had ended at secondary school level, the Calcutta Labor College was the first big institution I had experienced. But going to Oxford in October 1955 was still a greater eye-opener. It was my first opportunity to taste something of the atmosphere of an academic institution, to meet intellectuals and to read books. I spent a lot of time reading in the Bodleian Library and the library at Ruskin. I was keen to read biographies and the history of political institutions, rather than pure political science. My special subject of industrial relations I was able to cover quickly, because of my background and experience in the trade unions.

Although Ruskin is not part of the university proper, we took part in all the university activities, and I joined the Labour Club and the Socialist Club. But my main interest was in discussions I held with some of the Ruskin lecturers — Henry Smith, who took me in economics; Jay Bloemler, who lectured in political science; and Bill Hughes, the principal — and in discussions at Nuffield College. Margery Perham, who became a great friend of mine, invited me to take part in some of her classes and discussion groups at Nuffield. She provided one of the most important stimuli for me during my year at Oxford. Her knowledge of the colonial administration in East Africa and elsewhere was very useful, and she always asked me pointed questions about the Emergency situation and the problems of political development in East Africa. As a result of much provocation from her, I came constantly prepared to defend the African cause, and this led me to clarify my views and to read more about Kenya than I had ever read before.

One day she said: "Nobody has written about these things. The African point of view is unknown. Why don't you write something about it?" And this led me to begin work on my Fabian Bureau pamphlet *The Kenya Question: An African Answer*, for which Miss Perham wrote a foreword.

Through the Labour Party and Ruskin College I met Miss Joan Wicken, who in recent years has worked in Tanganyika. Each weekend I used to go down to her flat in London, and try to put down on paper the thoughts I had had during the week and to prepare notes for public meetings I had to address in different parts of Britain arranged by the Movement for Colonial Freedom, the Africa Bureau and the Fabian Bureau. Miss Wicken was then assistant to the Commonwealth Officer of the Labour Party at Transport House.

Two West Indians were at Ruskin in the same year I was: Miss Audrey Wooding from Trinidad and Dick Woodam from Jamaica. We went to the same economics and political science classes, and we traveled together to London at weekends. In their relatives' homes in London we discussed West Indian and Kenya affairs, and it was especially through discussions with Audrey and Dick that I formulated my ideas about how best we should approach the constitutional strug-

gle in Kenya when I went back. We discussed the Lyttelton
Constitution and the Coutts Report, which recommended a
"fancy franchise," by which a limited number of Africans
could qualify for up to three votes in the elections for the
first six African representative members. We wrote down
the steps to be taken in this constitutional battle, and all this
talk formed the basis of my Fabian pamphlet.

So, when I look back today, I feel that Oxford played a
major part in my life, giving me a year of unhurried thought
to help me decide what line of policies would be effective in
our struggle. The year at Oxford gave me more confidence
in myself, it gave me the time to read more, it taught me to
look to books as a source of knowledge. It led me to take
part in intellectual discussions, sometimes of a very provocative nature, and it helped me to think more analytically about
problems and work out on paper how best to meet them.

Before I returned to Kenya in November 1956, I traveled
a good deal outside Britain. In December I went to Ham-
burg to speak at a Liberation of African Subjects Day meeting, and I asked the West Germans: "How long will Africa
be free from violence if racial bitterness is not stopped immediately by reform?" I was able to give them a picture of
the Emergency and of general conditions in Kenya which
they had not read in the one-sided newspaper reports.

The ICFTU asked me to go to Brussels and work on the
preparations for an All-African Regional Conference, and
the American Committee on Africa invited me to visit the
United States. I arrived in New York on my twenty-sixth
birthday — August 15, 1956 — to start a two months' tour
of the country. On the flight from Britain the plane developed engine trouble, and we had to divert and land in
Iceland, where we stayed several days waiting for a replacement. I remember feeling excited about this, and I recall

particularly sitting in the airport lounge at Reykjavik and looking at the big map of the world on the wall and thinking how far away I was from my little island home and from Kenya.

As the guest of the Reverend George Houser and the American Committee on Africa, I traveled from the Eastern seaboard to the Midwest, to the Southern states and to Los Angeles. I lectured, made radio and television broadcasts about the Kenya situation. Toward the end of the tour I visited Toronto for ten days as the guest of the United Steelworkers of America, again appearing on television and giving press conferences. It was good to feel the growing interest of North Americans in Africa and in Kenya. But I was also dismayed to hear at various places of Kenya students who had been offered places at American colleges, but who could not afford the air fare to take up the offers. I discussed the problem with George Houser, and he introduced me to William Scheinman, a member of the executive board of the American Committee on Africa. Mr. Scheinman runs his own business, making airplane parts in New Jersey and California, and he offered to help a few students come to the United States. That year he paid for seventeen students to fly over, and in 1958 he paid for another thirty-six. When he and George Houser met Dr. Kiano and myself again at Accra in December 1958 at the All-African Peoples Conference, we began discussing how students could be brought more economically and systematically. Out of these talks came the "students' airlift," which I will write more about in Chapter 7. The airlift plan was further discussed when I went to the United States in 1959 for a tour, and later the same year received an Honorary Doctorate of Law from Howard University.

While I was touring the United States, there were some

politicians following my movements with disapproval from Kenya. Group Captain Briggs, leader of the right-wing group of settler politicians and minister without portfolio, asked in Legislative Council why I was allowed to make political statements in the United States, and why I did not come under the ban then in force against political parties. And on November 1, 1956, when I arrived back in Nairobi after thirteen months away, there were forty police on duty at the airport and all my luggage was carefully searched for "seditious literature." I felt at that moment I was fully back in the Kenya I remembered, but I also felt I was better equipped, because of my new experiences, to tackle some of the nastiness the old Kenya and its colonial administration threw in your path. I was equipped through the books I had read at Oxford, and the notes I had made in discussions with everyone from Margery Perham to George Houser and my West Indian friends. Perhaps that was the sort of "seditious literature" the customs officials vainly searched for at Nairobi airport.

FOUR

National Mobilization I:
The Mass Movement

FOR the effective struggle against colonialism and for the work of economic reconstruction after independence, it has come to be accepted that you need a nationalist movement. I use these words advisedly, as opposed to a political party. A nationalist movement should mean the mobilization of all available groups of people in the country for the single struggle. This mobilization is planned on a simplification of the struggle into certain slogans and into one distinct idea, which everyone can understand without arguing about the details of policy or of governmental program after independence. Mobilization is planned on the assumption that for the time being what is needed is to win independence and gain power to determine one's own destiny.

Everyone is taught to know the one enemy — the colonial power — and the one goal — independence. This is conveyed by the one word round which the movement's slogans are built. In Ghana it was "Freedom," in East Africa it is "Uhuru," and in Northern Rhodesia and Nyasaland "Kwacha" (the dawn). This one word summarizes for everyone the meaning of the struggle and within this broad meaning everyone has his own interpretation of what Uhuru will bring for him. The simple peasant may think of Uhuru in terms of farm credits, more food, schools for his children. The office clerk may see it as meaning promotion to an executive job. The apprentice may interpret it as a chance to qualify as a technician, the schoolboy as a chance for a scholarship overseas, the sick person as the provision of better hospital facilities, the aged worker as the hope of pensions and old age security. This interpretation of the goal is not immediately relevant or important when compared with the importance of mobilization of the entire population. This kind of approach is not unique to Africa: despite his spiritual approach, Gandhi used virtually the same tactics.

The people have to be organized so that they are like an army: they must have a general, they must have discipline, they must have a symbol. In many cases the symbol is the national leader himself, and it is necessary to have this kind of symbol of a heroic father-figure if you are to have unquestioning discipline among the different groups and personalities who should rally their followers behind him. The national leader needs an organization whose pattern allows him to lead and also to impose discipline and demand action whenever it is necessary. This must be therefore a mass movement taking in everybody and anybody, and an important feature of it is the series of mass political rallies held all over the country.

Some foreign visitors have expressed surprise at the political rallies they have seen in Africa. There is the huge crowd, streaming toward a stadium or an open piece of ground, sitting patiently for hours while a dozen politicians make speeches. The speakers do not seem to make many new points — or, at least, for every new idea there is a great deal which everyone has heard often before. The speeches are frequently interrupted by the speaker calling on the crowd to thunder back at him a series of slogans:

"Uhuru!"

"Uhuru!"

"Uhuru na umoja!"

"Uhuru na umoja!"

"Uhuru na KANU!"

"Uhuru na KANU!"

"Uhuru na Kenyatta!"

"Uhuru na Kenyatta!"

And so on. The crowd is good-natured and seems to look on the rally as a festival occasion. In fact, in the front is a women's choir whose members have bark-cloth dresses and painted faces and a curious mixture of Western ornaments like dark glasses, and tin cans round their ankles. But what is the point of it all? It may help to boost the people's morale a bit, but don't they get bored after the first once or twice? And why do so many leaders spend so much time at these rallies?

This is how some foreigners feel at first, but it is easy to show them the importance of these rallies. They are intended to have an impact both on the population and on the colonial power. They are intended to show the colonial power the strength and unity (umoja) of the people and the leadership, and the unanimity of the people in their demand for Uhuru. And, among the people themselves, they are intended to show the strength of the leader and the complete loyalty of his followers, and to persuade the few who may doubt the rightness of the cause that after all everybody else believes in it. The rallies tackle the task, in the early days of a national movement, of creating in each African a sense of self-confidence, a feeling not only that it is right to fight for his independence but that it is possible to win independence. Further, that it is not only right he should be free, but that he has a duty to free himself. The rallies are intended to create a revolutionary spirit, to wipe away the acquiescence he has shown before and the obedience which was expected of him.

For a nationalist movement faces the problem of changing attitudes inculcated by the colonial power. Schools have taught Africans to accept the inevitability of gradualism in the development of their countries and the attainment of independence. They have taught the never-never policy — independence cannot come in your lifetime, it is too complicated to hope to win, you cannot run a government unless you have reached a certain high standard of education. They have taught that certain traditional forms of government must be maintained if independence is to survive, and in many cases they have taught that the African is inferior to the white man and must depend on him for guidance. In Kenya and other colonies many people — and especially chiefs — were convinced through the administrative setup that the white man's position was indestructible and no amount of agitation was going to move it. Africans who had worked for years with missionaries, older African teachers and Africans employed by district administrations were all conditioned in this manner. They will always give you long sermons about gradualism, and they dislike every aspect of nationalist agitation as a threat to good order. In the initial stages of the struggle, their opposition is one of the big problems. I remember, when I had decided to become involved in KAU in 1952, how not only my father but other elders in my tribe kept telling me:

"We can never compete with the European. After all, he has airplanes, he flies about while we walk on foot. He has cars and he has guns."

I was told we were beating our heads against a brick wall. But I did not find it strange, because I knew various district commissioners who at barazas (meetings) had told the people they could not compete with the white man because they had not yet learned how to make a nail. To foster this spirit of inferiority among Africans, the administration had identified everything good with the European and everything bad or inferior with the African. Thus, first-grade maize or eggs or potatoes were designated European-type maize or eggs or potatoes, and all inferior maize or eggs or potatoes or even cattle were described as African-type ("Mahindi ya Kizungu" and "Viazi vya Kiafrika"). In overcoming this feeling of inferiority, the nationalist rallies play a vital part.

A nationalist movement cannot immediately be run on the same basis as a modern political party in Britain or Europe or North America, with committees and research workers and discussion groups on this and that problem. Such a system brings people too much into discussion of details and creates too many opportunities for differences and divisions. The mass movement must be organized on a foundation of strong membership, but the organizing machinery should concern itself with increasing membership and raising funds and not with too much study of aspects of future policy. When we organized the Peoples Convention Party in Nairobi in 1957 and 1958, we had on each housing estate an organizing cell with a committee of six whose task was to run a local membership drive. It was never intended that these cells should be intellectual discussion groups on policies, studying the problems of education and agriculture and so on.

The concentration on Uhuru does not date from the beginning of the nationalist struggle, it must be added. In the days of KAU, independence was referred to, but the main emphasis was on the struggle against the color bar and the reservation of land for white farmers. The British government did not in those days dream of talking about dates for independence. When a United Nations Visiting Committee spoke in 1956 of a target date of 1972 for Tanganyika's independence, the British government went nearly berserk; and for their part African leaders were prepared to accept the UN line because it stated the principle of independence, although it did not press for an earlier date. The main focus on independence came from 1957 onward, because Ghana set a precedent in that year for the rest of Africa. Before Ghana there were only Egypt, Liberia, Sudan and Ethiopia as independent states, and their history was so different they did not have a similar impact on postwar nationalist aspirations in the rest of Africa. The first Conference of Independent African States was held in Accra in April 1958, and it passed resolutions which highlighted the struggle for independence. Delegates to the first All-African Peoples Conference in that December could read on the plinth of Kwame Nkrumah's statue the declaration that the independence of Ghana was meaningless unless it was linked to the liberation of all Africa. The whole trend changed from emphasizing the struggle against piecemeal acts of injustice, and everyone decided to prepare the nationalist movement to fight for the independence within which all other problems would be solved. Once again Nkrumah's remark should be quoted: "Seek ye first the political kingdom and everything else shall be added unto you."

In this respect the position of our friends in Central and South Africa is no different from our own. We fought against the exclusive reservation of land, Southern Rhodesians fought primarily until 1959 against injustices done to farmers under the Land Husbandry Act, Nyasas and Northern Rhodesians have fought against Federation. In fact, in Northern Rhodesia it remains the prime target: during the elections in October 1962, when Kenneth Kaunda shouted "Kwacha!" at a rally, the answering call from the crowd was always "Federation must go!" These are slogans which mobilize and appeal to emotion on matters close to the ordinary man. But the issues change swiftly: when in Southern Rhodesia the municipalities opened the swimming baths to all races at the end of a tough struggle between reformers and reactionaries, Joshua Nkomo told officials: "We don't want to swim in your swimming pools. We want to swim with you in parliament." He had moved on to demand greater representation than just a few "lower roll" seats in the legislature.

So the slogan "Uhuru" only came into universal use in East Africa in 1957. From then on we were often criticized for being unrealistic when we called for "Uhuru sasa" (Freedom now). Our critics thought we were merely stating a date for independence. The slogan was coined to convey the people's sense of urgency and their conviction that freedom is a birthright and not a right to be acquired by qualification. It was a revolt against the colonialist argument that "You cannot be free because you are not sufficiently educated; you do not have enough doctors and engineers and lawyers." It was a refutation of those people who laid down criteria for voters, that they should be "responsible and civilized"; of the Capricorn Africa Society, whose leaders declared "a vote is not a right, but a privilege"; and of the Tredgold Commission, which in 1957 confined the vote in Southern Rhodesia to those who would exercise it "with reason, judgment and public spirit" — and these turned out to be (in the commission's judgment) only those earning more than three hundred pounds a year who had been at school for ten years. So "Uhura sasa" was our declaration in simple words that we had always possessed the right to be free, and freedom had nothing to do with riches or schooling or civilization.

In the process of mass mobilization, leadership is needed to act as a rallying point, and one problem which sometimes has to be faced is a clash of personalities when trying to create the national leader. The clash may come because of tribalist tendencies. It has been said that Nigeria is perhaps an example to quote in this respect, because each region has produced its own leader — Awolowo in the West, Azikiwe in the East and the Sardauna of Sokoto in the North — but I feel this is a simplification of the Nigerian position, because the country is too vast and communications were too undeveloped for a mass movement to be created. But Nigeria has been mentioned frequently in discussions of this question of tribalism — and so, in another sense, have events in Kenya; and I would like therefore to dwell on the issue of tribalism, and put it in the context of politicians organizing a national movement.

To anyone concerned with African unity, tribalism presents one of the major problems. We discussed at length this problem at the All-African Peoples Conference in 1958: the question of traditional rulers, the problems of language and customs. We concluded that if governments tried to destroy tribal culture and customs, language and ethnic groupings, such a vacuum would be created that the African might find he had nothing to stand upon and become a most bewildered person in this modern world. We thought it essential to isolate what you might call negative tribalism from tribalism in the form of customs and culture.

Let me state the positive contributions of tribalism first.

At this stage of economic emancipation, with many more Africans moving into the money economy, they have to decide whether to allow themselves to be completely uprooted from all their past beliefs. I believe it is unwise to destroy this African structure of interdependence within the community, where each man knows he has certain responsibilities and duties and where there are certain sanctions against those who do not fulfill expectations. There is, for instance, inherent generosity within a tribe or clan. From the moment a child is born, he is virtually the property of the whole clan and not just of his father and mother. He is expected to serve everybody and also to receive from everybody. As a young child he herds cattle in a group with other children of the clan. Later he will work with other girls and boys in other peoples' fields, or build a hut for a member of the clan without distinction of family. His own father may be poor, but when he comes to marry, if he has even only a distant uncle with property he does not hesitate to go ahead and contract a marriage. If that uncle refuses to part with cattle — for a bride-price — he is entitled to take them away without the support of the elders. If, on the other hand, he has not as a youth made his full contribution to the community, he does not stand a chance with the clan elders when he comes to the age of marriage. When he is in need, his demands will often be disregarded and the elders are bound to tell him he deserves nothing better until he proves himself. This is an aspect of the African tribal system I would hate to see die. It provides the discipline, self-reliance and stability needed in the new relations.

People have done their worst in attacking tribalism, and never differentiating what was positive and worth preserving. Missionaries taught Africans to despise their tribal culture, telling them it was in conflict with the modern world.

No effort was made to trace what was good, or point out to the potential leaders of a community how some customs could be modified to suit the changes in the world. Africans were simply taught European social behavior and the way European workmen lived their lives, without any reference to African customs. This tended to raise a serious conflict in the minds of an unsophisticated African as to whether he should remain entirely tribal or shift completely to the European way of life. Yet this is not a question which should be posed at all. The question is whether we can develop within Africa a system which reflects the African personality but is at the same time a growing system in which a man does not have to cling to tribal customs in the raw and primitive sense. For example, some people have told unsophisticated Africans that wearing clothes and washing with soap means moving away from African tribal life. "Wash with this piece of soap, and you will have reflected the European way of life!" You can imagine how this approach destroys his confidence in what is good in African society.

After the influence of schools comes that of money. When a man earns his own salary and begins to buy a gramophone or a bicycle or a suit of clothes, he ceases to look on certain things as belonging to the community and begins to regard them as personal. This is a main area of conflict with tribalism, where adjustment is most necessary. He asks himself: "Am I going to become individualistic like the European, or can I own something of my own and still belong to the tribe?" To a large extent, even African leaders and heads of African states have not succeeded in transforming themselves completely into individual personalities: they are still to some degree communal because their background and their relatives remain tribal, and so they themselves cannot afford to change at the risk of offending their family. In a European society I would expect that if people were coming to my house they would first telephone to say they were coming, or if they were coming to stay they would advise me in advance. But to expect this from my relations would be asking the impossible. I have learned to expect them when I see them, and I also know they may not telephone me even if they have a telephone. But I do not object to this: I regard it as part of the Africanism which I think can synthesize with what is modern to create something African.

I would never pretend, however, that there is not a negative form of tribalism, which is most harmful in Africa. The man who tries to live completely within the confines of his tribe, not so much revering its customs as discriminating against other tribes, represents the kind of tribalism of which Africa must beware. The Luo who thinks nothing good can come from other tribes or continuously protects a person merely because he is a fellow Luo; the Kikuyu who thinks it suitable to meet only other Kikuyu and disregards merit and ability in other people only because they do not belong to his tribe — this is negative tribalism which cannot allow for unity. That we are born of different tribes we cannot change, but I refuse to believe that because our tribes have different backgrounds and culture and customs we cannot create an African community or a nation.

The European colonial powers and even missionaries for a long time tended to build up tribal antagonism. It made it easier to influence the people if they could find an amenable tribe to use against another tribe which was hostile. This was the straightforward tactic of "divide and rule," and it cannot be excused as part of the British public school attitude of administrators backing "my team" against the "other chaps." We must also beware of people, including the colonial powers in these last stages, trying to re-create old tribal hostilities. In Kenya the Masai used to fight the Kikuyu, either for cattle or women, and the Luo had boundary clashes with the Kisii. Some political leaders have revived these old hostilities for their own personal reasons. When a leader feels himself weak on the national platform, he begins to calculate that the only support he may have will come from his own tribe; so he starts to create an antagonism of this sort, to entrench himself as at least a leader of his tribe.

Education is one weapon against negative tribalism: not bookish education, but practical civics and general sophistication — for instance, people working together to form a trade union and fighting for their rights as a workers' movement. The trade union movement can be a very useful instrument of education against negative tribalism, even among illiterate people. But perhaps the strongest weapon is the political party machinery, in which everyone is mobilized for the struggle regardless of tribe or language and in which leadership is given to the person who merits it regardless of his tribe. Again, there is education involved in the social intercourse which takes place in urban communities, where people of all tribes live together and go to the same beer houses and dances and football matches. A long time ago in Nairobi the antagonism between Kikuyu and Luo was such that they fought on sight. They did not even quarrel about anything, they just fought. As soon as a Kikuyu saw a Luo, the first thing he did was pick up a stone and try to brain him. We have come a long way since those days, and men like Kenyatta have done much to educate the people away from negative tribalism.

Nevertheless, tribalism is one of the basic differences between the Kenya African National Union (KANU) and Kenya African Democratic Union (KADU), and perhaps is the origin of these differences. Some will say the smaller tribes must be protected from the bigger tribes. Such people refuse to accept the challenge of tribalism, and instead of fighting it have given in and are actually promoting it. The difference between KANU and KADU over tribalism is this: KANU concedes that tribal feelings exist but say they can be eliminated by wise leadership and positive action; KADU is exaggerating these feelings to entrench tribalism. These were the dangers of tribalism to which we referred at the All-African Peoples Conference in Accra in 1958.

Closely tied to the question of tribalism is that of traditional rulers, like the Ashantahene in Ghana and the four Kings of Uganda. I do not agree with many Western observers who think these tribal rulers will always be in conflict with the setting up of modern political institutions. Some of our traditional authority can be worked in usefully with a local government system based on an African background. The conflict only arises if we try — as the British want us to try — to change the local government system drastically and make it into the British pattern. The British were the first to use these tribal authorities as tools in their own administration, but when independence comes they are the first to criticize the continuance of such authorities. There is danger that some tribal authorities will be swept away because they are known as mouthpieces of the old colonial government. But this will happen mainly to chiefs, who were created by the colonialists in place of the traditional councils of elders. The Kabakaship in Buganda is an entirely different institution, and we need to look at this problem in the context of each separate country. These institutions have been corrupted by colonialists and stand a danger if they fail to recognize the new forces in Africa.

Kenya has been afflicted a good deal with negative tribalism, although not more than some other African countries — consider the attitude of the Baganda people in Uganda, for example. I concede that the remedies mentioned — education and urban contact — do not work fast enough. One of the major problems has to do with the character and integrity of the leaders. It is therefore disturbing to see how tribalism is sometimes more common among the highly educated than among the illiterate. This bears out the view that ambitious intellectuals have been exploiting tribal fears. They can attract a good deal of attention because their appeal is emotional and couched in clichés the ordinary tribal man understands. Still, if he is given a choice, the ordinary man will usually choose strong, honest and dedicated leadership in preference to a tribal demagogue.

Certainly I was encouraged in believing the ability of the ordinary man to reject tribalism when, during the Kenya elections in 1961, in some constituencies (including my own) candidates of minority tribes were returned. I believe the ordinary African will always be influenced by the record of a leader or candidate, and he is not as foolish as many people would like to think. One important factor in the Kenya situation was the knowledge of events during the Emergency, when members of the same tribe had actually betrayed each other, while leaders of different tribes had worked ceaselessly for the affected people regardless of tribe.

During the Emergency I worked closely with the affected tribes in Nairobi and got to know some of the fighters and some of the leaders in the forests. I became one of the few members of other tribes to whom they spoke freely and discussed their intimate problems. After the Emergency most of the Kikuyu, Embu and Meru tribes would come to me for advice and help. They had no feeling of tribal differences. In their eyes I was an African leader who they believed was faithful to the cause. I think this played an important part in the 1961 elections.

Some of our present difficulties in Kenya and some of the suspicions against the Kikuyu and the Luo arise from the allegation that although many of their leaders condemn tribalism, they meet secretly behind the scenes and plan a Kikuyu or Luo approach to Kenya politics. The Kikuyu are especially accused of this. Fears of this sort have had effect on relations between the tribes and have sometimes produced tribalist reactions among other tribes. These fears have also been exploited by ambitious politicians for their own ends. Occasionally they have been used as propaganda to belittle good done by genuine Kikuyu leaders and even to try to keep them out of national affairs. The settlers and the British have used these fears deliberately to undermine African unity.

With the return of senior ex-detainees, whom the newspapers have dubbed "the Kikuyu old guard," these fears have been increased by some thoughtless individuals who have claimed that Kenyatta's leadership is Kikuyu leadership, which they must do everything to uphold. I have said publicly that any Kikuyu who looks on Kenyatta's leadership in that light will inevitably produce an anti-Kikuyu reaction from the other tribes: Kenyatta's leadership is in fact African leadership and not Kikuyu leadership. For those people who complain, "Why should we be led by Kenyatta, who is a Kikuyu?" I suppose we have to produce a tribeless leader, for in no other way can we ensure that such people will look at leaders on merit and not by tribe.

This distinction may not appear to be very important, but it is significant in the future relationships of Kenya's tribes. There is a clique whose members parade around as nontribalists but hope to be dragged to power on the coattails of leaders who come from the same tribe. These people create suspicions between some leaders and sections of the different tribes who are made to believe that one leader constitutes a threat to the leadership of another, who happens to belong to a different tribe.

In building up a mass nationalist movement in Kenya, we faced peculiar and extra obstacles. It was not until June 1955, after the Emergency had been in force for nearly three years, that the government allowed us to form political parties. And these were only allowed to be formed on a district basis; not until after the Lancaster House conference in 1960 did the government allow an African party to organize nationally. The official explanation was that this would encourage a "simple and orderly development of African political life." It was promised that at a later stage, a "convention" of these district associations would be permitted. Of course these restrictions produced the opposite of orderly development and greatly aggravated tribalism. It was clear from the outset these district organizations would be a threat to national unity, because we could see district loyalties building up and reflecting tribal loyalties (since district and tribal boundaries were often the same). District chairmen became kings in their own rights in their own areas, and this has been the major part of our problems of disunity, both between KANU and KADU and for some time inside KANU itself. We have never been able to escape completely from the district consciousness which developed during that period. No other country under British rule has started off with such difficulties in forming a national movement as we faced after the Emergency. It might be added that the British insistence that there should be no national parties from 1953 until 1960 is the best refutation of Corfield's argument that KAU was really only a Kikuyu party: it was precisely because the British had had a taste of the strength of a national movement with KAU that they tried to avoid the experience a second time. In doing so they harmed national unity immeasurably.

The first African district parties were formed while I was away at Oxford. I returned to find that the Nairobi African District Congress had been formed. I took over my old position as General Secretary of the Kenya Federation of Labor and immediately was under strong pressure to stand in the elections four months hence, in March 1957, as a workers' candidate. For a month I resisted, because I thought we should all agree on one candidate nominated by the Congress if we could work out a comman policy. This proved impossible. When I said I would stand in December, I put three basic demands: political freedom, human dignity and economic opportunity.

My KFL friends were keen for me to stand so that I could improve the conditions of workers through taking part in the legislature and could give the labor movement an effective say in the country's affairs. This influenced me in deciding to stand for Nairobi rather than for my home district of South Nyanza. If I had chosen my home district, I could not have continued my active interest in the trade union movement. But the organization of my election campaign in Nairobi was difficult, because the KFL was forbidden to take an active part in politics — it had nearly had its registration canceled on these grounds in February 1956. So I had to set up independent committees all over Nairobi.

Those were exciting days — and nights — during that campaign. Many friends worked with me round the clock organizing committees and addressing meetings. There was a good deal of malicious talk and propaganda I had to face,

I was attacked for being too young (I was twenty-six), for not being married, for not having a university degree. I answered that youth provided the dynamism a revolutionary country needed; that I had never heard of a wife's being taken into Legislative Council to help a husband with the debates; that men like Churchill and many American Presidents had done well enough without a university degree. These arguments seemed to carry weight with my audiences.

I was lucky too in the voting symbol I was given on nomination day. My main opponent had the symbol of the lion, and I of the cockerel. There were humorous exchanges about our symbols. At one meeting I found an audience hostile because some Congress man had told the people they couldn't vote for a jogoo (cockerel) because it could so easily be eaten by a lion. My bright lieutenants retorted:

"According to African custom, you never set up a new house without a cockerel. Kenya is our new home, for we are going into the legislature for the first time. A lion would be mistrusted as a domestic animal. You never know when it will become hungry and eat you up."

And on polling day my followers crowed like cocks, while my opponent's roared like lions. It was all good fun, and there were no ugly incidents. The only time the police had to act was to protect me from enthusiastic supporters when the result was announced. I had won the election.

Throughout the campaign I had pondered how we could bring about national unity. My hope was to establish without delay a close working relationship with the other seven African elected members. Mine was the first result announced, and as the others came over the radio I sent off telegrams of congratulations to the winners and at the same time invited them to a meeting in Nairobi. When we met, we found we all felt alike about the urgency of breaking up the Lyttelton Constitution, abolishing the exclusive reservation of the "white highlands," desegregating schools and bringing in adult suffrage. We gave ourselves a target of independence within five years, and coined the phrase "undiluted democracy" to express our demands in the simplest terms. At that meeting, on March 13, 1957, the eight of us launched Operation Freedom.

When we took our seats we came face to face for the first time with the hypocrisy of the British in the colonial legislatures. It was obvious our presence there was only to add color. There were many issues on which we knew we had a strong case — the ending of the Emergency, freedom of assembly, ending of restrictions on African national parties, social discrimination — and we introduced motion after motion, but were always defeated. We faced too the racial problem, as the result of communal elections. I cannot remember a single instance in which any of the fourteen European elected members of those who sat with us on the opposition benches supported any of our motions; they were usually the first to oppose us.

By June it was clear we needed to do more than simply introduce motions in a legislature heavily loaded against us. So we decided to send to Britain a delegation consisting of Ronald Ngala and myself to put pressure on the Colonial Office and to create more sympathy for our case among the British public. We met the Colonial Secretary and several members of Parliament, and returned convinced that success in our struggle would lie more in the effective organization of a political party than in delegations to Britain. Britain and Lennox-Boyd needed to see action by us before they would acknowledge that our people were determined in their struggle.

Ronald Ngala and I therefore urged our colleagues to join the different district associations so that we could use them in the struggle. We argued that although the restrictions on these associations made national organization difficult, we were united in the center and so could coordinate the policies and programs of these associations.

We then set about organizing leaders' conferences at which we could synthesize and formulate common policy. We also planned to invite office-bearers from one association to address meetings in other districts and promote national unity in that way. This strategy began in October 1957, and in the following May we formed a Convention of African Associations to foster unity further. But the Convention was refused registration, because the government was hostile to any countrywide organization and in other ways too the government moved to break up the beginnings of African unity. A new regulation made it illegal for us to hold leaders' conferences unless we had a license and listed the agenda we planned to discuss. We were stopped from holding meetings in each other's districts: in January 1958, for example, the administration refused to let Julius Nyerere and myself speak to the Mombasa African Democratic Union. All these restrictions put our group of eight elected members of the Legislative Council, who were trying to hold the cords together at the center and plait them into a strong rope, under terrific strain. Inevitably, too, with eight individuals having no party discipline among them there developed disagreements and jealousies. And so frictions arose, which were perhaps not important at that time. But national unity suffered.

The government became worried about the activities of the Peoples Convention Party, which had been formed in Nairobi after the elections and of which I had become presi-

dent. It was a party with more discipline than many others
I have worked with. We were sure decisions would reach
everyone's notice and they would be carried out in the way
the leaders wanted. As I said earlier, we built the PCP on a
system of six-member cells in each Nairobi location: thirty-
two cells in all. Attached to each cell was a woman and a
youth, to act as the spearhead in that location for the
women's and youth wings of the party.

The PCP was built on these lines with the intention that
if the government proscribed the party it could survive
through the cells, with only the top leadership removed.
It could also transmit information, if necessary, without the
use of newspapers and radio. The PCP did, however, start
its own newspaper, *Uhuru*, mainly with the object of making
the revolutionary spirit, which was already there, more co-
herent and giving it fuller meaning in slogans. Also, all African newspapers had been banned with the Emergency and
the English-language papers gave little African news. For
instance, a speech, however trite, by a settler leader, to
fifteen Europeans would be given a front-page column,
while a speech by an African leader to ten thousand people
might get an inch in an obscure corner. So our little cyclo-
styled paper was launched as a nationalist mouthpiece, to tell
everyone what we were doing and what they were expected
to do. We used it to bring the name of Kenyatta back into
the limelight, to campaign for his release, and to restore
him as a symbol the people could carry around. In March
1959 *Uhuru* was banned and thirty-nine members of the
PCP arrested; which was, I suppose, the government's way
of paying tribute to our effectiveness.

But meanwhile we had decided the PCP should begin to
have influence throughout Kenya. The party's secretary,
Josef Mathenge (later member and now Senator), and the

organizing secretary, Omolo Agar, toured the country meeting the district leaders to discuss possible mergers with the PCP. In a number of cases joint statements were signed by which these district leaders undertook to comply with PCP policy and discipline and to adopt PCP organization, and we started the same cell system in those areas. Cells were formed in many parts of Central Province, in several areas of Nyanza and also in Coast Province. So, although the PCP was legally just a district association registered in Nairobi, it had a countrywide following.

Many times the government came close to proscribing the PCP. We were warned for our speeches, and particularly for our activities in Central Province, where the government alleged we were raising funds. In Central Province the law then laid down that no member of the Kikuyu, Embu or Meru tribes could join a political party unless he possessed a government loyalty certificate. This caused a big problem in the later development of the nationalist movement, for Kikuyu leaders were prevented from taking part in politics during that period and became suspicious that the other tribes were exploiting this period of Kikuyu restriction to build themselves up. It was widely said that a "Luo clique" was trying to rule all Kenya in the absence of the Kikuyu. When the restrictions were at last lifted, suspicions and unnecessary fears were created by the tribalists who did not want unity. Fortunately the tribalists failed.

With the policy of loyalty certificates, there arose a problem of political division between the so-called Kikuyu "loyalists" and Home Guards on the one side, and on the other the former "terrorists" and detainees. In 1960 this division inside the Kikuyu seemed one of the biggest problems Kenya had to overcome. Fortunately, through the efforts of many Kikuyu leaders, the divisions were quickly healed and unity in Central Province has steadily increased. The Central Province Consultative Committee played a useful part in this reconciliation, although it fell under suspicion by some people of becoming a tribal focus for Kikuyu ambitions.

Another strain upon national unity came with the return, after long years of detention or rustication, of many of the earlier political leaders. Some people were quick to sow fear and suspicion between them and the men who came into leadership after the Emergency was declared. The press increased this suspicion by dubbing the younger leaders "moderates" and the older leaders "extremists," who they suggested were irresponsible. This was quite unfair and created two fictitious camps. I am not saying there are no differences between African leaders, but I think the differences center not so much on ideology as on the ambitions and personalities of the leaders. Some of those who returned from detention feel they have fought and sacrificed themselves for their country, and now the country is nearing independence they should be given due recognition for those hard years. This necessarily raised the question whether recognition of the old leaders meant the discarding of all other leaders, who had also made a contribution to the nationalist effort and brought the country so far. Those who have suffered — and many did suffer — are entitled to recognition and deserve a place in the new setup. But the country also recognizes that while they were away others did not stand still, and they must also understand how much advancement has been made since the Emergency. In other words, both had made a significant contribution and there should in fact be no conflict, since they both contributed to the achievement of the same goal. The press and enemies of African unity tried to represent this situation as a conflict of ideology or policy. Events in Kenya since the return of Kenyatta and during the pre-election period in KANU prove in fact that unity has been achieved and that in fact the groups or camps created by the press were a mere attempt to disunite the nationalist movement.

The attempt to hold the district associations together through leaders' conferences lasted far into 1959. By then we had increased the number of African elected members from eight to fourteen, after Lennox-Boyd had visited Kenya in October 1957 and had agreed in April 1959 to a constitutional conference to be held in London early the next year. About the same time, the idea of a multiracial national party had grown. Such a party was allowed under regulations which forbade an African national party. Discussion on this idea only served to increase the dissensions between the fourteen African elected members and in July 1959 led to an open split. The Kenya National Party was formed with Masinde Muliro as president and the backing of Ngala and two Kalenjin members, Arap Moi and Arap Towett. Most of the African elected members of the Legislative Council identified themselves with the KNP, but four of us refused to join this multiracial body. We insisted that the African people's right to organize on a national basis must first be acknowledged before we would agree to work with Europeans or Asians. We formed the Kenya Independence Movement with Oginga Odinga as president and myself as secretary, and Dr. Kiano, who had just been elected to one of the extra six seats in 1958.

The KIM had the dynamism of a radical party, but the government restrictions on a countrywide organization meant it could not be registered and so was hampered by many disabilities. Before we went to London for the Lancaster House conference in January 1960, all fourteen African elected members agreed at a leaders' conference in

Kiambu to cooperate during the London talks. We unanimously chose Ngala as delegation leader and myself as secretary. During the Lancaster House talks we secured agreement on the lifting of the ban on national parties; when we came home we discussed the need for unanimity, and most members wanted to form a single party. A meeting was called at Kiambu near Nairobi for the end of March, but two days before the meeting the differences among the African elected members came into the open. James Gichuru, a schoolteacher who had led KAU before Kenyatta, had just been released from restriction. A few leaders went to ask him to lead a new political party, the Uhuru party. They tried to exclude from it some of the elected members, including myself. There was antagonism against me, it was said, because in the reporting of the London talks in British newspapers I had been given too much prominence.

When we went to Kiambu, there were hostile placards and heckling, especially against me. Youths organized by some leaders accused me of being too close to the United States, mainly because of my connection with the students' airlift. But by the end of the day, the idea of the Uhuru party was dropped and we had agreed to form the Kenya African National Union. Gichuru was made chairman of a committee of nine to draft the KANU constitution; among the committee members were Ngala, Odinga, Argwings, Kiano and myself. When we met again two months later to ratify the constitution and elect officers, Gichuru became acting president (it was hoped to register Kenyatta as president), Odinga vice-president and myself secretary. While they were away in the United States and Britain, Ngala was elected treasurer and Arap Moi assistant treasurer. But when they returned, they refused to accept these posts and their refusal led to the split out of which came the formation of

the Kenya African Democratic Union at the end of June.
The leaders who agreed to form KANU undertook to
convert their district associations into branches of the new
national party. In Nairobi both Congress and the PCP agreed
to merge as the new local branch, and we similarly dissolved
all the PCP organizations around the country which we had
built up alongside the local district associations. But while
we were moving in this direction of unity, the leaders who
eventually formed KADU were busy building up tribal organizations. After the first Kiambu conference, the Kalenjin
Political Alliance was formed of four district parties founded
by Arap Moi. The Masai United Front was announced at the
same time, and Ngala came back from the United States to
form the Coast African Peoples Union. With Muliro, who
had refused from the first to join a single mass movement,
and his Kenya African Peoples Party (a skeleton of his old
KNP), these groups eventually came together to form
KADU. I think this shows the essential difference between
KANU and KADU which I indicated before: KANU set
about eliminating tribalism, while KADU was formed by
men who had, in the weeks, before, rushed off to entrench
their tribal positions by spreading fear of the Kikuyu and
Luo leaders who had been elected to head KANU on a
basis of merit rather than of tribe.

Just as the emphasis on tribalism through the banning of
national parties before 1960 led to the formation of KADU,
so did the formation of KADU lead in its turn to greater agitation for "protection of minority tribes" within the independence constitution which we went to London early in
1962 to discuss. The cry before these London talks was that
there must be a federalist state which would guarantee each
tribe a certain amount of autonomy. From this developed

the theory of regionalism. But the origins of regionalism go further back, to the theories of white settler groups like the Federal Independence Party of Major Roberts and Major Day. These groups had realized Kenya was heading for independence but were determined there should be a settler area preserved in the "white highlands" with a degree of autonomy which allowed them to plan their own taxation. KADU simply borrowed from their thinking, and from the statements of the late Group Captain Briggs when he led the United Party right-wingers at Lancaster House.

Regionalism is very difficult for any Kenyan to regard dispassionately at the moment. Some people (in KADU) embrace it emotionally in the belief it will protect them as a minority tribe, because seven regional assemblies have been set up deriving their existence from the constitution. Others (in KANU) are appalled by it, because they are sure it will destroy the chances of national unity with too many powers devolved from the central government to regional assemblies. My own view is that regionalism, as KADU first conceived it, could never have worked; for instance, eight entirely separate civil services would have brought administrative chaos. Regionalism in its present form cannot stand in the way of a strong central government, unless there is a complete break and a region follows Katanga's example and declares itself autonomous. Gradually it will lose its significance by the sheer force of such things as the control over finance and economic planning and the control over defense and foreign affairs, all of which the central government is bound to exercise fully. The whole concept of nationhood and identification of sovereignty will work to diminish the importance of regionalism. If a man is proud of being a Kenyan citizen and being part of an independent Kenya, he will think of the country and not his region. Regions as at present constitute an irritant and nuisance which cannot survive.

Until the new constitution has proved itself, it is not possible to give an accurate estimate of the danger of regionalism except to state emphatically that it is contrary to our idea of unity. We have all along made it clear that we never believed the setting up of regions was necessary. We have never thought the fears voiced were genuine, but rather that those who spoke for the KADU type of regionalism or federalism were mainly interested in securing a constitution which would allow them to be bosses in their own tribal areas, because they had failed to achieve national recognition. As it is, not all of the seven regions will have a homogeneous tribal grouping, any more than the six provinces set up by the old colonial administration had. At least four of the regions contain more than one tribe, so that tribal problems have not been eliminated; the boundaries were to be drawn so that tribes willing to live together could do so, but this aim cannot be carried out beyond geographical possibilities. All the talk about regions which followed the London conference created false ideas about the power these regions were going to have, and this may lead to much disillusionment later on.

Not only was a group of right-wing settlers the original inspiration of KADU regionalism, but the brains behind most of KADU's arguments and papers on the subject have come from the so-called "liberal" Europeans in the New Kenya Party, which became associated with KADU in the minority government of April 1961 to April 1962. Prominent among them have been Reggie Alexander, an accountant and ex-mayor of Nairobi, Wilfred Havelock, and Roddy Macleod, brother of the former Colonial Secretary.

Apart from Muliro, very few KADU politicians are convinced regionalists — the others are tribal leaders. I do not see regionalism setting a pattern for other parts of Africa: the Congo, for instance, has to choose between being a federal or a unitary state, and regionalism as Kenya is trying it could hardly be applied there; most regionalists in Kenya, who used to regard Moise Tshombe as their inspiration, look around anxiously now that Katanga's "strong man" has been defeated!

In the years immediately after independence, the period taken up with consolidating that independence and with economic reconstruction, a state needs to maintain unity as the basis for all development. It needs a national symbol in the form of a popular head of state who is at the same time head of a political party. As far as is possible, it needs a single, strong and effective party to mobilize the full potential of the population for the task of translating independence into meaningful terms of development to meet the peoples' hopes. The single party can best mobilize the new force of a population ready to work with their hands and sweat to reconstruct the economy. In Tanganyika, years even before independence, Julius Nyerere made popular his slogan "Uhuru na kazi" (Freedom and work); and in the months after Uhuru came the great self-help movement when Nyerere, Rashidi Kawawa and other cabinet ministers showed by example, by going out into the fields to hoe and by digging trenches for the foundations of new houses, that the period after independence was the time for work and not for celebration. This is only possible where you have popular leadership and a strong party machine. It is impossible where you have a multiparty system with the opposition party waiting for the day it can replace the government. We cannot overemphasize the importance of national unity in this crucial stage of postindependence development.

Many people who declare democracy consists in having a two-party or three-party system ask whether a country like Kenya or any other African state will be able to maintain democracy after independence. Democracy, in their terms, involves maintaining Western parliamentary institutions.

Will we disappoint them if, having developed a strong nationalist movement and mobilized the whole mass of the people to support a single leader, we do not attempt the impossible task of changing it all overnight? Even though independence has been reached, the emotions and loyalties of the people will lie in the same place. The symbol of leadership which was created during the independence struggle remains the same. The leaders who worked together for independence are going to work together after it, unless there is a crisis of personalities. It is logical to expect the emphasis after independence to be still on unity, and the magnitude of the problems which a new state faces makes unity vital. The colonial power may have retreated, but the inheritance of colonialism has still to be fought, in the shape of poverty, ignorance and disease. Also, the new states are becoming independent at a time of great tension in the East-West struggle, and the dangers of this struggle to the integrity of a new state have to be faced immediately. Even where there is a general desire to form different political parties, these internal divisions may end up by being interpreted as taking sides in the East-West struggle. All this underlines the need for continuing unity after independence.

The British, of course, turn somersaults over this question of one or more parties in a state. Before there were two

African parties in Kenya they said a one-party system was a threat to democracy and would lead to dictatorship. Now that in Kenya we have three, they say this is extremely dangerous, as it means there is no unity and Kenya may well end up in civil war. We find it all very amusing.

A nationalist movement has no time for arguments about ideology or for differences in economic and social programs. Society in Africa — at least north of the Zambezi — is not divided between the capitalists and the workers, the landlords and the landless. The basic differences which create class distinctions in Europe are absent in Africa. Instead, you have in newly independent states a government which derives its strength from the masses, and talks in terms of universal education, more hospitals, better food, more opportunities for a better standard of life for everybody. The areas of division are very limited — at least at the outset, until you have created new interests which may clash — and it is difficult to form genuine political parties. The divisions there might be would be those of tribe or individual ambition, but very rarely could there be genuine ideological or class differences. This is why the British are wrong in asking about democracy in terms of their own parliamentary institutions and political party setup.

The safeguards for democracy in Africa lie elsewhere. They rest upon the integrity of the leaders, who have enormous power for good or evil because of the confidence the masses place in them. The risk that a leader may do great evil is the biggest risk democracy faces, but it is a risk these states must logically and inevitably take if they are to face the challenges of independence.

Another safeguard lies in the proper working of the party machinery, which should ensure the opportunity for full and frank discussions, so that decisions are taken democratically. Take KANU, for example. It has branches and district committees in which certain decisions should be taken. But the supreme body is the Governing Council, on which each branch or district has a representative, and these representatives must reflect together the whole country's structure and interests. Power should lie with the Governing Council, which should be able to bring together the views of the people from all over the country and should also be able to control the leadership. The Governing Council, in which these local representatives and the national officials combine, is the best point at which to check the leadership. It can ensure that the leaders respond to the general wishes of the public, and yet it cannot itself become completely dictatorial because of the interests it represents and the personalities which constitute it, I use the word "completely" advisedly, because views differ about what dictatorship means. The Governing Council should provide firm government in the country and pursue its economic objectives resolutely; this may mean stronger government and more discipline than some people like, but it should not be confused with dictatorship.

Clearly, the Governing Council must meet regularly if the party machine is to work effectively. Its members must also know the party constitution thoroughly and make sure it is respected and discipline is enforced. It must also be explicitly stated that the parliamentary group of the party should work together with the Governing Council and under policies agreed to by the party. Any policy which the parliamentary group feels should be put forward must be ratified by the Governing Council; otherwise, the Governing Council becomes redundant and the parliamentary group takes over not only the party work in parliament but control throughout the country. This coordination is essential to keep the government and people together and ensure national mobilization after independence.

We have to avoid what happens in Britain, particularly in the Labour Party. Despite annual party conferences, it is clear the parliamentary leader and his members decide what they are going to do, and it does not matter what the annual conference decides. This was only too clear in the two great Labour Party controversies over "Clause Four" nationalization and unilateral disarmament. If you had had a Labour government at the time, you would have seen the government doing exactly the opposite of what the party at the annual conference wanted done. If we allowed this, the parliamentary group could defy the Governing Council for the period of their time in power and do virtually what they liked. So we need to make clear the relationship between the two groups and the coordination of their actions.

The Delegates' Conference, with six representatives from every branch, has been regarded as the supreme authority to decide every issue and ratify every policy. But this is nearly impossible when you have hundreds of delegates — thousands, in some countries — gathering for one week in a year. They cannot be expected to be involved in the detailed working of the machinery by which the leaders, the national executive and the Governing Council run affairs. The best purpose of the Delegates' Conference is to give a foretaste of popular opinion on some issues, to bring the national leader back to his colleagues to renew their confidence in the party's program, and to get the other leaders and the members of the party machine, who are usually widely separated, to come together so that they know each other better and have greater confidence in the whole machine. To some extent the Delegates' Conference is the popular symbol of the party — a symbol of unity. It does not deal with details except to establish policy.

A common feature of national movements all over Africa has been the part played by women's and youth groups. The age limit for "youth" varies in different countries and parties; in some it goes as high as thirty-five, but with KANU nobody over the age of twenty-five qualifies. The youth wing acts as a vanguard in the struggle for independence: they sing party songs; they dance at the rallies; they express themselves adventurously; they help organize; they are prepared to take positive action when it is called for; they are in the forefront of the pickets when there is civil disobedience; they contribute most to the pool of volunteers when there is a military situation, as in Algeria, or in Kenya during the Emergency.

Women have similarly played a most important role, and the illiterate women contribute as much as, if not more than, the literate. African women are one of the most important supports a nationalist movement can have. They are more amenable to discipline and readier to accept leadership than the men; once a leader is accepted, most women will give him undying loyalty and confidence. Their ability to propagate the party's views in the homes and marketplaces and everywhere else is the greatest asset a national leader possesses; in the months before the Emergency, Kenya women showed their skill as public relations "men." When youths failed to get donations for KAU the women invariably succeeded. Later on they became important as messengers, and during the "terrorist" movement were nearly always the messengers between one group and another. We who were not detained received most of our messages through women messengers. Women can endure much suffering, and can in certain situations sacrifice much more than men would.

They may not have their usefulness reflected in parliamentary representation very swiftly, however. This is because the politically minded women have mostly been illiterate. Literate women have been more concerned with social advancement and welfare — with teaching home economics and hygiene, with nursing and teaching school. There is no prejudice among men against voting for women, but to be elected a woman candidate must make a name in the party and gain a reputation for being as strong a fighter as anyone else. Unfortunately in Kenya no woman was nominated for election to parliament this year. In Tanganyika, however, the women's leader Bibi Titi Mohamed by her own efforts raised herself to a position of leading and then into the National Assembly. We have to bring some women into parliament as nominated members, as Uganda and Tanganyika have already done.

Once the youth are organized, they have to be disciplined and — what is even more important — they have to be kept occupied, for otherwise discipline disappears. When they are on full-time party work, they must be properly looked after. Otherwise, whenever there has been a clash between leaders, the temptation to buy their services is great. There have been many allegations in Kenya that youths have been bought this way to do jobs for quarreling leaders, jobs which were not necessarily in the party's interests. Before independence it is difficult to give the youths constructive work on a day-to-day basis, because what work is available depends on the party's plan. But after independence, it is easier to employ them on useful projects. The way in which the Ghana Youth Pioneers are organized is an example of a good means of exploiting the full potential of the country's manpower; it can, it is true, be a dangerous weapon if it is misused and if the youths are not taught to believe in a certain type of discipline. In Israel I have seen youths trained so that they are a source of pride to the nation, and they are readily available for all sorts of national work programs. We must plan this way. We cannot leave them entirely on their own to find jobs on the normal labor market, because in our newly developing countries there will not be enough ordinary employment for all of them, and they could become a liability to the nation.

In the general mobilization of the people into the national movement, such organizations as the trade union movement, the farmers' associations and the cooperative movements have an important part to play. In Africa it is clear that the trade union movement cannot stand aside from the national movement without being accused of "consorting with the imperialists" and without forfeiting the opportunity to influence the changing of policies on behalf their members. In some countries these groups have representation in the highest councils of the nationalist movement by virtue of their being a separate interest group. But other countries believe it is better they should have representation because their leaders happen also to be national leaders. It is sometimes argued that if you have communal representation of these groups in the national movement, there is danger of conflict and danger that these groups affiliated to the party may begin to feel they are strong enough to challenge the parent body, or even to break away and form their own political group. Whatever form is adopted, I feel there must be close consultation between these various groups to ensure that in their individual activities they all move in the same direction. You find this close liaison in every country where you have a strong trade union movement, and in many cases the individuals who are prominent in the trade unions are also prominent in the political field.

Perhaps, in closing this chapter, there is no better way of underlining its main theme than by quoting the motto of Milton Obote's Uganda Peoples Congress, which took this neighboring country of ours into independence. It is "Unity and independence." The UPC put unity first. The problems of unity which we have faced in Kenya and to which I have referred briefly are a lesson that helps to bring out clearly some of the dangers to be avoided.

FIVE

National Mobilization II:
The Challenge of Nation-Building

THE second stage of national mobilization concerns what is perhaps best called "nation-building." It is a phrase which Sir Edgar Whitehead did his utmost to discredit in 1962, when he launched a "Build a nation" campaign in Southern Rhodesia in the hope of enrolling as voters fifty thousand Africans to give some justification to an undemocratic constitution. His campaign failed dismally, and he persuaded only one-tenth of the number he had hoped to win over. But for all that, "nation-building" is a good phrase with a suggestion of hard and worthwhile work, a phrase which Whitehead should not be allowed to spoil. The chief challenge in nation-building is in regard to those persons or groups who need to transform their attitudes, to conform with the new sense of urgency and the new values which the young state wishes to establish. The most important group is the press.

At a meeting of the International Press Institute in Paris in May 1962 I made a speech on "Relations Between Press and Governments in Africa." Since editors are as sensitive to criticism as any politician, I provoked several counterattacks, including a leading article in *The Times*. But perhaps my criticisms found their mark and did some good.

I pointed out to these leading journalists in Paris "the strange but simple fact that in many countries, especially in East and Central Africa, independence has been achieved, or brought within easy reach, despite a general press hostility." I included among the hostile ranks the newspapers printed in Africa with expatriate technicians and settler capital and some of the "overseas" newspapers published in the metropolitan cities, but I excluded of course the small nationalist and African-owned press.

I said the attitudes of the established press in Africa, being so rooted in overseas traditions, had expressed themselves in three principal ways. Editors had shown a fundamental dislike and distrust of change, and had indeed given a grim reception to British Prime Minister Macmillan's "wind of change" speech. They had been outraged, and said it "wasn't cricket," when African leaders demanded self-determination and human dignity and "answered palliatives with impatience, intrigue with rebuff." And thirdly, there had been a campaign, rooted in some superiority complex and conducted with maddening paternalism, designed to show that the people of Africa were incapable of controlling and enjoying freedom; for years the press in East and Central Africa had argued that the "grant" (as they called it) of liberty would extinguish freedom, and I added:

"It is difficult to work out, in all this, just what the press was hoping to accomplish. If their campaign had succeeded, it logically follows that a sense of inferiority might have crippled the energy and zest of our people. There is little doubt that constant gloomy prediction about the fate of major industries and services has contributed greatly to the uncertainties of ordinary families, to lack of confidence and flight of capital, factors which have magnified difficulties out of all proportion to conceivable hazard."

Nevertheless, we had all arrived at an open gate leading to the years of independence, and there were heart-searchings on both sides about future relationships between governments and the press. "The African leaders," I went on, "realize full well the advantages of having a free and professionally competent press, carrying out an informative function, a critical function, often an educational function, and with some of its columns providing outlet for eccentricity or inventiveness or grief. The established newspapers in East Africa can be confident they need not be suppressed or be absorbed into some government propaganda machine. But they will need to find their feet."

I suggested these newspapers and reviews would find a new set of values if they were public companies with a good deal of local participation both of capital and staff, and if they therefore approached their task with the realization that they had to live with the results of their proposals or condemnations. Many of the staffs of these papers are still recruited overseas and think it amusing to spend a couple of years in Africa without any real interest or commitment in the country. I complained that the standard of reporting among these men was low and sometimes slanted, "splashing a sentence out of context, preferring a story about failure or fear to a story of achievement or endeavor; stressing every day the clash-of-personality angle rather than common purpose and dogged advance." And I ended with some advice to the world press, that "Africa today is something new. We are building a society that is pledged not to distort the cherished values of dignity and freedom, is committed to justice and effort and effective independence. This should be a story of compassion and construction, a story that has never yet appeared in print. If at any time you think this rates a column, and you'd like to come and cover it, we should place no restriction on where you'd be able to travel, or on whom you'd like to see. We'd rather have your shrewd appraisal, and be jolted at times by constructive ideas."

In a speech of that sort, one can speak only in generalizations, and journalists a few thousand miles away from the parts of Africa where a colonial press has operated challenge you for specific instances. The only difficulty in answering their challenge lies in remembering the most glaring instances. But, for example, when we were fighting the Lyttelton Constitution, the Kenya press persistently stated we were moved not by nationalism but by emotionalism, and this led Europeans into doubting whether there was such a thing as African nationalism — until in 1960, when Iain Macleod said Kenya must eventually be an African state, they were shocked into realizing their press had never told them the truth. The press made — or tried to make — African leaders into objects of scorn and encouraged European readers to regard them as "irresponsible agitators." As for Kenyatta, the press led Kenya Europeans to believe he would never return; and later, when this was proved false, that no European would serve under him. What sort of service to the future or to the readers was that?

If these are explained away as "honest mistakes of short-sighted men who will learn better with guidance" (I don't accept such an excuse, but people may make it), here is an example of inexcusable slanting of a news event through the use of colorful words. It was the lead story in the *Northern News* of Ndola, the only daily newspaper in Northern Rhodesia and one of a newspaper group with a parent company in South Africa, a group which has a virtual monopoly throughout the Rhodesias. The story deals with the return in December 1962 of Dr. Kamuzu Banda from the smoothest and most good-tempered of London constitutional conferences:

Dr. Hastings Banda, leader of Nyasaland's ruling Malawi Party and probable Prime Minister after self-rule, returned here in triumph today to be greeted by a sobbing, chanting crowd officially estimated at 40,000.

Shortly afterwards he thundered: "We are in control now. We are the Government in name and in fact." After strutting up and down the airport apron, waving his fly-whip to the throng, he mounted a dais outside, to be garlanded and have a lion skin thrown about his shoulders.

Dr. Banda's speech was fiery but typical of a party rally. He did not go into detail about his London talks, nor did he make direct reference to independence or secession.

In a voice that became so high-pitched that he screamed at times, Dr. Banda called for an all-out effort in the future for investment, party discipline and solidarity. He repeatedly made bitter references to individual journalists and certain newspapers in the Federation and overseas, accusing them of spreading lies.

He welcomed — and warned — Europeans, including civil servants, when talking about Nyasaland under self-rule.

Dr. Banda, who is known for his abruptness with journalists, was true to form. He snubbed journalists in Nairobi, Dar es Salaam — and even in the air.

This is only a selection of paragraphs from a long news story, but in no phrase does the reporter come within miles of honoring the first principle the press needs to follow in its relationships with new African governments: to reflect the dignity of the indigenous people, their sense of pride and achievement. There is certainly preoccupation with the press's own dignity, and one can detect a martyr complex or death wish in the writing, the complacent belief that Uhuru in Nyasaland will mean the destruction of all "Western" values, including freedom of the press. Unless such journalists transform their attitudes, one can confidently predict a clash between them and a Malawi government. If, one day, some youthful journalist is deported from Nyasaland, I hope that before the international press rushes to condemn the new state's dictatorial attitudes the world's editors remember the tone of such a news story, and reflect that this was only one of hundreds.

How "free" can the press be in Africa? In the earliest days of journalism in this area, when the *Gazette of Zanzibar and East Africa,* edited by men like Cowpin and Magerditch (who was also deputy jailer at Mombasa Prison), was competing with the *East Africa and Uganda Mail,* freedom meant all forms of license and the *Mail* was often libelous. I would certainly wish to see the press maintain enough freedom to carry out its historic function of protecting people against corruption and the abuse of law by junior officials. Most new countries begin with commitments to that freedom of the press but become disenchanted when the press becomes unnecessarily critical — unnecessarily in the sense that the criticism shows no attempt to understand the problems of the governing party or the country. As an example, one of the daily papers in Nairobi published a leading article on the threatened teachers' strike in August 1962, making seven points which were either exaggerated or mischievously misleading. I asked the senior editorial staff to come and discuss the article in my office at the Ministry of Labor, and they all agreed it was highly misleading but argued they had not been told the facts before writing it. This I could not accept as an excuse, for the facts were available all the time, and if the editors had made a proper attempt to understand the country's problems they would have found them out from me or my colleagues.

The *Nation* group of newspapers, which came to Kenya in 1959 and has now spread into Tanganyika and Uganda, ought to be a good press — it has enough financing and technical experts to do an excellent job. Their initial problem seemed to arise from an effort to write on English standards. They were accused of sensationalism. They must recognize their responsibility in the task of nation-building. Among Africans there will always be suspicion as to their motives until they demonstrate a new look and genuine cooperation with the new government.

Because African leaders are trying hard to create unity, they become sensitive to anyone who appears to act as though he constituted opposition and did nothing but criticize the government's efforts. Freedom of the press in a new country has, therefore, got to be limited — not so much restricted by legislation as deliberately guided; for its main functions include not only giving news but also taking part in the national effort and contributing toward the building of a nation. If the press is to be guided for this task rather than restricted by law from the more destructive forms of criticism, confidence must be built up between press and government. When we joined the Kenya government in April 1962, we found this confidence totally missing, and rarely would any minister hold a press briefing to give editors and reporters background information for their guidance. The government was worried that the press would not respect confidences and the press was worried that these private briefings were simply to keep them in line and supporting government on various issues. But if the press gives a positive reaction, they will see that they win friends in government.

African leaders have often been critical of the overseas

press. Some newspapers, especially in the metropolitan countries, have adopted unhelpful attitudes toward the former colonies and join the chorus of people who wait hopefully to see mistakes being made by the newly independent states. They exaggerate these mistakes, generalize from them, and make them appear as the rule rather than the exception. They refuse to understand the problems and forget to mention the achievements of the new nations. Ghana becomes front-page news everywhere when a member of the opposition is arrested, but is it ever mentioned how school attendance rose from 50 percent to 85 percent in the first five years since independence? Again, Julius Nyerere caused an uproar of overseas press criticism when he said in a speech that Britain had left Tanganyika poor: papers like the *Daily Express, Daily Telegraph* and *East Africa and Rhodesia* hastened to justify the colonial period by reciting how many schools had been built, how many miles of road had been constructed. But Nyerere had never said the British had done nothing — he said they had left his country poor. This is the sort of mentality, rooted in opposition to change and defense of the status quo, which should be avoided.

Another danger in the overseas press is its tendency to judge each African nation and every African leader in the context of East-West power politics. To many journalists from such countries, Africans are either pro-West or pro-East; they are rarely pro-African. When President Nasser nationalized the Suez Canal, he was "going to the East"; when he attacked Russia in a speech, he was "returning to the Western fold"; nobody seemed to realize Nasser might be just pro-Egyptian with his own genuine African policies. Smith Hempstone, of the *Chicago Daily News*, who should know better after his years in Africa, defended the breakaway policy in Katanga on the basis that Tshombe is the "most pro-Western leader in the continent"!* I once told an American audience that I thought the first enemy of the United States in Africa was the American press itself, because it so often represents the American position in Africa as one governed by the American interests against communism. The reaction of African states is to avoid being represented as associating with the United States in her efforts to establish American influence against the East. Because of attitudes of this sort dominating press thinking, people in Africa begin to wonder whether freedom of the press is helpful for those newspapers or for the people whom those papers are supposed to be serving.

News in Africa used to be covered in overseas newspapers by correspondents who flew in overnight from New York or London. In my speech in Paris to the International Press Institute, I criticized those correspondents who "after twenty minutes in Africa write pungent stuff which seeks to turn back the clock of history at a time when the production of our history needs sympathy, sagacity, cold reason to help it to reality and make it all worthwhile." Recently there has been a tendency to station staff correspondents in Africa, many of them being based in Nairobi. This should certainly mean they write from wider foundations of knowledge, and one hopes their sympathy also expands. Another good trend has been the setting up of training courses for African journalists. The temptation for a good African journalist to find more rewarding employment in government or politics has meant that standards among African newspapermen were low. After an IPI survey, a six-month training course for sixteen journalists from several countries was planned, to be attached to the Royal College, Nairobi, and

* In Hempstone's book *Katanga Report*, London, 1962.

supervised by Tom Hopkinson, former editor of *Picture Post* and *Drum*. It is too early to see how this course, excellent in theory, works out in practice; an important factor in its success or failure will be the degree of encouragement the tutors show with the main theme of this chapter: that journalists must write from a basic sympathy with the national effort. A second IPI course is being started in Lagos and soon West Africans may also judge this venture.

If independent newspapers are unsympathetic, new states tend to resort to government newspapers. They may also take this step if private investment is too small for an independent newspaper to be set up effectively. The scope of a party paper is limited, because it has to aim at serving the party membership and spreading party propaganda. There is room for a government-sponsored press, although the danger in a government-controlled press is that it reports only what the government ministers want to read. I would have thought that in the circumstances of all our countries, we could best have the press run on the basis of a public corporation, in the same way that Kenya's radio and television services are run. This does not exclude, of course, the establishment of private and independent papers when there is sufficient private investment to set them up.

Just as the press must be founded on a basic sympathy with the national movement, so must the universities and other academic institutions. It is sometimes suggested that in one-party states, as many countries in Africa will be, the universities and the press should serve an extra role as institutions which focus constructive criticism of government policies. I cannot agree with this: I do not think any institution should be set up with the aim of focusing criticism. Universities should be politically independent, certainly. Education should be available to everyone regardless of his religious faith or his politics, and there should be academic independence so that he can obtain his knowledge in any form he wants it. What he does with this knowledge is another question. But academic independence should be there for this reason rather than for the university to become a focus of criticism.

Freedom to analyze and expose government policies at a university is important, if clear thinking is to be done. Intellectual freedom must be maintained for the sake of the country's future. This may bring some lecturers into the position of supporting an opposition, if they feel this is where their logic takes them. But that is very different from a university's organizing itself into a continuing opposition; if a university begins to do that, it ceases to be the independent institution it should be. I wholly agree with some African leaders that it is wrong for any university to set itself up as an alternative to a political opposition and for lecturers there deliberately to begin organizing themselves into groups which are intended to oppose the government.

A. L. Adu, Secretary-General of the Common Services Organization, made several wise comments when moving the bill to set up a University of East Africa* in 1963: "The role of the university in developing East Africa is immense. It should not follow the Oxbridge tradition of pursuing knowledge for its own sake, but must tackle the problems which are facing East Africa and contribute to their solution. It should imbue its students with a sense of urgency, and

---

* Makerere College in Uganda has been East Africa's "university" for thirty years; the Royal College in Nairobi converted itself from a technical college to a university college in 1961; and the Dar es Salaam University College began the same year with a small law school. In 1963 the three university colleges were drawn together as the University of East Africa.

should be an African university in the sense that it reflects the needs and priorities of Africa, not a pale reflection of alien universities."

And he went on to warn that if these objectives were not pursued, the university would move in one direction and the East African territories and their needs would move in another. This would be the point at which academic freedom would begin to be questioned. Neither he nor I intend any threat to universities that academic freedom "is all right as long as you support the government." It is simply that if universities are to be appreciated by the people, they must be attuned to the national mood.

One of the biggest challenges of nation-building is set when you have immigrant communities. This problem is most acute in East and Central Africa, in the Congo, and in Algeria. Fears about the future of an immigrant minority have been played up often in the hope of delaying independence. When we have asked British ministers why Ghana should be independent and not Kenya, we have been told more often than not that there is a big difference between the West African and the East African. I have failed to see any difference — except for one: they have more mosquitoes than we have.

The lack of mosquitoes led to Kenya's being called a "white man's country" by Sir Charles Eliot. Since his day, we have gone through other stages of relationship with the immigrants and have had other titles given to this relationship. The 1923 Devonshire Declaration said that when there was a clash of interests between the indigenous and the immigrant people, the interests of the indigenous people should be paramount. But paramountcy of African interests was never upheld. Only when the nationalist movement became

organized and effective did the white settlers and the colonial powers recast their supremacist policies, and their reaction to the nationalist onslaught was to introduce new
slogans in Kenya and Central Africa. These countries, it
was hastily said, were "multiracial" states, dedicated to the
"partnership" of the races.

They tried multiracialism first. White supremacy was
dead, but multiracialism was soon qualified to mean that
each race was contained in its own compartment and that
from the European compartment should come the leadership, since the experience and "civilization" were there.
When we rejected multiracialism and said we stood for non-
racialism, the compartments were broken down a little and
the theory of partnership of the races was produced. It was
given its longest run in the Federation of Rhodesia and
Nyasaland, being written into the preamble of the Federal
Constitution as the basis of policy; but the first Federal
Prime Minister, Lord Malvern, gave the game away when
he explained it was "the partnership of horse and rider."

Partnership was accepted by those Africans to whom I referred earlier when I said colonialism had created a group
with an inferiority complex, a group which accepted that
for their lifetime the African status would be that of a junior partner. But Joshua Nkomo of Southern Rhodesia ridi-
culed the whole idea in front of Sir Edgar Whitehead when
he asked why, if the Europeans had been "trustees" for the
Africans, they had now suddenly chosen to be partners.
The logical development, he told Whitehead, should be for
the trustee to remain only so long as he is needed and then
surrender his trusteeship.

After multiracialism and partnership had both been repudiated, a number of Europeans came up with the idea of
"liberalism." Among them were Sir Michael Blundell in

Kenya, Sir John Moffat in Northern Rhodesia, and Garfield Todd when he was still in power in Southern Rhodesia. They came forward to try to create a halfway house between white supremacy and what they called "extreme nationalism." They could not be accepted fully by any nationalist, but they served a purpose in helping their own people face the realities of the change which was taking place around them. They were courageous enough to recognize the coming change but not brave enough to acknowledge its full impact. They wanted to leave an emergency exit and refused to give up the past completely. They always pleaded for time and talked of the need for preparation, the need to "develop the African sufficiently so that he can take his place, his rightful place . . ." They also spoke (more quietly) of the need for Africans to recognize European participation in government as vital for development.

So the European "liberal" is often mistrusted, because he will not completely accept the new order. It was this mistrust which led to the failure of Michael Blundell. When he formed his New Kenya Group in April 1960, overseas newspapers interpreted this move not only as a stride toward greater understanding between Europeans and Africans but actually as the only means which could safeguard European interests in the new Kenya. Some papers even went to the extent of saying Blundell could become the unifying force in Kenya and emerge as the first Prime Minister. But this was a clear underestimate of the strength of nationalism, and of its sense of urgency.

There is no real room in Africa for European "liberals" of this sort. What Africa needs is the man or woman who as an individual adapts himself or herself completely to the new system. In all the constitutions of East Africa there is provision for immigrants to become full citizens of the new independent states. As citizens they will have equal rights with everyone else, but separate European representation on development bodies and in the legislature is a feature of the past.

Some Europeans and Asians become alarmed because they find that although they are allowed to become full citizens, they cannot for an initial period join the political party of the nationalist movement. This was, for instance, the case during Tanganyika's first year of independence. Such people must try to understand African feelings in resisting certain changes, just as the immigrants once pleaded with Africans to understand their feelings in resisting changes. Many Africans feel they cannot completely accept with implicit confidence every European as a fellow citizen. This suspicion will be resolved not only by the passage of time but more effectively by the actions of the European settlers themselves.

Julius Nyerere once posed in a pamphlet the question "What would I do if I were a European in Tanganyika?" His answer, in effect, was "I would stop worrying about my future. I would say to myself that I had certain advantages over my fellow citizens, certain talents more developed. I would make those talents available in the general interests of the country, and my presence would be felt through my contribution. I would make myself needed, rather than keep asking whether I would be needed."

There is a good deal of worthwhile advice in those remarks. The European has to help the African forget past indignities and racial discrimination. He cannot afford to leave this to the good nature of Africans, because, being human, there are bound to be Africans who will want after independence to teach the European a lesson. It is the same human feeling which existed in Europe against the Germans after 1945. The challenge of acting in such a way that Africans can bury the past really faces the immigrant minorities.

One test Africans will apply is that of how many Europeans and Asians apply for citizenship and prove they are serious about staying in Africa. The figures in Tanganyika, so often held up as a model of race relations, are not very cheering. After nearly a year of independence, only forty Europeans and twenty-five hundred Asians had applied for citizenship. This must lead Africans to doubt the sincerity of immigrants who continually talk about being Tanganyikans.

For this reason, I do not think the offer of "dual citizenship" is a wise move. It does not help our kind of societies to integrate rapidly if some hold back from considering themselves as part of a single nation. If a European insists that he must retain dual citizenship, Africans are bound to think: "This man says he is a Kenyan but wants to keep an emergency exit which I as an African citizen do not have." The test of sincerity is, has he given up everything else to become a Kenya citizen? Is he with us in the same melting pot?

The ownership of land must, in my opinion, be tied to the taking of citizenship. Land is such an important asset and such an emotional issue that it should be given only to those who have declared their faith in the country and not to those who merely want to use it for business speculation. I made this point to an audience of white farmers at Eldoret in July 1962, and their Convention of Associations published a circular calling me "brutally frank" and arguing that:

Convention has always maintained that anyone who changes his citizenship should do so from a sense of conviction and from a desire to identify himself with the new state, and not merely in order to retain certain rights and privileges.

They had clearly misunderstood my point. In my view, the taking of citizenship is the test of identification, and identification is the prime consideration, to be placed far ahead of any calculation that a man should take citizenship to hold on to his land.

The economics of the big coffee and tea plantations present a slightly different case, but an exception over citizenship for plantation owners should be only temporary. There was a good deal of alarm after my Eldoret speech, and we had to emphasize two points in the following week: first, that people would be given three to five years to decide whether to take out citizenship, and second, that citizens of another Commonwealth country should enjoy the privileges which were fixed by such reciprocal arrangements. Also we made it clear that the maintenance of urban businesses and suburban small holdings would not be tied to citizenship. But in any event, absentee landlords, owning large farms run by a manager while the landlord lives in London, cannot be tolerated. A KADU spokesman replied to my speech with the question, "How do you expect people to invest in agriculture if they have to become citizens? We simply ask that such investors be obedient and loyal to Kenya." My answer is that we should not want agricultural investment of that sort. The best way to ensure they are loyal is to stipulate that they become citizens.

Another question to face during the process of nation-building is how long the policy of "Africanization," both in the civil service and elsewhere, should continue and how soon it can be replaced by the criterion of merit. We must recognize that Africanization is bound to go on for some time, until we have resolved the problems of citizenship and social integration and adjusting the artificial imbalance created by deliberate policies of race discrimination during colonial rule. Any African state which wants to have a loyal and disciplined and sacrificing public service will insist that the important positions are manned by Africans, certainly in the early years.

I told the Kenya Indian Congress in July 1962: "There is no intention to replace present privilege with African privilege, but a true Kenyan — irrespective of his race or creed — must be entitled to some degree of privilege in his mother country. In the past the African has been underprivileged and therefore, in the early stages at least, 'localization' is bound to give the appearance that it is primarily Africanization, as indeed by force of numbers it is."

At that same meeting it appeared I had put a cat among the pigeons by telling the Indian Congress that "cocktail integration is not enough. You must be prepared to revise some of your long-established conceptions. For instance, an integrated community can lead to intermarriage between the members of that community — and why not?"

There was widespread reaction from Asians against these remarks, but I was not disappointed in that. The more people speak publicly about such matters, the better. There will be more intermarriage during the next twenty years or so, and I welcome the prospect. We have to break the myth that there is something wrong with different races marrying each other, that intermarriage leads to an extinction of values and civilized standards. The example of the West Indies should be enough to convince us that this is a false argument. On the other hand, intermarriage is not intended to be a goal or policy or a subject on which to legislate. It remains a matter for free and voluntary and natural decision. What is in fact referred to is that group of people who pretend to be Kenyans but want to live in social and racial compartments. Such people are hypocrites.

The feelings aroused at the Indian Congress meeting brought out more clearly than anything I could say myself the problem we face of bridging social gaps between the races before we can claim we are a united nation. Again, most of the white farmers at the meeting in Eldoret had lived for a generation in Kenya, yet it was the first time that Europeans in that area had ever listened to an African leader. The correspondent of the *Kenya Weekly News* ended his account of the meeting by saying: "On the grass, outside the Town Hall, stood the Van Rensburg trek wagon. Like that wagon, we have all come a long way on a stony, hard track." I hope, for their sakes, that the Afrikaner and English farmers around Eldoret and everywhere else in the Kenya highlands realize that there is still much of that stony track ahead of them.

The Asian community, which in Kenya is twice the size of the European and in Uganda and Tanganyika many times the size, does not receive the same agonizing appraisal from newspapers, presumably because the newspapers are mostly European-owned and the administrations have been subject to European influence. But their need to integrate swiftly and wipe out the memory of discrimination is probably greater than among Europeans, many of whom can leave East Africa if they cannot adapt to change. The majority of Asians here have no other home.

For this reason, I think the leaders of the various Asian communities have often in the past betrayed the interests of their people. The overwhelming majority of the Indian community in Kenya supported the African stand and wanted to adhere to the standards set by Nehru and Gandhi as friends and allies in the struggle for freedom and democracy. Yet when the Kenya Indian Congress in 1955 declared its support for a common roll and adult suffrage, it hastened to add: "It will take time to achieve these ends." In 1958 the President of the Kenya Muslim League was quoted in *Drum* as saying: "As long as the Colonial Office has control, we have little to worry about." He was answering his General Secretary, who had said: "We have to worry about preserving our position against the Hindu; about our personal rights; and about African nationalism."

The Asian Muslims particularly have given too much time to their differences of religion with other Asian groups and have appeared to be sitting on the fence politically. The first Muslim to jump uncompromisingly down was the late Ibrahim Nathoo, when he startled other Asians by backing adult suffrage and a common roll (with no "It will take time . . .") at the 1960 Lancaster House conference. Later that year, the Kenya Freedom Party, which accepted members of all religions and races, was founded and allied itself to KANU until KANU opened its doors to non-Africans in 1962, when it dissolved with its job well done. It had set a proper example of identification with African nationalism. But those others still crouching on the political fence, and perhaps sending their profits out to India, must realize the time is late. As I said at Eldoret: "Either you are with us, or you are not even on the field of play." That is a friendly warning, not a threat, to men who I hope will become fellow citizens in a new Kenya.

It is no easy task, nation-building in new African states. But I see it as the most exciting and stimulating challenge anyone can face in the modern world. If the effort is successful, the power of human enthusiasm and the strength of mass effort can be overwhelming; it can indeed shift mountains. But success cannot be achieved by a few leaders. Every group in the country — political parties, trade unions, cooperative societies, women's organizations, business associations, youth movements, the press and the universities and cultural clubs — must play a full part, with no hesitations and no reservations. Men who look for others to give a lead, minorities who think their best policy is a passive role confined to immediate daily objects, will not be proving their worth. Every individual counts, even though this is a mass effort. And with the speed with which Africa is moving, every week counts and none can be wasted in idleness or quarreling. At my eve-of-poll rally in Nairobi before the 1961 elections, I read out to the great crowd the whole of Rudyard Kipling's poem "If." When facing the challenge of nation-building, nobody can claim to be playing a manly part if he (or she) does not:

> . . . fill the unforgiving minute
> With sixty seconds' worth of distance run.

~~~~~~~~~~~~~~~

SIX

Political Tactics in the
Freedom Struggle:
"Growl Now, Smile Later"

A S January 1960 faded into February, the talks at Lancaster House in London had gone on for nearly a
month. The ingenuity of the Colonial Secretary, Iain Macleod, had already been strained to the utmost to prevent
them from breaking down. There had been the early battle
over the admission, demanded by the African elected members, of Peter Mbiyu Koinange as an adviser. Macleod solved
the deadlock by giving us a blank pass into Lancaster House,
for us to put Koinange's name on; and Group Captain
Briggs had staged an afternoon's boycott to show it was
"morally wrong" to let "a Mau Mau" into the neighborhood
of the conference. For weeks in those early days of 1960
each delegate had aired his reactions to Macleod's opening
statement, in which the Colonial Secretary defined Britain's
ultimate objective for Kenya as independence and said he
now wished to see the introduction of "a wide franchise."
When tempers were rising, he had divided us into committees. When opposition to his first proposals grew, he had the
delegates working late into the night, so that anger simmered

down in weariness. He made his second big statement, and the next day was entertaining all the delegates at lunch on the deck of S.S. *Kenya* in the Royal Albert Docks.

Despite all these tactics — cajoling, wearying, charming, patiently listening to every repeated viewpoint — he had not succeeded in getting agreement on a new constitutional formula for Kenya. Then, on February 13, he called each group of delegates in to him separately. First went the right-wing United Party. He told the delegates his new formula and asked them what they thought of it. They told him they rejected it completely. He did not say anything in reply except "Thank you very much, gentlemen."

In the lounge after they came out, we heard Briggs say: "What exactly do you think that man meant? He didn't say anything to us. He treated us like little schoolboys."

Michael Blundell's New Kenya Group went in next and were asked the same question. "We cannot accept this formula," they replied. "It is premature to move this far."

Macleod looked at them and again said merely, "Thank you very much, gentlemen." They came out just as puzzled as Briggs had been.

Then the Asians went in. They said they would accept the proposals if the African members did. They were courteously thanked.

Finally the African elected members went in. We told Macleod we had reservations on four points: we had wanted adult suffrage and an overall majority in the Council of Ministers, and we disliked racially reserved seats and multimember constituencies. He looked firmly at us and said:

"Gentlemen, I did not ask you to comment on the proposals I have put to you. I only asked you to accept them or reject them. I understand that you reject them. In the circumstances I propose to withdraw the proposals and

send a commission to Kenya in six months' time. It will report to me in maybe a year's time, if that is what you would
like . . . Thank you very much."

Odinga, Kiano, Ngala, myself — nearly everyone almost
simultaneously — said: "No, sir, you misunderstand us!" He
used these tactics to shock us, and certainly succeeded. This
was the one reason why he got a "Yes" from us. After we
accepted his broad formula, he agreed we should discuss
the details. The next day, Blundell was accepting the formula and ten days later the conference was over.

Macleod was a master in the tactics of running a conference, and it was a pleasure to watch his skill. For three
years, from the time we were first elected to Legislative
Council in 1957, tactics had been a major preoccupation
with us, too. It is all very well to lay out the broad strategy
for a nationalist movement along the lines already described
in the previous chapters; but it would have counted for
nothing if we had not chosen the right tactics with which to
fight Britain and our opponents in Legislative Council to
gain our strategic ends. And some of these tactics needed
the most careful consideration, because decisions made pre-
maturely could easily have led to the undoing of the whole
nationalist movement.

The nationalist movement in each different country must
clearly choose its own tactics for itself, to suit particular circumstances. There are obviously no hard and fast rules for
nationalist leaders to follow, to gain majority rule for their
people. But a description of the tactics we had to use in
Kenya may, nevertheless, be interesting or perhaps instruc-
tive to friends in other countries.

The first decision we had to take came in 1954 when
Oliver Lyttelton as Colonial Secretary produced his famous
Lyttelton Constitution. The first African member had been

nominated to Legislative Council ten years before, and by 1954 there were four nominated Africans. The Lyttelton Constitution brought an African into the Council of Ministers for the first time, as well as increasing to six the number of Africans in the Legislative Council. It came at the height of the Emergency, when all the KAU leaders were imprisoned; so that it fell on the Kenya Federation of Labor to express the African reaction. We had no hesitation in rejecting the plan on two counts. First, there was no direct representation of Africans (the Governor was to appoint the six members to Legislative Council "with the approval" of African organizations). Secondly, the African minister was clearly going to be used to make the world believe Africans were participating in government, although in fact he was a tiny minority with no policy-making responsibility. The situation was similar to that in Rhodesia much later: the Federal government said it was going to appoint an African cabinet minister, and all that happened was that Jasper Savanhu was made a parliamentary secretary — not even a minister!

The African nominated members could not agree among themselves, and finally passed a mild resolution saying they rejected the Lyttelton Constitution but would not stop any of their group from taking part individually. So B. A. Ohanga became a minister and Jimmy Jeremiah a parliamentary secretary. Through the KFL and through *Habari za Dunia* (*News of the World*), a newspaper James Gichuru, W. W. W. Awori and I were then running, we campaigned strongly against the Lyttelton Constitution. It was the first time Africans had had the chance to deal with the positive side of our struggle and decide whether or not to take part in the colonial government.

Lyttelton had promised, during a visit to Kenya, to appoint a committee to work out methods of election for African members, and Walter Coutts (later Governor-General of Uganda) made his recommendations in 1955. He recommended there should be direct elections, but the franchise should be limited to Africans over twenty-one with any of seven qualifications: an income of one hundred and twenty pounds a year; long service in the army or the police or government; membership of a local government authority; "meritorious service," marked by either possession of decorations or a certificate from the provincial commissioner; and a long employment record in industry or agriculture. Multiple voting was allowed, and one African could have as many as three votes.

The Coutts recommendations provided a "fancy franchise" we obviously did not like. We had to decide whether to reject them completely and wait for the day of full adult suffrage, or to accept them to the extent of using them as a stepping-stone toward our objective. We decided to condemn the franchise but to use it nevertheless as a lever in our further efforts. The Lyttelton Constitution was scheduled to last until 1960; the Coutts franchise was designed to bring four hundred thousand new voters on the rolls; an extra two African seats in the Legislative Council were added in 1956, bringing the total to eight: so we decided to participate in the March 1957 elections and get a platform in the legislature from which to fight our case. We stipulated that candidates should be supported only if they condemned the Lyttelton Constitution in general and pledged themselves not to take part in government and be used by the British. The eight of us who were elected acted swiftly to form the African Elected Members Organization, with Oginga Odinga as chairman. We had organized a meeting for all eight in the same week as the elections, and before anyone could capture or inject ideas into the group we met and made a firm decision about tactics.

We announced that we considered the Lyttelton Constitution null and void, as there were no African leaders with whom he could have negotiated it; he might call it an agreement, but we regarded it as an imposition. Having established our attitude to the constitution, we went ahead to use the legislature as a platform. It should be remembered that in early 1957 there was no proper African political party in existence and public meetings were forbidden. So we used the LegCo as the main platform for African demands: demands for the release of the detainees, for the removal of bans on parties and meetings and movement, and for the removal of many other restrictions on our freedom. We moved such motions as a vote of no confidence in the Kenya government; we knew the motions would never carry, but we wanted to use the legislature as a platform.

We moved motions on every conceivable subject on which we thought we would embarrass the government, and by these tactics we mounted enough pressure to worry the British government and the white settlers and gain good space in the newspapers. At the same time, we adopted another approach. We sent a delegation — Ronald Ngala and myself — to England in August 1957 to tell the British public what was really going on in Kenya and what Africans wanted. We were particularly anxious to explain why we had boycotted the Council of Ministers. Lennox-Boyd, who had taken over as Colonial Secretary, had referred to our refusal to accept ministerial office as "a sterile challenge which is bound to fail," and in other circles our refusal had been badly misrepresented. We wanted also to explain to Lennox-Boyd why Africans stood firmly against the Lyttelton Constitution. These tactics succeeded, and in October Lennox-Boyd was forced to come out to Kenya, to try to find out what was wrong with the constitution.

Lennox-Boyd was strongheaded, with firm ideas of his own, and a difficult man to argue with. He came and said what he wanted us to do with a take-it-or-leave-it glare. After he had been a week in Kenya, the talks had come to a deadlock. We were asking for fifteen more African elective seats, which would give us twenty-three, or three more than the European and Asian elected members together. He wanted us to accept his "package deal," by which we would gain six more seats, and would accept the innovation of twelve specially elected members, four of each race. These twelve were to be chosen by the whole Legislative Council — Governor's nominees as well as officials and elected members — sitting as an electoral college; the plan would mean a selection of four more Africans by a predominantly European legislature. In view of Lennox-Boyd's toughness, we decided we would be equally tough, and when after four weeks he imposed his constitution, we rejected it.

Our tactics had been that as our first target we should win a voice in the legislature, and then effective representation in government. The slogan of "Uhuru sasa" did not enter the picture until 1958, although we had begun using the slogan of "Undiluted democracy." At that time all we were demanding was a declaration of British policy. When Lennox-Boyd arrived, we told him:

"If it is a bus ride we are invited to join, let us have in clear terms the destination, for unless we are agreed on this we shall certainly not agree as to the route."

But Lennox-Boyd would not accept our call for a round-table conference, at which we hoped a declaration of policy would be made. He kept saying that Lyttelton had made a "wise settlement" in 1954, and that there was "no prospect in the foreseeable future" of the Colonial Secretary's abandoning his responsibilities for Kenya. He said he was prevented by a "standstill" provision in the Lyttelton Constitution from initiating changes, but he found his hands untied when the three European elected ministers (Blundell, Havelock and Briggs) and the two Asian ministers (Nathoo and Madan) resigned. He sat down in his shirt-sleeves in Government House and wrote out his new constitution, which was thereupon imposed on us. We had to decide whether, having rejected this new constitution, we should accept the six new seats he had created for Africans. It took us some time to decide that we should accept them under protest but reject the two ministries we were offered and stay out of government altogether. At one point we considered whether we should not all resign our seats, but we decided we should fight on from inside the legislature.

A fortnight after the Lennox-Boyd changes were announced, Blundell was warning white farmers at Kitale to prepare for "an era in which the uneasy and untutored forces of African racialism will become apparent for the first time, and in which it will be the task of Europeans not to repress Africans, but to guide them." He was on his way to becoming the "liberal" leader we discussed in the previous chapter. Other European members were jubilant about the Lennox-Boyd Constitution. "It means," they said, "the common roll never, and no Ghana here."

They saw this system of specially elected members chosen by the whole Legislative Council as a way to avoid having a common roll. We led a campaign against these special seats, and seven of us were sued for criminal libel when we called the Africans who announced their candidature for them "quislings." We were fined seventy-five pounds each, and a great crowd outside the court greeted the news as a victory for us. What was not so happy in its outcome was that in the election of the specially elected members, Sir Ernest Vasey was defeated. Vasey had been Finance Minister and put up for one of the new seats (as did Blundell) to gain the extra standing of having acknowledged support from all races. We boycotted these elections, and so could give no backing to a man we knew was sympathetic toward us. He ended with the same number of votes as Humphrey Slade, and the farcical if very English procedure for resolving this deadlock was to draw one name from a silver bowl. Slade's name came out of the bowl. Vasey remained as Finance Minister after we proposed a vote of confidence in him, but we had decided we could not compromise our principles as to the boycott for the sake of voting for an individual.

The six new African members who were elected in March 1958 were all "rejectors" — men pledged to fight against the Lennox-Boyd Constitution and to refuse a ministry. At their election we began the universal use of the slogan "Uhuru" for the first time. It was time, we had decided, to fight firmly for a definite declaration about the future objectives for Kenya. I had attended Ghana's first anniversary of independence celebrations that month, and to a meeting of four thousand people in Nairobi I showed a flag with Ghana's date of independence on it and said: "No one will hand us freedom on a silver platter. We must be prepared to use our powers — and I don't mean guns and pangas — to achieve it."

Later in 1958 we decided to switch our tactics to a boycott of Legislative Council, because we felt our presence there was being used to give the impression that we blessed the constitution and were not firm in our opposition. The step was taken when we learned what Governor Sir Evelyn Baring proposed to say when opening the new session in November. By certain means we had secured a copy of his speech in advance, and we took especial exception to a passage in which he said the Lennox-Boyd Constitution was going to stay and the government would govern, regardless of what the African members thought. "The government is always open to suggestion," he ended. "However, as it is now constituted, it can and if necessary it will carry on the administration of the country." We were angry both at the content of this statement and because it seemed to embody an official reply from the Colonial Secretary to our request for a round-table constitutional conference. To receive a reply in this indirect, and therefore insulting, way was an annoyance heaped on our opposition to the present composition of Legislative Council.

When the Governor delivered this speech, we waited until, after three minutes, he reached this passage, and then all fourteen African elected members walked out simultaneously. Sir Charles Markham at once gave notice of a motion condemning our "discourteous conduct," and the next day Chief Secretary Walter Coutts moved that we all be suspended for three days, after Speaker Sir Ferdinand Cavendish-Bentinck had complained to Legislative Council of our "grossly discourteous conduct . . . insulting behavior to the Queen."

Our tactics were deplored by the *East African Standard*, which wrote:

What they have gained is a momentary blaze of publicity and the proper censure of the House, expressed in three days' suspension. What they have lost is respect, both at home and abroad.

Yet, when the three days' suspension was over, the *Standard* seemed to be showing doubts about whether our tactics were not, after all, rather effective. For its next editorial suggested "A New Deal" and said:

Who will deny that the art of politics is forgetting and the art of good government is forgiving? Why not try [the editorial advised us] another approach — through co-operation? What the 14 members apparently fail to grasp is the abundance of goodwill waiting to be tapped among those of liberal views in all the communities for legitimate African aspirations.

What the editorial did not discuss was just what "legitimate African aspirations" were or who was to have the main say in this matter of "aspirations." Our aspirations were then for a round-table conference, which would produce a one man, one vote franchise. But the *Standard* was writing for readers who were still living in the age of paternalism, well-meaning parents who knew just what we Africans should legitimately want.

Within eighteen months, Lennox-Boyd must have seen that his constitution had failed, because when we sent a delegation of African, Arab and Asian representatives to London in April 1959, he agreed that a round-table conference should be held. He was clearly worried that his plan, of gentle changes carefully controlled by himself and the Governor, was not working. Our boycott of the Council of Ministers had been one blow: Musa Amalemba, chosen predominantly by Europeans as a specially elected member, had become Minister of Housing, but the other ministry set aside for Africans had not been taken up. Since the beginning of 1959 we had boycotted Legislative Council completely. And the defeat of Vasey for a specially elected seat, after he had angered Europeans by saying over the

BBC that an African legislative majority was inevitable, be-
lied Lennox-Boyd's claim that this system would bring in
"liberal and moderate men."

Although Lennox-Boyd agreed that a round-table conference should be held later in 1959 (it was eventually post-
poned until 1960 because of the British elections), it was far
from clear what would have been its outcome if he had still
been Colonial Secretary when it gathered. We had, from the
time he instituted it in November 1958, been suspicious
about the Council of State, which was given power to delay
the passing of laws it considered racially discriminatory but
had no power to review existing laws. While the Colonial
Office ran Kenya, such a council was redundant, so we
could only assume Lennox-Boyd had set it up against the
day when Britain began handing over her powers to the settlers. Indeed, this is what happened in Southern Rhodesia
in 1962, when Britain surrendered most of her "reserved powers" and a similar Constitutional Council of a dozen Southern Rhodesians was established. Again, the Colonial Office
had clearly given its support to the founding, in May 1959,
of the New Kenya Group under Michael Blundell. Of the
forty-six members of Legislative Council who signed the
Group's first statement, twenty-one had been nominated by
the Governor and twelve were the specially elected men.
The rest were mostly European elected members. Just as
had happened earlier in Tanganyika, when the Conservative Central Office sent out a man to organize the "multiracial" United Tanganyika Party at the Governor's request
for a moderate party to push aside the Tanganyika African
National Union, so the Colonial Office encouraged the starting of the New Kenya Group in the hopes that a "middle party" could take charge. The NKG was very careful
not to offend European susceptibilities on such subjects as

school integration and the opening of the highlands to non-European farmers; and its ideas on a franchise for nonracial seats centered on systems like an electoral college, the Capricon multiple vote and (a few months later) an obscure "national register on a qualified roll." If the New Kenya Group was reflecting the thinking of the Colonial Secretary, as we thought, we were going to have a hard battle at a conference held under the chairmanship of Lennox-Boyd.

But so much else was working in our favor through 1959. The All-African Peoples Conference in Accra in December 1958 had turned the world's eyes to Africa and the liberation movement there. In the same month the United Nations formally entered Africa with the setting up of the Economic Commission for Africa in Addis Ababa. Within two days of returning from Accra I flew to Addis for the ECA founding conference, at which Dag Hammarskjöld spoke. This illustrates the speed at which events began tumbling on top of each other from 1959 onward. In July 1959 came the publication of the Devlin Report on the Nyasaland uprising and the revelation of the murder of eleven detainees at Hola Camp. Lennox-Boyd's position in the Tory Party was shaken by the Labour Party attack on him during two debates on these subjects on the same day. As well, we had by then almost perfected our international propaganda: after the impact of the Accra conferences in 1958, the American Committee on Africa organized an Africa Freedom Day rally in New York in April 1959, the anniversary of the first Accra conference. I was on a six-week lecture tour of the United States and, as I have mentioned earlier, spoke at the rally alongside Mennen Williams. Toward the end of 1959 came the British elections and the replacement of Lennox-Boyd as Colonial Secretary by Iain Macleod. Finally, before the Lancaster House conference began, Prime Minister Macmillan set out on his tour of Africa which culminated in his "wind of change" speech to the South African Parliament in Cape Town.

The five weeks of the Lancaster House conference in January-February 1960 not only brought the declaration we had sought, that Kenya was to be "an African country"; it also reversed the whole constitutional process. Whereas before, the Europeans always had a lead in the government and legislature (four ministers, fourteen elected members and the preponderance of nominated members to the offer of two African ministries and fourteen elected members), under the Lancaster House Constitution the Africans would have a majority in the legislature and a four-to-three lead in the Council of Ministers. The constitution also introduced for the first time a common roll, although we did not get adult suffrage. We eliminated the multivote franchise system and the unnecessarily high franchise qualifications which had operated under the Coutts Plan. The New Kenya Group had the new Colonial Secretary's brother as its executive officer, but Iain Macleod was not beguiled by kith and kin into accepting the Group's halfway house ideas.

Together with the gaining of more power by the liberal section of the Conservatives went a decline of Kenya Europeans' influence in Britain. During 1959 there had been a heavy traffic of European leaders journeying from Nairobi down to Salisbury to consult Sir Roy Welensky. He had won their admiration with a thundering speech about "never forget what the white man has done in Africa" at the 1958 Nairobi Royal Show, at which he arrived driving a railway engine. Briggs, for instance, came back saying, "Sir Roy Welensky is determined that the position of the European in East and Central Africa shall not be sacrificed." I think this scared the British a bit as to what might happen. They began to think there might be a point of solidarity between the white settlers in Kenya and those in the Rhodesias. Indeed, some of the Kenya Europeans began to talk openly about their association with Welensky and about how he would supply them with arms to fight Britain if Britain tried to change the constitution to their detriment.

The African elected members decided on one further tactic before leaving Lancaster House. On the eve of our departure, we presented a paper to Macleod and the British government in which we said we considered that this new constitution had come many years too late and would be out of date even before it was implemented, especially if the elections took a long time. This paper raised a good deal of controversy later, because when I repeated a summary of it on our arrival at Nairobi, people thought we had repudiated the constitution. What we had done was to draw Macleod's attention to the fact that although he had made a declaration of the ultimate objective for Kenya, our struggle was still going on and had lost none of its momentum because this matter of "the objective" had been settled. I think he understood our motive better than people in Kenya did, and told us the issue was by no means closed and he would, at the appropriate time, be happy to receive further representations from us about another constitution.

Tactics had to alter after the Lancaster House conference yet again. A big new question we had to face was: Who should cross to the government benches and accept the four ministries allotted to Africans? As I said at the start of this chapter, a wrong decision over timing can wreck the whole nationalist movement. Julius Nyerere had earlier had to face the same problem, at a time when TANU was offered three ministries among a majority of officials: he had decided to stay himself in opposition and sent across the floor Chief Fundikira and two other lieutenants. In our case, there were many weeks of negotiations. In the end, we asked Ngala and Muliro to join, together with Muimi and Dr. Kiano. This was still a colonial government, in a "caretaker" stage before elections which would give Africans a majority for the first time. The place for most of us, then, was in opposition, using the Legislative Council as a platform for general harassment of the government. There was a great deal to be done to organize before the elections, and this would be difficult if one were attending to a ministry at the same time.

When, and on what basis, to join the government in a colonial territory is one of the more difficult decisions for a nationalist leader to make. Our four colleagues would have been in great difficulties if we had not defended them at public meetings and made it clear that we had all asked them to join the government benches.

As I trust I have made clear by now, our tactics were varied because this was a way of keeping up the pressure on Britain. But these tactics would not necessarily work in another setting. For instance, some Africans thought they were using the platform of the Federal Assembly to broadcast their hatred of the Central African Federation but were later disowned by their people. We were using the Legislative Council to bring into the open accounts of atrocities committed during the Emergency by security forces, and in many different ways supplementing the efforts of others to build the nationalist movement. In Central Africa every African was against the Federation and against cooperation with it, and it did no good for any leader to cooperate with the Federal Assembly and bring motions before it when the only opposition that could be effective was being organized outside it. On the other hand, I feel that Joshua Nkomo did right in 1962 to reject the offer of fifteen seats in the new Southern Rhodesian Assembly of sixty-five. We accepted seats when we knew we could be effective. It can be argued that had Nkomo taken those fifteen, he would simply have been cooperating with Sir Edgar Whitehead (or, as the election turned out, Winston Field), and his cooperation would have been used as a weapon in the white government's campaign for full independence. In boycotting the elections he has highlighted the problem and — we hope — delayed the giving of independence to the settlers.

We learned during our struggle that the only way to get anywhere with Britain was by being tough, although of course this meant we were usually accused of being intransigent, obdurate and extreme. It was the only language Britain understood, because Britain was being frightened on her other flank by settlers threatening an open clash. I have had the impression about several colonial secretaries we have had to deal with that they would have come forward with more positive programs but hesitated because of their own backbenchers. Colonial issues only became hot matters in the House of Commons when settlers went over and spoke to Tory backbenchers, and then the ministers were subjected to heavy pressure. It became evident that the fate of East and Central Africa depended more on the atmosphere inside the Conservative Party than on any logical analysis of the African case as such. And if action in one colony, say Kenya, were to cause a bad reaction in another place, say Rhodesia, where Welensky might protest at its unsettling effect, then there would be pressure from backbenchers to do nothing. The number of contradictions — the way British Somaliland was handed independence almost overnight, the way the Wild Committee provided a liberal franchise for Uganda, which had no settler group

— shows that the only consistent factor in the Conservatives' colonial policy was a yielding to the greatest pressure.
They would not take the initiative in advancing the colonies: we had to be tough, vary our tactics, pile on the pressure, appeal to international bodies; and only in that way
did we slowly begin to move forward.

Neither Sir Evelyn Baring nor his successor, Sir Patrick
Renison, who took over the governorship just before the
Lancaster House conference, seemed to understand African
nationalism at all clearly. They behaved very much as would
any white settler in Kenya. Baring never seemed to appreci-
ate the force of the nationalist movement nor the determination of the African elected members. This led him to
believe that people like Blundell had more support in the
country than our group; and when we boycotted the Council
of Ministers, he was sure that within a few months some of
us who wanted a big salary would come forward and ask for
a ministry. He was quite shocked when no one came forward. Renison also mistook the mood of the African people after the general elections in February 1961. Instead of
calling together the newly elected members and discussing
future plans privately with them, he took it upon himself
to make a national broadcast in which he emphasized he
stood by every word of his earlier statement when he had
called Kenyatta the "leader to darkness and death."

I believe it was this single broadcast, in which he said the
new government would not change the policies based on this
attitude to Kenyatta, which really ruined the chances of
forming a popular and stable government at that time. He
did not understand that having an African majority in the
legislature meant taking them into his confidence and con-
sulting them before making such statements of policy. He
invited James Gichuru and myself from KANU, and Ngala

and Muliro from KADU, to Government House and asked
us to be there at 8:55 P.M. We arrived and sat down, and the
Governor came in with his transistor radio and said: "Gentlemen, I have made a statement which I want you to listen
to."

He turned on the nine o'clock news broadcast and we
heard his voice over the radio say:

"In spite of the great difficulty of conscience after the
Mau Mau horrors, it is not my view that Jomo Kenyatta
should be kept in restriction indefinitely. I don't however
propose to release him until the new government is working
well and until I think that the security risk can be accepted
and contained, and that the danger which his return presents
to the economy and administration and to our whole constitutional progress towards early independence has been
minimized.

"I care for Kenya too much to contemplate his stepping
from restriction to a position of authority. . . . I accept
that the responsibility is mine, and mine alone."

At the end of the broadcast, he asked us what we thought
of it. We said it was no use asking us our opinion because it
was already published: we completely disassociated ourselves from it. We asked that representatives from our two
parties be allowed to go to Lodwar and discuss the situation
with Kenyatta before the Governor formally called on any
of us to form a government. He refused this the first night,
and the next day called us and said we four could go, but
not Odinga. Gichuru and I replied that we certainly could
not go to Lodwar without Odinga, the party's vice-president. Later still he agreed that Odinga might go, but by
then it was too late, since KANU had decided not to go in
any case. Renison thought that it would be an embarrassment if he let us all go to Lodwar to consult Kenyatta

before the new government was formed; it would mean conceding that the man he was still calling the "leader to darkness and death" was the real leader of Kenya. He showed
great lack of appreciation of the thinking of the African
elected members. Had he behaved more tactfully, Kenya's
history could have been very different and the date of independence could have been very much advanced. Five
months later Kenyatta was released; within the year he was
a senior minister alongside Renison; fifteen months later he
was sworn in as Kenya's first Prime Minister. Yet for the
sake of a stand in March 1961, Renison turned Kenya's constitutional advance topsy-turvy by having to rely for a year
on a government with minority support.

From the start we had told Sir Patrick Renison he should
emulate Sir Hugh Foot in Cyprus, who had taken it on himself to meet the EOKA leaders and discuss with them the
island's future. We said Kenyatta was definitely going to be
the leader of Kenya, and he should fly to Lodwar and talk
to him. During all the time we were asking for Kenyatta's
release, the Governor kept telling us he did not know what
was on Kenyatta's mind — "No one knows what he is
thinking," he would say — and our view was that as Governor he should have arranged an early meeting to discover
for himself what Kenyatta was thinking.

Perhaps basically Sir Patrick lacked confidence in Kenya.

Nationalist tactics in the period before independence have
to take account of the problem of confidence. Everybody
seems suddenly to be talking about the need for confidence.
The investor talks about the need for security, the expatriate civil servant wants assurances. We have had to face this
call perhaps more than any other country because of eight

years of Emergency, with the dislocation and political instability which those years brought.

In general, every African leader agrees there should be stability and foreign capital should be encouraged and offered normal protection. But it has become obvious in Kenya that many people try to exploit this reasonable demand and use it as a political weapon and not simply as an economic argument. Some who stress the need for confidence are not strictly foreign investors at all but local investors (such as resident farmers) who make this call in order to defend their political position — for instance, to delay independence by calling for an "orderly" (meaning gradual) transition. Our reaction is: Do these people need to call for confidence, or should they not be taking part in the whole exercise of creating confidence? How can they expect foreign investors to come to Kenya and explore its great potential when they — the local investors — are crying to the world there is no confidence in Kenya? This is why we have called on them to express their confidence and put Kenya in a different light abroad, rather than tour the world exhorting African leaders to give greater confidence and stability to the country.

Some of the expatriate civil servants, also, tend to indulge in blackmail threats along the lines of "Do this and do that — or else we go." They make it clear they are prepared to desert the country which has done so much for them in their careers at the hour when it needs them most. This creates the reaction among African leaders: "How far can we rely on such a civil service? Is it wise to give in at all to their demands when tomorrow they may dream up new demands and begin to threaten afresh?" It is one reason why African leaders begin to advocate rapid Africanization of the civil service, even at a speed that seems reckless. At least by that process there will be a public service which will not desert the country when it is most needed, and by that approach there will be time to train a number of indigenous administrators before the colonial power departs.

The expatriates tend to think they can hold the country to ransom, and lay down conditions about their compensation money* — how much they want, where it should be paid and in what form. In the end we find ourselves in the position of paying out millions of pounds, some of it having come as a loan from the British government to the newly independent state but none of it being spent inside that independent state. In other words, the money is given and taken out at the same moment, and the independent state pays the bill in the end. The expatriates' behavior also leads to the need for having, during the period before independence, an expensive administrative machine: you have to create shadow posts and in some cases almost double the establishment, because you are unsure when your expatriates are going to leave and you must have local people working side by side with them, ready to take over at any time. This hinders the planning of a normal training program of the local people.

For these reasons, African leaders come to the state when they feel bound to ignore this question of "creating confidence." Most of us believe the only time confidence can be completely restored is after independence, and no action can be taken before independence which can give complete stability or confidence. The investor is going to say, "I shall

---

* Compensation for "loss of career" is calculated on seniority in the civil service together with the number of years by which the career was curtailed. On this sliding scale a man of forty-two gets the handsomest "golden handshake" — ten thousand pounds in a lump sum.

wait and see how it settles down," and the white settler who has decided to go will never change his mind, however much the British government tries to spin out the period before independence to make it appear "orderly" so that confidence may be restored. The real answer is to move swiftly to independence, once the decision about the ultimate objective is made, as it was made for Kenya at Lancaster House in 1960.

Kenya has suffered from having this period stretched out to the extent that a lot of money has left the country and little has come in to replace the loss. One of the biggest mistakes we made was to be fooled into believing it would be to our disadvantage to impose a certain degree of control over the movement of money. I know our enemies would have used the imposition of controls as a propaganda point, and might have thereby discouraged some new investment. But when the Central African Federation faced a small crisis in 1962, they immediately imposed controls, and so have many other countries, such as Nigeria, which like us were going through the period of transition to independence. When we talked of imposing some safeguards, however, Britain and the white settlers at once condemned the idea as disastrous and certain to drive away investment and undermine confidence. But we know now that the settler who decided to go after he heard about the Lancaster House decisions was never to be dissuaded by these tactics of the British government. He was only interested in how much compensation he could get for his land. Britain has agreed to advance nineteen million pounds for the buying and developing for African settlement of a million acres of the highlands, and the African farmers are to pay back the purchase price over a lengthy period. On principle, we insist that Britain should be the one to pay the compensation to the white farmers she brought to the country, and so there are large points in this matter which are still doubtful even today.

To anyone looking for a moral or a lesson in tactics from this chapter, it may seem my message in brief is: Be tough. I suppose it does boil down to that. The pressures to which the British government has responded in the last dozen years, the presence in Kenya of a settler group with influence among the Tories, the braking effect that Welensky, the ex-engine driver in Salisbury, had on British policies in this whole area of Africa, all these dictated our tactics. After independence we hope and intend to be good friends with Britain, and we trust the Commonwealth will survive and that we can play a worthwhile part in that unique community. Perhaps then "Be tough" is not the whole message of this chapter. Perhaps it should paraphrase the famous advertisement and read: Growl now, smile later.

SEVEN

Preparing for Independence

AIRPORTS in Africa are always exciting places. Even the biggest of them have not grown so large as to create an impersonal and casual atmosphere, like the outsize bus stops which American airports have become. The big and small have equal place in Africa: the tree-hopping aircraft of the Desert Locust Survey nudge up against the great jet airliners. It is the place to receive important guests, or for friends from all over the continent to cross paths on their varied journeys. It is the place, too, where thousands gather, singing and cheering and waving placards, to welcome back their political leaders from conferences and tours abroad, expeditions which may have had a historic effect on the future of everyone in the crowd. Buses tumbling down dirt roads, laden with passengers inside and bicycles on the roof, used to be the symbol of Africa, but airports have taken over that role. They symbolize Africa-on-the-move, in a hurry of course, but a haste that is good-natured and allows time to make a celebration out of the occasion.

Among the most exciting occasions there have been at African airports were the departures from Nairobi of young men and women on the "students' airlifts" to the United

States and Canada. In Chapter 3 I told a little of how the idea of the airlift grew out of conversations with William Scheinman and George Houser of the American Committee on Africa, after I had found that many Kenyans could not take up the scholarships they had been offered at American institutions because they could not raise the travel money. In two years (1957 and 1958) Bill Scheinman paid out of his own pocket for fifty-three students to fly from Kenya to the United States, but by 1959 we began talking of the possibility of chartering an aircraft so that it would be far cheaper per student. We formed the African-American Students Foundation, based in New York, to raise money for charter aircraft. With the help of Sumant Patel and P. K. Jani of Equatorial Travels Ltd., we organized one Britannia aircraft. I toured the United States in 1959 to get more scholarships. The United States government insisted no student should go without first getting three hundred dollars in cash; so families of hopeful students worked furiously to raise money by giving tea parties and in other ways and we added to their efforts with money raised centrally in Kenya. The first charter aircraft, taking eighty-one students, flew off in 1959. One of the students on this first airlift was Pamela Odede, who came back after two years' studies with a degree in sociology. We were married in January 1962.

During 1960 and 1961 the numbers soared as enthusiasm grew all over Kenya and down through East and Central Africa. I had been at first the only African director of the African-American Students Foundation, and there had been criticism that nearly all the students in the first airlift came from Kenya. Since I was then chairman of the All-African Peoples Conference, some people thought I had used my position to help my own country and disregard the needs of other countries. So we decided to broaden our representation. Julius Nyerere, Kenneth Kaunda and Joshua Nkomo became directors of the Foundation and we made the airlift an East and Central African effort. In the enlarged programs of 1960 and 1961 we sent 295 and 322 students respectively, although most of them continued to come from Kenya. From having only about sixty students in the United States in 1956, by January 1963 we had 1011 and another hundred in Canada. We laid much emphasis on women's education in our airlift plans, and there are now 132 Kenya women in the United States, half of whom are taking degree courses or other professional studies.

A good description of the atmosphere at Nairobi airport when the airlift students left has been written by Gordon Hagberg, East African representative of the Institute of International Education, who did a great deal to help coordinate the 1961 airlift. Mr. Hagberg headed a team which helped 147 students with a hundred thousand dollars granted by the State Department, through the Council for Educational Cooperation with Africa, a group of six American educational bodies. Of the task of selecting students, Mr. Hagberg wrote in his report on the CECA project:

They came in a seemingly endless stream. In persistence they outdid any Washington lobbyist. For me privacy was becoming a thing of the past, with students finding their way to my hotel room, waylaying me in the lobby, or gently enveloping me on the sidewalk.

He goes on to mention the problems of rounding up in a few days, students from areas nearly two thousand miles apart, the uncertainties of passport and visa issuance, the hazards of medical clearance and the general unfamiliarity of African students with travel requirements. Add these together, he writes, and:

. . . you get an idea of the complexities besetting a short-order mass movement. Making a list is one thing; producing the students is another. The reason for nonappearance is sometimes trivial, sometimes tragic. One student who failed to show up, we learned quite casually, had died. More often, however, the excuse was not quite so absolute, and one had little choice but to exercise patience and have a few "standbys."

The self-designated standbys were perhaps the most pathetic. They were unsuccessful candidates who nevertheless persisted in standing around hoping for a last-minute change of fortune. Their tearful vigils were sometimes punctuated by more dramatic pleas, such as that of one boy who got down on his knees and begged to be allowed to go.

Another student — a three-time loser — stood on the sidewalk, tears streaming down his cheeks. "Get a good night's sleep," I said, trying to cheer him up. "You'll feel better in the morning."

He stared straight ahead and replied, "I do not think I will live till morning."

Mr. Hagberg speaks also of how the airlift meant "involvement, on a much broader scale, of friends, families and benefactors," and pays tribute to:

. . . the sometimes tremendous sacrifices made by families to send a young member overseas to school. Selling a prized piece of land or incurring a heavy debt was not uncommon in the efforts of fathers or brothers to raise needed money. It was estimated that the students themselves, through friends and relatives and district councils, raised about 50,000 dollars. Add to this what the governments contributed and what was raised from merchants and business concerns, and it becomes evident that the State Department's grant for this project was well matched by local funds. This is in the best "help those who help themselves" tradition cherished by Americans.

Such large-scale involvement came into exuberant display when the planes departed. It was especially true of the second plane, which was the first jet to be used on a student charter and carried the largest number to go on a single plane — 136. Despite the awkward hour of 4 A.M., there were thousands on hand at the airport. Spontaneous singing and dancing, and the excited chatter of old and young, made a happy bedlam of the otherwise austere airport building.

When the students walked out to the plane, there came a cheerful roar from the crowded observation deck, topped by the shrill ululating yell of the Kikuyu women. A student walking beside me grinned and said, "That makes me feel good."

Mr. Hagberg (as you might expect from someone who was so sympathetically involved) has caught the spirit of Kenya's people as they face the task of preparing for independence. In this task of preparation, Kenya is at some advantage in that we are becoming independent after so many other African states have won their freedom. We are able to see from their examples what we need to take into account just before independence, and what we need either to avoid or to work for in the early stage of independence. But even without their examples, it has always seemed clear to me that the most important matter is the education and preparation of the personnel who will be needed at all levels to man the new institutions, the administration and the professions where responsibilities will fall on the indigenous people. Hence our concentration on a crash program of education, sending students overseas in far greater numbers than the British government was doing. Too often during the nationalist struggle our critics informed us the African people were not ready for independence because they would not have enough doctors and engineers and administrators to take over the machinery of government when the colonial power was gone. This criticism has never been justified. At no time has a colonial power deliberately educated the mass of the people for the day of independence. In nearly every case, education has been denied the top priority, since it was not a really lucrative investment. Too often the colonial power planned for education only to give an appearance to the outside world that it was concerned for the welfare of the colonized people; the other motive in promoting education was to train enough people to help the colonial power in the administration and the industrial and commercial concerns in their efforts to exploit the human and natural resources of the country.

In Kenya, nevertheless, a broader basis of education has been laid than in many African states — and probably credit for this should mainly go to the missions. In 1960 the percentage of boys attending the four-year primary course out of the potential enrollment in the seven-to-eleven age group was 107, and the percentage of girls was 55. (The percentages are inflated because children above or below the age level attend these courses, and others have to repeat courses. But the figures do give some idea of the spread of primary education.) In 1962, 918 boys and 154 girls passed their Cambridge School Certificate. For a comparison, in Northern Rhodesia, a country with half the population but many times the wealth through its copper mines, only an estimated 165 passed school certificate that year.

The really depressing part of studying the school "pyramid" in Kenya — or anywhere in Africa — comes when you see the numbers who have to drop out after four and eight and twelve years because there are not the schools, much less the teachers, to take them through the next stage. In 1958, of those completing eight years' schooling, 13 percent were able to go on to secondary schools; since then the percentage has dropped slightly because expansion of secondary schooling has not kept pace with the growth further down. In 1963 the percentage of students able to go on from intermediate to secondary schools had fallen to 12.3 percent, and one education officer Nyeri district, for instance, had the sad job of allocating twenty-five secondary school places among pupils from more than forty intermediate schools. The United States government has done much to help broaden this bottleneck. After the Princeton conference in 1960 on Educational Needs of East Africa, one hundred and fifty American teachers arrived the next year, and one hundred in 1962, to fill the gap, on two-year contracts throughout East Africa. Britain through the Department for Technical Cooperation has joined in as well. Such a program needs to continue for several years until East Africa can provide enough graduate teachers of her own to take over.

Higher on the pyramid, the situation is worse still. In 1958, the year we were planning the first airlift, there were only seventy-four Kenya Africans taking higher education (i.e., post-school certificate courses) in Britain and seventy-five in India and Pakistan. It was against this background of lack of preparation for independence by the colonial power that we planned the airlift.

When we began the airlift, we were criticized from many sides, from British civil servants in Kenya and from American foundations. The foundations had been in the field of African education for many years, but were helping only a few students each year: they criticized us for tackling the problem wholesale, and said we would lower standards by sending students to low-standard colleges. Looking back, I believe all this criticism was based on a realization that our airlift was a challenge to them, to the institutions which had paid lip service to the African struggle but had done until then virtually nothing to help. It was a challenge to the British government, which financed only fourteen students to go to Britain in the year we organized eighty-one to go to America.

Our reply to this criticism was an amused offer to come and help. "Well, if you think you can do it better, we welcome you to join us. Or would you like to take over?" And in 1960 the African Scholarship Program of American Universities was begun, drawing together 213 of the best colleges and universities in the United States. These universities are prepared to offer free tuition for four years, while the American government provides funds for boarding and the African government concerned raises, with local help, the transport money. By 1963 ASPAU had brought to the United States 503 students from twenty-four African countries and plans to bring another 300 in 1963. Britain, too, has begun to wake up. By the end of 1962, there were nearly 4000 students from East Africa there, and 1592 of them from Kenya. Most of these, however, were Asians getting higher education by private means, and the number of Kenya Africans had only risen to 195 in higher education. There were only 13 Kenya Africans studying law in Britain, and another 13 at the University College in Dar es Salaam. Uganda had 218 studying at British universities and Tanganyika 150, and again a good number were Asians. Another 110 Kenya Africans were studying courses of higher education in India and Pakistan.

While in no way decrying the efforts of many institutions and foundations which have begun to produce this improvement — and in particular the efforts of David Henry, former Admissions Director of Harvard and now administrator of ASPAU — I believe much of this better result is due to the earlier effort of the African-American Students Foundation. The Foundation had to do pioneering work in facing many different problems: it had to help students desperate for money, it had to find suitable candidates when an institution wrote offering places, it had to sort out social troubles. The importance of this work hardly needs underlining, but one might nevertheless recall that Dr. Azikiwe, Governor-General of Nigeria, came close to committing suicide under a train when he was a student in the United States years ago, and no institution existed to help him out of money difficulties. The Foundation became a universal adviser, financier and virtually an academic screening agency. So we put in as executive director a very active American, Mrs. Cora Weiss, daughter of an industrialist and wife of a New York lawyer. She became the mother-confessor to the students.

The African-American Students Foundation spurred on the Ivy League colleges to set up ASPAU, and it also stirred the Institute of International Education, which is a private agency handling educational exchange for the United States government on a contract basis, to expand its then small program. The African-American Institute, which has been active in African education since its formation in 1953, decided to open an office in Accra and another later in Dar es Salaam. Our challenge helped to bring these changes about. And other foundations helped greatly. When we were having difficulty in 1960 in raising the fare for the 260 students offered places, I flew to the United States at short notice. Bill Scheinman had arranged that we should meet John F. Kennedy, who was then still Senator from Massachusetts and a candidate for the presidency. I had met him the year before, and the plan was to appeal to him to find money for us from the Kennedy Foundation. A difficulty was that the Foundation originally concerned itself primarily with mentally retarded children. I went to Senator Kennedy's home at Hyannis Port, and we spent the whole morning discussing the airlift. I explained to him the airlift was a people-to-people program, very dependent on individuals in America and Kenya. He was very sympathetic, and promised to ask his brother-in-law, Sargent Shriver, who looked after the affairs of the Foundation, to see what money could be given to us. And so we received a hundred thousand dollars, which enabled us to pay for four DC-4 charter planes and also to provide some money for students who could not find enough by themselves.

This hundred-thousand-dollar gift caused a lot of controversy, since 1960 was a presidential election year in America. We had already appealed to the State Department and been turned down. Bill Scheinman had been to many State Department officials and had spoken to Vice-President Richard Nixon. The year before, I had met Nixon and also appealed to him to help the airlift. He had been sympathetic, but nothing had been done, and the answer we received in 1960 was that the State Department could have nothing to do with a private program. However, when word leaked out that the Kennedy Foundation, at Senator Kennedy's request, was going to give us one hundred thousand dollars, Nixon immediately instructed the State Department to find one hundred thousand dollars, even though we had just received a letter saying the Department had no money available for this kind of activity. Bill Scheinman and his colleague Frank Montero were called to Washington at once to be given the one hundred thousand dollars. But by then we had committed ourselves to accepting the Kennedy Foundation offer, and I had anyway advised Scheinman and Montero not to accept the State Department offer, because I was resolved we should keep the airlift a private program rather than turn it into one sponsored by a government.

The Aga Khan, who has many Ismaili followers in East Africa, helped the airlift program considerably in its early days. Several times I found myself appealing to him to help students who were in every other way ready to go but did not have the pocket money (one hundred and five pounds) the American Consulate required them to have. On the first occasion the Aga Khan contributed five thousand pounds to help the students, and he has given similar help several times since.

It was inevitable that something so unorthodox as the airlift should run into criticism at many stages. Perhaps Albert G. Sims, the American educationalist who was a member of the Kennedy Foundation team which visited Kenya in 1960, summarized these criticisms best in an article he wrote for *Harper's*. He set out the objections of the Kenya government in these terms: the program was political rather than an educational enterprise; the students were financed for only one year; the selection of students was faulty and would result in a high wastage rate; the students had chosen the receiving American institutions without guidance and many would be disappointed; and the airlift would cut the supply of secondary school graduates to East African institutions — Makerere, teacher training colleges, technical colleges and sixth forms.

Mr. Sims adds his comment:

There is point to these criticisms. In the main, however, they are probably irrelevant to the real issues.

African management of Kenya's affairs is coming at a rapid pace. A country with 8.6 million Africans about to be entrusted with the governance of their own affairs must arouse itself to the consequences of a system producing but 750 secondary and some 100 college graduates a year. In this situation the spirit of radical innovation rather than of cavil or complaint can be a last act of wise leadership by the colonial government.

But even Mr. Sims slipped into the camp of the cautious in the end, for he finished his article by saying:

Neither we nor the Africans can long afford the random mating of our people and institutions in the style of the "crash" program for East African students.

Writing in the *Atlantic* soon after Mr. Sims's article appeared, I said:

Most of these objections would be well taken if this were just another student-exchange program. But they miss the fundamental point. This is not an "exchange." We propose to send you over the next few years thousands of our young people because our countries desperately need the training which your colleges are able and prepared to give them.

The pioneering, shoestring, crash-through quality of our approach, our free-enterprise solicitation of scholarships by going to the donor college directly — these have been interpreted as unwillingness to coordinate our efforts with those of other foundations . . . While favoring coordination and cooperation with all bodies sincerely interested in African education, I sometimes detect in the American foundation world a surprising lack of confidence in the freewheeling spirit of American education. I would suggest that nothing short of such educational daring will do in the present circumstances of African independence.

Looking back, I gave more validity to those objections than they deserved. The Kenya Education Trust, set up in 1960 to raise funds locally, had representatives from both political parties and all main tribes. The great majority of students who went to the United States or Canada were not in the academic stream at all, so the supply to local institutions was not affected. In his CECA report, Mr. Hagberg analyzes the occupations of the 1961 group of students, and writes that the largest section were clerks and primary

In 1950 (age twenty) at the Royal Sanitary Institute, Jeanes School, with the principal, Tom Askwith.

October 1953, the Emergency. A patrol of Inniskilling Fusiliers frisking Africans in Kariakor Market, Nairobi. The African in the center holds a pass book.

April 1954, the Emergency. Police and three hooded men "screening" suspects at Langata Camp near Nairobi during Operation Anvil, in which thirty-five thousand men and women were detained — and Mboya himself arrested. *East African Standard Ltd.*

At the 1958 trial for criminal libel of African elected members of the
Legislative Council. Left to right: Mboya; their lawyer A. R. Kapila;
and Bernard Mate (who later switched to KADU and became Minister
of Health 1961-1962 and Minister of Lands 1963).

With Thurgood Marshall, of the NAACP, at the time of the 1960
Lancaster House conference.

At Howard University, with Dean William Stuart Nelson, after receiving
an honorary Doctorate of Laws in 1959.

The first students' airlift to the United States — students waving good-by to a crowd of over seven thousand at Nairobi Airport, September 7, 1959.

With Iain Macleod, then Colonial Secretary, at the end of the Lancaster House conference in February 1960. The whites in the background are Colonial Office men, not Kenya politicians.

At Embakasi Airport, Nairobi, on return from the conference. Mboya was secretary-general of the Kenya Federation of Labor (K.F.L. on placard).

With John F. Kennedy, then Senator, at Hyannis Port in 1960, when Mboya requested a grant from the Kennedy Foundation for the student airlift.

Speaking at KANU election meeting in January 1961.

Election scene; Mboya's face is on the placard.

Africapix

Crowd at election meeting in Nairobi. Mboya is wearing Luo elder's cap popularly worn in Kenya since 1957. His robe is not Kenyan and was presented to him on the occasion of his visit to Liberia in 1961 when he was made an honorary Tribal Senior Chief and a Knight of Humane Order for the Redemption of Africa by President Tubman.

At opening of Legislative Council in May 1961 (after six-week constitutional
when KANU refused to help form a government), showing support of all race
KANU. Left to right: K. P. Shah (with spectacles); Mboya; Bruce Mackenzie (
ister of Land Settlement 1962-1963); Derek Erskine (deputy chief whip for K.
group when they were in opposition); Fitz de Souza; Dawson Mwanyumba.

With Julius Nyerere in Dar es Salaam during Tanganyika Uhuru
celebrations in December 1961.

With his bride, Pamela Odede, and his mother and father at his wedding
in January 1962.

The wedding. The woman at the left, carrying flowers, is in Kikuyu dress.

The Mboyas, on their wedding trip, at audience with Pope John.

Meeting with Premier David Ben-Gurion in Israel on their wedding trip.

East African Newspapers (Nation Ser

KANU ministers in the coalition government in Government House grounds, July 1962. Left to right: James Gichuru, Minister of Finance; Mboya, Minister for Labor; Lawrence Sagini, Minister of Education; Jomo Kenyatta, Minister of State; and T. M. Chokwe, Minister of Works.

Signing the Industrial Relations Charter, October 1962. Left to right: Sir Colin Campbell, president of the Federation of Kenya Employers; Mboya, Minister for Labor; and Peter F. Kibusu, acting secretary-general of the Kenya Federation of Labor.

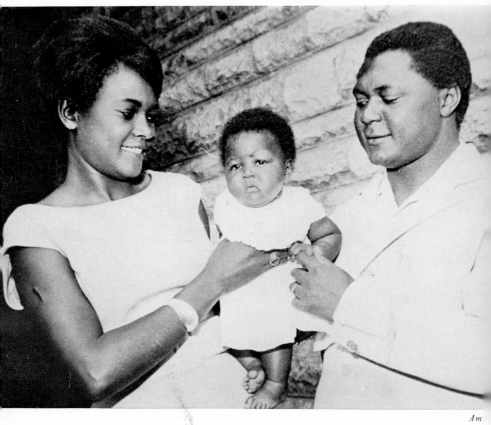

The Mboyas, December 1962: Pamela, daughter Maureen, and Tom.

school teachers, followed by secretaries, draftsmen, laboratory assistants, surveyors, postal clerks, salesmen and health inspectors. There has been a certain amount of financial distress, it is true, but reports have generally been exaggerated; and the argument that no student should be allowed to go to the United States unless the expenses for his entire four-year stay are provided in advance betrays a lack of faith in the students' resourcefulness as human beings. The opportunity to work during the summer and be dependent on their own efforts is an important part of their character training. Finally, in answer to the criticism that many were going to inferior colleges and so wasting their time, there came from officials of the Kenya government in 1962 what amounted to a recantation. A Kenya government committee toured the United States, interviewing 470 Kenya students to find out what jobs they might best fill on their return, and these officials reported they had been impressed (and surprised) by the standards achieved by the great number of those they had seen.

A humorous sidelight on the whole airlift project was cast during the 1961 general elections. Since the vote was given to (among other groups) people over thirty who were illiterate, each candidate had to be identified on the ballot paper with a symbol, drawn by lot on nomination day. Some of the symbols drawn were appropriate to the candidate: one well-known European reactionary of considerable girth drew a hippopotamus. I drew the ndege — an airplane. By this happy chance I was able to dramatize the work I and my colleagues had done for Kenya students. We chartered an aircraft to circle above my eve-of-poll rally, and we added the slogan "Uhuru na ndege" to the list of popular cries.

Early in this chapter I said that no colonial power had deliberately set about the task of educating the mass of the people for the day of independence. Yet education is the most important field of preparation for a country's independence. In every case an independent state at once begins to give greater emphasis to education. Within five years of gaining independence Ghana raised the numbers in primary and middle schools from 571,000 to nearly a million. Obviously there are difficulties in the way of introducing compulsory and free education immediately after independence: not enough schools have been built, not enough teachers produced. The process of moving toward compulsory and free education may have to be taken at three stages. The first stage is to ensure a place for every child for a minimum of seven years. The second is to set up a system of free but not compulsory education through secondary school. And the third is to offer free and compulsory education. Such a plan requires much money and work of expansion, but it can be done.

The need for educated people is so great that I often marvel at those persons who suggest expansion will produce *too many* educated people; there will therefore be nothing for them to do and so a worse problem will have been created. If we are to keep pace in necessary economic development, we must have a far more enlightened population. By educating the people we not only help their chances of getting better jobs and create a more skilled labor force; we also produce a better market for a country which is expanding economically, since with greater education come greater demands and desires among the population. There are also those who argue we should not be especially interested in having Africans fill particular fields at this stage; for instance, they say, don't bother about training African lawyers in Kenya since there are plenty of European and Asian lawyers there already. My view is that no field in Africa today is saturated, and to try to slow down the African desire for education or for specialization in various fields would meet strong resentment.

There is some criticism that by sending so many students overseas we are starving the three colleges of the University of East Africa of men who would help not only to raise standards there but also to further the hopes of an East African Federation. The ideal for East Africa is to educate many more at home; but even so, it would still be desirable for a good number to go overseas for further education. The experience broadens their minds and helps them to be able to interpret the thinking of foreign nations to their own people when they return. Such students are also needed as ambassadors-at-large, to bring closer to other peoples the ideas and problems of our countries. This two-way traffic should continue to flow. Traveling abroad for studies has also helped African unity, for many African leaders have made their first friendships with each other when overseas — the first postwar Pan-African Conference was, after all, held in Manchester in 1945, and Kwame Nkrumah, Jomo Kenyatta and Kamuzu Banda all met first in England. At the same time, the University of East Africa is one of the most important institutions in encouraging closer association between the three territories, and the graduates are bound to think in East African — rather than Kenyan or Tanganyikan or Ugandan — terms when they return to their own countries to work. Of course, while appreciating opportunities given to our students overseas, we must beware of attempts to use such scholarships for propaganda on behalf of the country giving the scholarships.

I have written at length about expansion of schools and

university opportunities. Adult education tends to be neglected, but it is quite as important. If we were to concentrate only on expanding the school-age educational system during the ten years around independence, we would leave out many adults who had passed school age. Adult education institutes — like the Jeanes School in Nairobi, teaching farming and cooperative and other technical courses, Kivukoni College in Dar es Salaam, and the Kikuyu College of Social Studies, concentrating on civics — have played a worthwhile but restricted part. But to create a more enlightened population in the shortest possible time, what is needed is a mass program of adult education.

Part of such a program must be a literacy campaign. To teach an adult the elementary skills of reading a newspaper, signing his name, writing a letter to a friend, is as important a provision as sending children to school. Someone who can read a newspaper makes a greater contribution to his country's development than his brother who cannot. A person who has to ask a young boy to write a letter to his wife for him, and sends it off without knowing what has been written, and then has to find someone else to read him any letter which comes back, suffers inside himself whenever he has to stoop down in this way. The fact that we can release him from this kind of embarrassment and shame helps him to grow internally and acquire self-respect and confidence. And this is a necessary part of the forces we must generate in facing the task of building a nation.

There is nothing like enough activity in adult education in East and Central Africa. Makerere College runs extra-mural classes with tutors spread over the territories, but these are not helping the illiterate people. The Literacy Organizing Center in Nairobi, generously supported by the Laubach Fund, put forward a plan for a five-year campaign to teach literacy to one million people. The plan suggested using five thousand primary schools out of school hours and working through a hundred and fifty-five youth centers where adolescents who have missed their schooling are now taught rather haphazardly. But the Kenya government, facing a demand from Britain to cut back on expenditure in 1961, actually reduced its social services vote and the Literacy Organizing Center's £1,200,000 scheme was stuffed at the back of a pigeonhole. However, the picture is growing brighter now. Tireless work by an American, Mrs. Helen Roberts, in organizing workshops for literacy teachers, writing Laubach primers in vernacular languages, and preparing literacy lessons for television should soon bear fruit. In Tanganyika, government initiative came at an early stage, with Julius Nyerere ordering one hundred thousand literacy primers as soon as he entered office. In Uganda the government launched a campaign offering free literacy "kits" and popularizing the campaign with the slogan "Be literate by Christmas." In Southern Rhodesia, a group of anonymous women who had run a successful "courtesy campaign" to break down racial discrimination in shops turned to the battle of literacy and joined forces with the Girl Guides, who had begun working in that field. Then, in 1963, the University College in Salisbury set up an Institute of Adult Education, which took as one of its main tasks the organizing of a mass campaign. It is too early to see how this will develop: one hopes they will heed the example of Ghana and Tanganyika, which set up bush schools, literacy classes under trees. In a short time this urgent approach helps create a new sense of purpose among the people, and gives strength to the government effort to establish self-help schemes.

Another part of adult education which has had even less

attention is the teaching of civics to tens of thousands.
During the Second World War the British Army showed
the way for Africa with the Army Bureau for Current
Affairs. ABCA instructors lectured all training units, and
the fact that Conservatives later blamed these men for their
1945 election defeat, when soldiers overwhelmingly voted
for the Labour Party, is an unwitting tribute to the effectiveness of this system. Adapted for Africa, such a system
can help transform ordinary villagers into active participants
in their own development, deciding for themselves where
they want to go and how they can get there.

In the previous chapter I mentioned the need to replace
the expatriate civil servant as soon as possible with a local
man. To do this, various institutions are necessary. Each
country builds up its agricultural and veterinary schools, and
most have set up, under one name or another, an institute
of public administration. We are thankful to the friendly
nations who have come to help establish such institutions.
In Nyasaland the United States government has financed a
polytechnic, and a New Zealander has come to head the
Public Administration Institute. In Northern Rhodesia the
Oppenheimer College of Social Service is supplementing
the work of the Staff Training College. In Kenya the
Agency for International Development has contributed
$830,000 to transform Jeanes School into the Kenya Institute
of Administration, Syracuse University has sent five spe-
cialists out on two-year contracts, and the Kenya government has matched these contributions with funds of its
own.

While we are grateful for all this help, the pattern of in-
struction at some of these institutions has its faults. In Kenya
the administrative course, six months long, was originally

designed to produce blueprints of the old British officials. They had their Mess Nights, when they punctiliously passed the port to the left (or is it to the right?). They spent three weeks at an Outward Bound course under Kilimanjaro, clambering along ropes and finally up the mountain, to "test character." They did military drill in the early morning. This training may have been designed to reform the bodies of the aging participants — one victim was a forty-five-year-old chief and chairman of a district council — but is that the main point, to turn out replicas of the British "officer and gentleman"? The system took little account of the fact that the past administration was a colonial one governing by indirect rule, imposing laws which often ran counter to the wishes of the people. With independence, the people begin to have a greater say in their own administration and their local government. The pattern therefore must change to an emphasis on direct rule, with the people taking an active part in making decisions from the lowest level to the highest. The district commissioner will have to be a different sort of person, no longer the little tin god we knew whose orders were law. He is likely to become instead the executive officer — or secretary — of the local authority, like the town clerk in Britain who coordinates a team responsible for different services. And the once almighty provincial commissioner has already been transformed into the civil secretary responsible to the regional assembly.

These changes are far from unique. In Tanganyika the change has already taken place, with provincial commissioners giving way to regional commissioners who not only ensure that the administration is running smoothly but as political appointees see that the party and the ministers are kept in touch with the work of the government in the region and with the thinking of the people there. Perhaps the best example to study in this respect is Guinea. There the system of administration was drastically altered from the French model, and a great effort was made to adopt a system by which village committees decide what the village shall do and what jobs each person shall be given. This system works best in a one-party state, where the village committees are a part of the party structure and the chairman can explain to villagers the details of government policy. There may be minor problems when, in a country with more than one party, the local chairman belongs to the opposition party. If election by villagers does not work in such a case, perhaps one would need to resort to appointment by central government. The colonial system produced a chief who was neither really elected nor appointed: he was usually a mixture, chosen by the district commissioner from a local "short list." His successor in an independent state needs to be either a civil servant, properly appointed and free to rise by normal promotion in the civil service, or else a locally elected representative and spokesman of his people, cooperating with central and local governments.

It is most important that the best men be selected and properly trained for the job of commissioner. For they can play a crucial role in seeing that the government's efforts to mobilize the population for certain projects in the economic plan are successful, and that self-help schemes do not falter after the first enthusiasm. In Kenya, as elsewhere, we talk too much about unemployment, about the lack of capital and the need for overseas investment and industrialization. We have done very little until now with the resources at hand: the two main resources of land and labor, which are abundant and far from fully exploited. There are estimated to be in Kenya five and a half million acres of good but undeveloped

land. And much labor lies idle because of the attitude of
mind among our people that the work they have been asked
to do during the colonial period has not been in their immediate interests. A new spirit has to be created, so that
people feel they are laboring for themselves, and that the
government's economic program is a challenge not to the
government but to themselves and the country; that they and
not someone else will reap the benefits of whatever sacrifices
are made.

This approach cannot go hand-in-hand with the attitudes
of the old administration, and this is an important consideration when planning the future pattern of the provincial administration. Clearly, therefore, the Institute of
Administration must be geared to produce the kind of administrator who will fit into the new setup, and the selection
of teachers is a matter of importance. You may need one or
two of the old colonial administrators to give the Institute
some idea of the past, but generally you have to rid the Institute of these old mentalities if the new pattern is to be reflected. Some short courses for senior African civil servants
and trainee-diplomats, administered through the political
science department of Makerere College in 1962, showed
the way for many institutes, with imaginative case studies
and stimulating informal discussions which were far removed from the semimilitary approach of the old administrators.

For much the same reasons, the control of Africanization
should be removed from the hands of expatriate officers as
far as possible and placed under a separate Ministry of
Training, with a fully Africanized Civil Service Commission. The expatriates cannot do their job objectively because they are invariably the ones affected by Africanization. They would not agree, for instance, that the top jobs,

like that of permanent secretary, must be the first to be Africanized; yet this is so, if the decisions of political ministers are not to be obstructed by old-style civil servants, some of whom will be sticking to past colonial ideas and methods.

In the period before independence, the Ministry of Defense, comprising the police, army, special branch and prisons, must be marked out for rapid Africanization. The lesson of the Force Publique in the Congo is too bitter to recall. After a slow start, the process has been reasonably speedy in the three Kenya battalions of the King's African Rifles, and eighty-four (exactly half) of the officers were Africans by April 1963. In a Legislative Council debate on the KAR the previous December, the Minister of Defense, Sir Anthony Swann, gaily admitted he had been "guilty of racial discrimination" by having four African officers promoted to the rank of captain ahead of the normal schedule of promotion. I replied that "It is not a question of creating captains overnight. We want an effective army and not a lot of pretty uniforms." And I proposed a government amendment to the motion of general dissatisfaction which expressed the hope that the training program would be intensified, and attractive terms of service offered to draw the best candidates into the army.

The last departments to be Africanized should be those staffed by technicians and professional men. Such departments as Medical, Legal and Works should not be disturbed unduly in the period before independence. Departments such as Agriculture, Education and Forestry will fall in the intermediate range.

In the changes of personnel during this period, there crops up the problem of the chiefs. Sometimes they are modern-minded and well educated, and can find important places in the new administration. Others among them have had their views molded fast in colonial times and are out of sympathy with the new spirit. Either these have to change drastically or else they are removed from office, as has happened in Ghana and Tanganyika. Some may remain as ceremonial symbols rather than active administrators, as in Nigeria, where chiefs were traditional heads before the British came. In Kenya that can hardly happen, since the chiefs are the creation of the British and enjoy no traditional authority. They will be replaced at location level by elected chairmen who are the activists needed to explain government policy and secure local cooperation. And the chiefs will be left to find their own level in the future society on the basis of individual merit.

One of the tasks of preparing for independence is to lead the people on from the political struggle to the more prolonged economic battles against what Julius Nyerere has called "those very real enemies — ignorance, poverty and disease."

President Nkrumah once pointed out that the struggle of the African people came in four phases. First came the struggle for independence, the building of the mass movement and the fight against the colonial power. Then followed the consolidation of independence, when the struggle was to ensure that foreign interests did not undermine the new-won freedom and that the government was truly the government of the people and not just a stooge of the former colonial power or other money interests. Thirdly came the struggle for economic reconstruction, where the biggest challenge is faced. And lastly came the phase leading to Pan-African unity. To some extent, these phases overlap, and economic reconstruction, with which we are concerned now, should begin even before independence. "Uhuru na kazi" was a slogan in Tanganyika long before December 9, 1961.

The first task in this phase is to disabuse the people of the attitude to employment they possessed in colonial days: "This is not my job: I only work and get a wage at the end of the month and that is that." There is no feeling of involvement or of being needed. People have to begin to regard their part in the national economy as a major contribution toward the survival of their own country. This can be achieved by ensuring satisfactory working conditions and the wages they deserve, so that they feel they are not simply tools taken for granted, but that the government and industry have regard for them. They begin to feel recognized as partners in the national effort. In fact, that nation-building is their duty.

We must also change the attitude of government and investors. Colonial governments concentrated on extractive economic activities and paid little regard to social aspects of development. Rarely did they believe in participating in development themselves: an exception is Uganda, which through the Uganda Development Corporation "primed the pump" for many different concerns from hotels to tea estates. As a rule, though, there has been too much reliance on private investment and private enterprise. To secure economic reconstruction, the first step is to plan for maximum active participation by government. This involves producing a realistic economic plan — as Nyasaland pre-eminently did in 1962, before Dunduzu Chisiza's tragic death — and being able to guide investment in areas vital for the country's development. The government must also set out its money policy and make clear its views about the movement of currency. It needs to concern itself at the earliest stage with building the infra-structure of power lines, roads, markets and all the other organization necessary to attract investment in various areas.

To face this challenge, we need the cooperation of all the country's institutions: political parties, trade unions, businessmen's groups, farmers' societies, and schools, to name only the most obvious. The challenge must be properly defined for them, so that they know the part they are to play. For this reason, we began in 1962 addressing different groups in Kenya — white settlers, Indian traders, the press and the trade unions — in terms of the challenge of nation-building. I was very happy with the result of some of these meetings: for instance, the trade unions and the employers' federation certainly see the shape of that challenge much more clearly than before. Businessmen accept more readily now the idea that their part of the challenge is to take responsibility for creating conditions which will attract further overseas investment, rather than to go moaning abroad about the lack of confidence or threatening the Kenya government with their departure. And, on broader fronts than business, the challenge has to be met of doing more locally and talking more of how, with limited local resources, we can best develop our own economy. Naturally we will still go out to borrow from other countries and will hope investors come in. But we must create the base at home, so that our economy does not depend on the whims or interests of foreign people who may fold up their tents and leave us any day, deserting us when we need them most.

Lastly, we should consider the role women can play in the preparation for independence. They have a part to fill in education, in agricultural development, in business, in the taking over of the civil service, in the trade unions, in the political parties, where they especially can generate the spirit of challenge. I see the role of the African woman not only in terms of her own individual challenge in the task of creating an enlightened family and community, particularly in rural areas, which many men have left to move to the towns; she has also the job of taking part as any other citizen in the overall development of the country.

A touching story, illustrating the enthusiasm for learning and advancement among older women, I heard about in Northern Rhodesia. A sixty-year-old grandmother with thirty grandchildren, Mrs. Anna Chilumbi, had had only one year's formal schooling when she was a girl. But in 1961, after all her eight children had been through school, she decided to recover lost time and enrolled in a night school where one of her sons-in-law was a school councilor. She explained that her main reason was "not really to catch up with my children and grandchildren, but to speak English so that I can mix freely with people away from my own home." Within two years Mrs. Chilumbi had gone ahead to Standard 5. That is the spirit which will ensure a country's development.

In Ghana and other West African countries, the retail trade is mainly in the hands of women: although the 1960 Ghana census showed that only five thousand women had gone to secondary school, more than half the country's women (a far higher proportion than in either Britain or America) were recorded as actively working and earning money. Most of them were producing and selling food, but forty-seven thousand were dressmakers, and there were even eighty who described themselves on the census forms as "quarrymen" and another ten as "deck ratings"! In East Africa our women can be encouraged to enter the sphere of economic activity more and more. Already they are playing an important role as agricultural instructors and have proved to be some of the best teachers of improved farming methods. They are moving into the cooperative societies and many of them are working in community development: the setting up with Israeli help of a rural social workers' training center at Machakos under Dr. Hoffert and Mrs. Ruth Habwe is an example of how far they have gone in this direction.

There is room for a mass movement of women, not as a separate political entity but as an enormous pressure group for advancement in a certain field. There was a very successful Kenya Women's Seminar in 1962, and the Uganda Council of Women has been a most lively body in the field of adult education. Its "Knowledge Through English" course of reading and discussion on such topics as "Sharing Responsibility for the Family Budget" and "Nutrition — or Feeding the Body-Engine" may be described as pious and worthy by people who affect sophistication or hanker for crime stories. Personally, I found the tales of Mary Mukasa, the schoolteacher's wife, who looked after four young children, kept her house spotless and put on a clean dress before her husband returned home, and who pleaded with him at budget sessions for an increase in the milk vote, both charming and worthwhile. I would agree with the description of her coined by her husband Augustine — "Flower of the Home." If there were many such Flowers in East Africa, we could revolutionize the homes of twenty-five million people. I hope it may still be possible to form a mass movement of women, who will challenge the government and the men in each district to give them greater facilities, and who will seek out every woman in a gigantic campaign for literacy and self-improvement. That will be the best preparation of all for consolidating independence.

EIGHT

African Socialism

Mgeni siku mbili; siku ya tatu mpe jembe. (Treat your
guest as a guest for two days; on the third day give him
a hoe.)

— SWAHILI PROVERB

IN Africa the belief that "we are all sons and daughters of
the soil" has exercised tremendous influence on our social,
economic and political relationships. From this belief
springs the logic and practice of equality and the acceptance of communal ownership of the vital means of life —
the land. The hoe is to us the symbol of work. Every able-
bodied man and woman, girl and boy, worked. Laziness was
not tolerated, and there were appropriate social sanctions
against it. There was equality of opportunity, for everyone
had land — or rather, the use of land — and a hoe at the start
of life. The acquisitive instinct, which is largely responsible
for the vicious excesses and exploitation under the capitalist
system, was tempered by a sense of togetherness and a rejection of graft and meanness. There was loyalty to the society, and the society gave its members much in return: a
sense of security and universal hospitality.

These are the values for which, in my view, African socialism stands. The ideals and attitudes which nourish it are
indigenous and are easily learned, for they have been ex-

pressed for generations in the language of the soil which our people understood, and not in foreign slogans.

All African leaders who have written on this subject are agreed on these points. President Nyerere has said: "My fellow countrymen can understand socialism only as cooperation." And President Senghor of Senegal, speaking at the Dakar conference in December 1962 on "African Roads to Socialism," said: "Socialism is the merciless fight against social dishonesties and injustices; fraudulent conversion of public funds, rackets and bribes."

I have, I hope, given some idea already of the reason why Africans call these attitudes African socialism and not just socialism. But there are other motives, bound up with the African reaction from colonialism. The African is anxious that his attitude of mind, his approach to problems, be identified as an African approach. After independence is won, he wants to see that Africa is recognized in her own right and on her own merits. This desire has led to a determination to establish the "African personality," which we shall discuss at greater length in Chapter 11. Briefly, it is a reaction from colonialism, intended to wipe away the constant references by people in other parts of the world to Africa in terms of British Africa, French Africa, Belgian Africa or Portuguese Africa. Africa has her own history, her own culture and even her own philosophy. There is a positive desire, arising out of what may start as a negative reaction, that whatever is of value in Africa's own culture and her own social institutions be brought out to contribute to the creation of the new African nation.

I wrote earlier about the task of reconstructing the economy in the days after independence. In the effort to do this, new values have to be established in place of the old colonial values, and we have to decide what part the traditional

African social and cultural structure can play in the country's economic development. Its main difference from the European structure, which was of course the one officially favored during the colonial era, is that it is communal by nature. Most African tribes have a communal approach to life. A person is an individual only to the extent that he is a member of a clan, a community or a family. Land was never owned by an individual, but by the people, and could not be disposed of by anybody. Where there were traditional heads, they held land in trust for the community generally. Food grown on the land was regarded as food to feed the hungry among the tribe. Although each family might have its own piece of land to cultivate, when there was famine or when someone simply wanted to eat, he merely looked for food and ate it. It was not a question in his mind as to who owned it. In many parts of Africa it was thought quite natural for a traveler to walk into the nearest garden (shamba) and pick some bananas or maize and eat it. Nobody would interfere with him unless he went in and started taking loads of food away. Then he was of course contravening the laws of hospitality and generosity, and exploiting the clan through whose land he was passing.

The same attitudes prevailed in marriage customs. Brideprice had to be paid, but if a man did not own cattle, it did not rule out marriage for him: as I have said earlier, cattle owned by an uncle or a distant cousin or by any member of his tribe could easily be acquired to provide the amount. In such cases, the tribal elders usually ruled that several people should provide cattle for the man who had no wealth of his own. It was not expected that he should repay them; instead, it was expected that he would do the same in years to come if somebody else's son found himself in a similar position.

When money was introduced, the African came to work for wages; but he still maintained contact with his native land as the only source of security to which he could look in old age or in sickness. He was secure in his mind that he could go back to his home and be taken care of by his people. It was a social security scheme with no written rules but with a strict pattern to which every one adhered. If someone did not adhere to the pattern, and did not take on the obligations inherent in the system, he found that when he next got into trouble he received little or no attention.

He was expected to live harmoniously with others in his community and make his contribution to work done in the village. When a hut had to be built, everyone was expected to go out and cut the trees and erect the frame. The women would bring the cow dung and the earth to make the floor, and draw water and make the plaster for the walls. Then the men would bring the grass for the thatching, and the work would be done together. The owner of the hut would cook food for everyone and the work would be finished in a day. If someone refused to take part, he would find that when his time came to build a hut, few people would come to help him and he might be completely boycotted. This was the kind of sanction which operated against the lazy man. If he persisted, and refused to help when there was harvesting to be done or weeding during the rainy months, he could be disowned and left to wander about alone. This was a strong sanction, because it meant he lost his whole source of security in life. Many of those who were disowned saw how foolish they had been and asked to come back into the clan; ceremonies had to be performed before they were taken back.

This communal spirit was part of the tradition of the early American pioneer — the customs of barn-raising and other group efforts which the eighteenth- and nineteenth-century frontiersmen respected as they moved West towards the Pacific. But in Africa it was never properly translated by the colonial powers into their terms of economic development. They tried to exploit it in the form of communal labor, imposed by an outside authority; they misunderstood the whole basis of this African custom, which is founded on common understanding and consent.

Another important part of the African social structure is the division of the community into stages of development. The young men belong to different groups: hunting groups, warrior groups and so on. Then they graduate into the pre-elder status, become married men, and began dealing with matters nearer home. Finally they become elders and wise men, who decide what the tribe should do. At every stage there is opportunity for contact with the group above and for joint action between three different age groups.

The practice of African socialism involves trying to use what is relevant and good in these African customs to create new values in the changing world of the money economy, to build an economy which reflects the thinking of the great majority of the people. Few Africans are so Westernized and detribalized that these attitudes no longer have their hold on them. Even most of those who have moved to work in towns still understand these values, and still behave in the same fashion as they did in their original homes and land units. The challenge of African socialism is to use these traditions to find a way to build a society in which there is a place for everybody, where everybody shares both in poverty and in prosperity, and where emphasis is placed upon production by everyone, with security for all.

African socialism has an entirely different history from European socialism. European socialism was born of the agrarian and industrial revolutions, which divided society into the landed and the capitalist on one side and the landless and the industrial proletariat on the other. There is no division into such classes in Africa, where states came to nationhood through the pressure of mass movements and where governments are made up of the leaders of the workers and peasants rather than the nobility who have ruled in Europe. So there is no need in Africa to argue over ideologies, or to define your actions in terms of doctrinaire theories. There is no need to quarrel, as the British Labour Party did over their famous Clause Four, about basic doctrine. African socialism consists in practice, not in theory, and one cannot argue its merits in terms of communism or British or Italian socialism. For some years it was said in the West that Guinea was "going communist." But all the time Sekou Touré was trying to interpret and implement African socialism in a form in which ideology is not important. He saw it as a question of getting his villages to work together and defining the self-help programs, in the same way that clans cooperated on their common program of hut-building, harvesting and so on.

It will be a difficult task keeping Africa clear of ideologies. There will be the Cold War growling its thunder around us. There will be professional communists and professional capitalists finding their way into Africa and preaching their irrelevant ideologies. This is why the newly independent states here are battling to define the African goal without being drawn into the Cold War, why they demand that Africa be left alone in these formative years to develop her own personality and her own brand of socialism. Nehru foresaw these same dangers threatening India. He never spoke of just being a socialist but always called himself an Indian socialist; this meant someone who lived by

Gandhian teachings about the welfare and security of the community. So it is with African socialism. In his booklet *Ujamaa: The Basis of African Socialism,* Julius Nyerere brings out clearly the essential difference between African and European socialism:

The foundation, and the objective, of African Socialism is the Extended Family. The true African Socialist does not look on one class of men as his brethren and another as his natural enemies. He does not form an alliance with the "brethren" for the extermination of the "non-brethren." He rather regards all men as his brethren — as members of his ever-extending family.

UJAMAA, then, or "Familyhood," describes our Socialism. It is opposed to Capitalism, which seeks to build a happy society on the basis of the Exploitation of Man by Man. And it is equally opposed to doctrinaire Socialism, which seeks to build its happy society on a philosophy of Inevitable Conflict between Man and Man.

Having sketched out the attitudes which foster African socialism, it is time to consider how they can be fitted into practice and how we can build an appropriate economy.

Perhaps the largest question to be settled is the degree to which government should participate in economic development, and indeed who should own the means of production. I look on government participation as absolutely essential, not so much because it is ideologically desirable, but because it is inevitable if there is to be the swiftest possible development and if the meager financial and technical resources are to be exploited to the full. Government can participate by owning certain parts of industry; or by creating the infra-structure which would guide the country into certain areas of development; or simply by working out an economic plan within which any development must be fitted. In any or all of these ways, government can maintain a course for the country, laying down the direction of development.

In a country like Kenya, there needs to be active government participation in most of these spheres. Government needs to lay out an adequate and effective economic plan and involve itself in producing power, providing education and health and social facilities, building roads and organizing marketing. It needs to canvass friendly countries for bilateral or multilateral trade agreements. It needs to set up a central bank to deal with financial and currency exchange problems. Nationalization is not a creed with us, as it has been with Britain's Clause Four socialists. But in practice African states find there are certain facilities which need to be nationalized in the public interest, such as minerals. In other matters, the best approach is to set up public corporations, and in yet others there should be direct government ownership or, again, private investment encouraged (and to some extent guided) by government. In other words, we will have practically every form of ownership, but all of them will work inside a development plan, with the direction set by government through its set of priorities. Our nationalization is not an ideology: it is aimed at providing services and opportunities for the community rather than at dictating who should own something and who should not. In practice in Africa, very few Africans individually own the means of industrial production; so these will — at any rate initially — be owned either by the new African states or by private foreign investors operating in the private sector.

The question becomes more complicated (although not much more complicated) when we intrepret African socialism in terms of ownership of land. I have already said that the possession of individual land title is an idea foreign to

Africa, which has only been introduced north of the Lim-
popo River during the last century. In the old African concept, land was the property of the tribe or clan and could
never be sold. This concept has been corrupted since the
introduction of the money economy: if you want bank
credit, you must offer security, and the kind of security
bank managers like best is a land title, it seems. So land titles
are bound to come, and in some places, such as Kenya's Central Region, where the process of consolidating land frag-
ments revolutionized the tenure system, they have come in
great numbers. But it would be a mistake to adopt this as the
standard system for all parts of Kenya or for all of Africa.
Among other agricultural tribes, like the Meru or Abaluhya
or Luo, it would be difficult to introduce land titles universally without destroying the sense of values which the communal system provides. Some may, no doubt, take the view
of the Kikuyu, to whom the possession of a title means a
good deal in terms of personal security. But this merely sets
government the challenge of finding a formula by which
people could be given title without destroying the communal system. The most obvious formula is one in which cooperative societies play a part.

Through cooperatives, a clan can translate the old tribal
structure into the modern money economy. Its members
can live and work together as they did before, but organize a
better accounting system and introduce a money market
without surrendering their sense of communal obligation
and security. There are three main types of cooperative
which African states and African farmers are busy assess-
ing for their appropriateness. There is the marketing cooperative, in which each farmer cultivates his own land separately but they all come together to market the product.
There is the cooperative in which each farmer owns his sep-

arate plot of land but they all work together, have a common accounting, and pool their resources of farming tools. And there is the thoroughgoing cooperative in which the farm is owned and worked communally. The marketing cooperative is now a universally accepted idea, and in some cases we are moving on to the second type of cooperative. The third type is possible, more perhaps among the Luo and Meru than among the Kikuyu, and the settlement schemes in the Kenya highlands offer us a unique opportunity to introduce cooperatives which might be of any of these kinds. With many large estates, totaling a million acres, to be bought and developed for African farmers over five years, there are existing nuclei for cooperatives in the outgoing white farmers' houses and sheds. A settlement officer is put in charge on an average of ten thousand acres, where as many as two hundred families may be given land. The schemes began in 1962, and from the start the materials were bought centrally and government loans controlled through the settlement officer. There is an easy transition from this state to a cooperative, with an elected committee of management taking over the job of the settlement officer as far as concerns marketing, buying and accounting. The process can be helped, as the Minister of Land Settlement has planned, by large commercial firms acting, for an initial period after the government settlement officers have been withdrawn, as agents and advisers to the cooperatives.

New African states have naturally shown great interest in Israeli experiments with different forms of cooperatives and Kenya has been fortunate in having the Israeli Deputy Director of Agriculture, Arie Amir, to advise us on what forms we could adopt. Any African who tours Israel cannot fail to be impressed by the achievements made in such a short time from such poor soil and with so few natural resources. We all tend to come away most excited and eager to return to our own countries and repeat all these experiments. It is thrilling to see such bursting activity, whether clearing boulders for farms or building schools, and to feel the sense of dedication and sacrifice, whether among girls doing military training or in middle-aged immigrants giving up all possessions to live in a kibbutz. But when you come to look at the Israeli systems coolly and dispassionately later, you find their introduction into Africa will not be as easy as you first thought. It would be hard, for instance, to get people to accept completely the kibbutz system: for the way everyone eats in a dining room and lives in scheduled houses while babies are left in a children's home from their earliest days would not appeal to Africans. More Africans are increasingly coming to want individual possessions, which they can dispose of at will and of which they can say, "These are mine." For myself, I doubt whether I could go so far in communal spirit as to enter a kibbutz for life.

Arie Amir explained in detail the workings of a moshav to the "The Kenya We Want" conference in Nairobi in 1962. He recognized that the African farmer was more individualistically minded than the Israelis who had formed kibbutzim, and concluded: "The basic solution, therefore, seems to be the moshav type of farming on individual holdings with very strong cooperation in all other activities like marketing, buying, machinery and credit."

Kenya has not been, until now, a good example of cooperatives working successfully. Only recently have marketing cooperatives, particularly in coffee and tea, worked well. Before then, government attitudes and administration virtually killed the cooperative movement. There was too much control and supervision, and very little voluntary initiative was allowed. There was much African suspicion that officers of cooperatives were trying to restrict African production, not so much so that farmers would concentrate on improving the quality of their crops, which in itself is laudable enough, but to ensure there was no unhealthy competition for European settler producers. The European maize grower, poultryman and dairy farmer had to be protected from African rivals in those days. So, when the growing of crops was not actually forbidden — as with coffee, tea and sisal — it was curtailed by government officials emphasizing the need for high standards all the time.

The record for Tanganyika is far better. Cooperatives have been encouraged by government there for thirty years, and the crops existed for organization through cooperatives: there were, for instance, forty-seven thousand acres of cotton being grown by Tanganyika Africans fifty years ago. The result is that the Victoria Federation of Cooperative Unions, grouping together nineteen cotton producer unions around Lake Victoria, sold £7,300,000 of produce in 1961 and own six modern ginneries worth £850,000. At Moshi the Kilimanjaro Native Cooperative Union, marketing bulk coffee grown on the mountain slopes by the Chagga people, sold its 1954 crop (when prices were at their height) for £3,700,000, and has built frrom union profits a school of commerce, a hostel, banqueting hall and library, as well as a secondary school. Tanganyika has more than seven hundred registered cooperative societies, and leading ministers like Paul Bomani first made their name as cooperative managers.

There are many products Kenyans could organize cooperatively. The fishing industry of Lake Victoria and elsewhere would thrive. There are possibilities for a textile industry based on cotton grown around our part of Lake Victoria. African sugar producers could cooperate to build and run a sugar refinery. The settlement schemes in the highlands offer scope for various vegetable cooperatives, and even the beef industry could be organized in this way.

Before I pass on from the subject of cooperatives and the example of Israel, it is necessary to sound another warning for those who think it possible to transplant to Africa all that has been achieved in Israel. There have been great experiments there which are useful for us to study, because Israel like Africa has been underdeveloped until recently. But Israel has enjoyed far more investment than any African state can hope to secure, and is probably the most highly capitalized country in the world. It is true she relies heavily on the sacrifice and hard labor of her own people, but she would nevertheless be unable to survive without the fantastic rate of investment, particularly from the United States. She has also enjoyed a supply of highly skilled professional and technical experts at a far cheaper rate than we can expect, for they came in as idealistic or nationalistic immigrants, whereas we will have to hire such people or train them expensively. Finally, there is missing in Africa the fanatical spirit of dedication you find in Israel. This has sprung out of the manner in which Israel was born, and the struggle which most Jews had elsewhere and which leads them on to a burning desire to struggle further and build a homeland for themselves at last. We Africans have had only one struggle: to remove the colonial power and the domination of the white settler before setting up our own country. We have not had to go round the world searching for a homeland.

Kenya has special problems in translating African socialism into practice because of its regionalist constitution. At the 1962 London conference it was agreed that a Central Land Board should control settlement in the parts of the former white highlands which were being bought for transformation into African farming areas. The Central Land Board has an independent chairman, and although each of the seven regions has a representative on the Board, each region decides the composition of the settlers for each settlement project. The Board merely selects and buys the land for settlement and supervises or administers the loans to the new settlers. This creates the risk that some regions may select settlers on the basis of tribe instead of need.

But outside the highlands and the other smaller areas of what used to be exclusively white settlement, it was agreed in London that the regional assemblies should control the transfer of land. So immediately we are faced with the problem of some tribes and regions (such as the Kikuyu in the central region) being exceedingly short of land, while others (such as the Masai in the Rift Valley region) have had great tracts of good land lying fallow for generations. Leslie Brown, the chief agriculturalist of the Kenya government, calculates there are four thousand square miles of high-potential and high-rainfall land within the Masai area which the Masai have never cultivated. In 1962 Arthur Gaitskell, while advising KANU on the outlines of an economic plan for Kenya, emphatically said that land settlement and development must be on the basis of need and not of tribal claims. He was writing as an economist and the pioneer of the Gezira cotton scheme in the Sudan. KANU leaders have to reconcile economics with politics. When KANU published the basis for its economic plan in July 1962, it said:

Land is Kenya's most significant national asset. To increase rapidly our national production and our exports to world markets, Kenya cannot afford to have unused land or good land being under-utilized.

And we went on to repeat our submission to the London conference, that a land survey commission be set up at once to classify all land in the whole country and recommend how the undeveloped and underdeveloped land can be better utilized. The next step would be for the national government to offer aid to the regional assemblies to help improve land in their areas, in the way the commission recommended. If the assemblies ignored the recommendations, because of some tribal feeling or some other local reason, we would consider that. But the assemblies in their turn would need to realize that they could not then expect the development funds which the national government would normally have allocated to them for the purposes they had now rejected. The national government would not think of taking over undeveloped tracts, such as the Masai areas around Mau Narok. This is simply part of the price we have to pay in Kenya in the cause of dissipating tribal fears. One hopes that after a period of paying this price, all tribes will come to look on land as KANU does, as Kenya's most significant national asset.

The KANU economic plan emphasized the need to diversify the economy further, a need made all the plainer by the problem of world overproduction of coffee and pyrethrum; it looked to the setting up of secondary industries in rural areas; and it pointed to the urgency of finding new cash crops. It was a general guide to the future development of Kenya's economy, and showed how a future Kenya government should fulfill the first part of the role of active participator, which I outlined earlier in this chapter, in its practical interpretation of African socialism.

NINE

The Neocolonial Threat

IT is clearly going to be impossible to put African Socialism into practice if African states, having secured political freedom, fall victims to neocolonialism. People produce different definitions of neocolonialism, but in general it means the continuing influence (sometimes political, but more often economic-political) of the former colonial powers, which effectively undermines the political independence of the new state. The object of neocolonialists is to make the new state respond to the wishes of the former colonial power and the money interests associated with it. Julius Nyerere broadened this definition when he told delegates to the Afro-Asian Solidarity Conference in Moshi in 1963: "Neither should we allow ourselves to think of this new imperialism solely in terms of the old colonial powers." This is certainly true, and neocolonialism is a real threat to African independence. African states have to tread cautiously in their economic and trading relations with outside countries. Their leaders have to justify in the eyes of their own people the way they have governed the country since independence: in other words, justify independence. So they have to find capital for development, skilled personnel, and also markets in the outside world. But all the time they have to ask themselves how far certain economic and trade agreements are likely to have political strings hidden in them, and how far these new influences might undermine the country's independence.

For instance, it used to be said that although Liberia was independent, the Firestone Rubber Company actually ran the country after buying a million acres very cheaply in 1925. And it is still said that some of the independent French-speaking states are victims of neocolonialism because, years after their political independence, they are still economically dependent on France. Joe Rogaly, writing in the *Economist* in August 1962, described the Ivory Coast, richest of the French-speaking states in West Africa, in the following terms:

A good way to get to the palace of President Houphouet-Boigny of the Ivory Coast in his capital city, Abidjan, is to stroll up the Avenue du Général de Gaulle and across the Place de la République. The President is likely to be out: he is abroad half the year, mostly in France. Perhaps one of his Ministers could help? The one required is likely to be on a trip seeking decisions from the absent President. A head of department? Sure, he is here, making decisions. Like the Minister of Finance, he is white, and French. . . .

The headwaiters in the cafés are French; so are the girls behind the counters in the smarter shops. Their fathers are French administrators; their lovers might be a soldier from the French base, or one of the petit-blanc electricians or motor mechanics who do the work of Africans. Like the 800 teachers (French) and the army officers (French), the administrators are paid in large part by the French Government; sometimes in French francs in Paris. . . . Like the shopkeepers and the factory-managers, all are making money fast, and sending it home faster. Perhaps this, and the fact that three-quarters of the country's imports come from the franc zone (and mainly from France itself), is some compensation to the French Treasury for the cash it must allow to flow towards Abidjan.

The cash flow is considerable; around £18 million a year comes from France in one way or another. Some is in direct aid; some in salaries paid; an important part in support of the price of coffee on the French market. Coffee earns half the Ivory Coast's living. It sells in France at an artificially high price.

Before I met President Houphouet-Boigny, this article had left me wondering about the Ivory Coast. It is obvious that the article is intended to dramatize the continuing French-ness even at the expense of the country and its President. Each country has therefore the task of asserting its independence and creating the proper image.

Some African leaders have thought that the best way to avoid the dangers of neocolonialism is to have all aid coming into Africa channeled through the United Nations Organization. This would be fine, if the resources of the UN were adequate to meet all Africa's demands. But UN resources are far from adequate, and this is to a great extent because the large powers, who could make their facilities and resources available to the UN, are more keenly interested in the political influences which they can wield as a result of giving such aid bilaterally. Each is eager to be able to make claims about how much aid it has given to a certain country individually, and how the other power either has failed (if it is the United States accusing Russia) to provide funds to the UN for the newly independent states, or (if it is Russia accusing the United States) has tied up the economic parcel of aid with political strings. So the new states are driven to making bilateral agreements for aid, and find that one way to avoid neocolonialism is to assert and use their right to trade with East and West alike. As an example: Egypt is receiving about $60,000,000 in aid a year from the US, while Russia provided $186,000,000 between 1958 and 1962 for industrial installations and to help build the High Dam at Aswan; it is ironic to remember that John Foster Dulles withdrew American aid for the Aswan Dam in 1956 because Egypt was doing its best to be neutralist, and Dulles thought neutrality was immoral. The second reason against exclusive use of the UN is that this in itself could constitute a negation of independence, which must include the right to decide with whom to trade.

There are broadly two types of bilateral agreement which a newly independent state can make. The first type is one with the former colonial power, and nearly every new state has retained certain economic and trading relations with the ex-colonial power, either the British Commonwealth or the French Community or later the Common Market. The new states are liable to regard these arrangements with some suspicion, for fear that neocolonialism will creep in. But the experience of most Commonwealth countries has been that such fears have not yet been justified. The second type of arrangement is with noncolonial powers, with whom the new state was probably barred from trading before independence. Countries like Ghana and Nigeria have developed new friendships and trade relations with countries like Japan and Yugoslavia and Czechoslovakia, and links with Latin American countries are likely soon. Again, these are areas where the new state has to look carefully to see that no political strings are attached to loan agreements, and — in contrast to multilateral arrangements — there is an especial danger here that political factors may intrude.

Multilateral arrangements through international agencies could help a lot. The only snag here is that Africa is moving onto the international scene at a time when most of the international agencies have been established, and no attempt is being made to reorganize them to take account of the emergence of Africa. So that for some time to come, they will presumably continue to function on the basis of what their original sponsors wanted them to achieve, without considering what is in the best interests of the newer nations. Until African states are given appropriate representation on these bodies, and can have a proper say in the running of the International Finance Corporation and the International Monetary Fund, as well as many United Nations committees and agencies, we cannot agree that this form of aid is completely free of dangers and entirely acceptable.

In seeking economic and trade arrangements, every African state will want to see industrialization taking place. In the colonial era, Africa was stamped as a producer of raw materials, and after independence one of the immediate tasks is to transform African states into manufacturing as well as producing countries. States where cotton is grown will want to build textile factories, agricultural states will want processing plants. Those with iron and coal deposits will want to industrialize more heavily, and most countries are examining hydroelectric projects and planning (at the least) car assembly plants. This is a logical development, for Africa cannot continue to trade with other nations without trying to put herself in a position to compete effectively with the highly industrialized world of today.

These proper ambitions are sometimes misinterpreted by critics from other nations, who speak scornfully of "prestige programs." There is a danger, of course, that some countries may be concerned too much in a prestige project, such as building a huge steel mill while ignoring more urgent priorities; but this is certainly not a general problem, for the simple reason that the experts of the countries which consider offering aid make a practice of testing with cold reason and technical sense the projects for which their aid is wanted, and few prestige plans which are uneconomical survive this test.

There could, however, be a greater amount of regional planning in such matters as hydroelectric schemes, trunk roads and airlines. We in East Africa are fortunate in these respects. Since the Owen Falls hydroelectric scheme was inaugurated at Jinja, Uganda, in 1954, it has supplied almost as much power to Kenya as to Uganda. East African Airways has continued to serve the three territories, without Uganda and Tanganyika thinking that independence should mean setting up their own airlines. And the Common Services Organization, made far more representative after Tanganyika's independence, has maintained the joint research and communications system which the East Africa High Commission had founded in 1948. In other parts of Africa, independence has brought an early stage of separatism, mainly because independence came at different times to the various countries and the newly independent country did not want to continue an association with the still dependent country. West African Airways began to break up when Ghana wanted her own airlines, and now Nigeria and Sierra Leone have to have their own. A move in the sensible direction has been taken by the twelve states of the Afro-Malagasy Union in setting up Air Afrique; and African states need to follow the example of the Danish, Swedish and Norwegian airlines in founding the Scandinavian Airlines System by combining their three airlines in 1948, and ten years later coming to an agreement with Swissair to pool traffic, cooperate in maintenance, and lease jets to each other. For instance, the Congo could provide hydroelectric power for many

surrounding states — and indeed, in 1959 the £1,000,000,-
ooo Inga project was started — but some African states
have insisted on providing their own schemes. However,
there are other encouraging signs. Through the UN Economic Commission for Africa, a committee with representatives from nine African countries adopted a draft charter
for the African Development Bank in January 1963. The
bank, with a minimum capital of $200,000,000 subscribed
by African states, will finance investment for economic and
social development. The management and direction of the
bank will be wholly African, and special attention will be
given to projects affecting several countries. Its planners
hope to raise capital from governments and other sources
outside Africa, but the uses to which the capital will be put
will be decided in Africa, so that the bank will achieve two
important objects: it will remove dangers of neocolonialist
strings attacked to this money, and it will encourage regional planning.

Another achievement of regional planning came at the
end of 1962, when Uganda, Tanganyika and Kenya combined to oppose the British government's idea that we should
apply for associate membership in the European Common
Market. It was clear from the start we had all to act together
if our own (and older) common market in East Africa
was to survive.

We look upon the European Common Market in this
way: it is Western Europe's effort at survival. After two
world wars which began in her midst, Western Europe has
lost control and influence in most of the world, from the Far
East to Latin America, from the United States to New Zea-
land, and she is now losing her influence in Africa. She faces
new nations which were once regarded as her sources for
raw materials and are now impatient to industrialize; i.e.,

Ghana building the Volta Dam and Nigeria planning to spend £676,000,000 in six years on development. She faces economic challenges from the United States and Russia alike, and is losing much of her oil revenues in the Middle East. So, finding her political and economic and military influence greatly diminished, Western Europe decided to create its Common Market. By the Treaty of Rome, political federation will be established later; and this may lead to military relations, a full-scale European parliament and a stronger voice for a United Europe.

African states, together with some of the West Indies and Latin American nations, have been offered associate membership. This status originated with the economic relationship between France and her former African colonies, which remained economically dependent on her after independence. Many other African states had thought this relationship amounted to neocolonialism, so associate member status was held in suspicion from the start. Associate membership was offered to countries which had not yet reached the stage where they could compete with Europe as manufacturers; countries which had passed that stage, like India and Pakistan, were not offered associate membership. The graduated tariff system, as well, was planned to suit the needs of the European countries rather than the interests of the African states. So it can hardly be said that the European community was planned to benefit Africa: the only points at which its arrangements do not seek to interfere directly in African plans are those where African interests are not in conflict with European interests. And there is provision for the withdrawal of associate membership from any state after five years, a penalty which could easily be imposed on an African state which had managed to industrialize and begin competing with Europe in manufactures.

Such an outcast would have to start from the beginning in negotiating commodity agreements, having lost five years' bargaining time. And if anyone had any doubts about the political nature of this relationship, they should have been dismissed early in 1963 when, because of a controversy with France on purely European affairs, Italy and Holland refused to sign the new five-year agreement providing £260,000,000 to eighteen African states. This brought home to us how dangerously insecure and subordinate a relationship associate membership was.

The Treaty of Rome suggests that associated states form their own parliamentary group, where they can consult and harmonize policies. It is added, as an extra attraction for this idea, that such a parliamentary group would serve to help the cause of African unity. But it is more likely to divide than unite Africa if only half the states are associated; and anyway, this group would only be allowed to act, at most, in an advisory capacity to the European Parliament. Decisions affecting them — and us — would be taken by the European states alone. We have had experience of decisions taken by Europe on behalf of Africa, and we do not rate very high in the value of the "African unity" they have imposed — for instance, in combining Nyasaland with the Rhodesias.

A good deal of play was made with the argument that if we became associate members, we could expect greatly increased aid through the ECM Development Fund. The Development Fund was made a very slow start, and by January 1962 had awarded only $50,000,000 in contracts and signed agreements for only $215,000,000 in aid. In mid-1962 the ECM Council of Ministers agreed to offer aid during the next five-year period totaling $780,000,000 to the eighteen associated African states (the fourteen ex-French colonies, the Congo, Rwanda and Burundi and the Somalia Republic). This sounds a handsome enough figure, but the new nations which were being invited through Britain to become associates could not draw from this capital: they could only hope Britain would add to the fund a proportionate amount, or that Britain would add a certain amount and persuade the other European countries to add more. These calculations led us to wonder whether African nations like ourselves had anything economically to gain from association. When Britain's application was rejected, any further overtures to us seemed to have died too.

Politically, we saw great dangers of neocolonialism. West Germany would certainly begin by insisting we create no links with East Germany. The neutrals of Europe — Sweden, Austria and Switzerland — refused to become members under the Treaty of Rome, to avoid political involvements, and have since been trying to negotiate terms of association which would allow them to stay neutral politically and militarily. Greece, presumably because she was "safe" as a member of NATO, was granted extremely favorable terms of association. When East African leaders went to London for the Commonwealth Prime Ministers' Conference in September 1962, we asked Britain to negotiate for us associate membership under Article 238, which would establish trade and economic relations without any political commitments. Alternatively, we asked for the same sort of protocol arrangement which Morocco and Tunisia were allowed to make, so that they derive the same benefits from their trade with France and the other ECM countries as they did before the signing of the Treaty of Rome. But Britain rejected these suggestions, and said Article 4 was our only avenue. So it should not be surprising that we found it difficult to accept the assurances of Professor Hans Furler, vice-

president of the European Parliament, when he came to
Nairobi in October 1962 and told us, "Association does not
involve any political ties whatever." All the signs pointed
the other way.

We had anyway by then made up our minds and had
taken our stand at the Commonwealth Prime Ministers
Conference. Britain had already had heavy shocks during
the conference, and when Mr. Menzies detailed the harm
which Britain's entry would do to the Commonwealth, the
Observer commented in a long account headlined "The
Commonwealth's Longest Week": "Never, even at Suez,
had the future of the Commonwealth looked more bleak
than it did that night."

We did not have the same objections to Britain's entry on
her own account, but we could not accept associate membership. Alongside Nigeria, Rashidi Kawawa as Tanganyika's
Prime Minister flatly rejected association and added that he
spoke for Uganda and Kenya as well. Efforts were made to
drive a wedge between members of our East African team,
but they failed. We all resented this tactic — that the British, who had already failed to drive a wedge between the
West Africans, were now trying to split us in East Africa.
We saw more clearly than ever that the most important concern for us was to preserve our own East African common
market and make unanimous decisions about any links with
the European countries. So we agreed to send an East African delegation direct to Brussels, to negotiate better terms
for various commodities on conditions other than associate
membership. My hope is that European nations will begin to
understand our desire for economic as well as political independence; for it is quite as strong as the European desire today for economic, political and military independence.

I think Mr. Macmillan and his ministers failed to take the trouble to learn our views beforehand, because they were filled with anxiety over the negotiations on their own and Britain's account. France had brought her former colonies into association with the Common Market as part of their own political evolution rather than as part of an economic plan. Britain overlooked the fact that our background and the Commonwealth evolution were entirely different, and that we looked forward to complete political independence in accordance with the whole Commonwealth concept. This development had not been the case with the French-speaking territories, apart from Guinea. The task of negotiating separate agreements over commodities with the European Common Market may not be an easy one for East African leaders, but we happily accept it; for we have shown other countries how we work together, and how we are jealous enough of our independence to reject something which may at first sight seem beneficial but which is almost certainly concealing political snares. To the extent that the offer of associate membership had some political motivation, to that extent we in East Africa have been true to the principles of African socialism and positive nonalignment in rejecting such association. Later, when Britain was refused admission, events seemed to bear us out.

TEN

Broad Horizons for the Workers

IN Chapter 2 I told a little about the growth of the trade union movement in Kenya. This is an appropriate point to pick up again the threads of this growth, and to show how our experience made us diverge from the British model. Particularly our different experience has made us think out how best to tackle a problem which is peculiarly acute in young states: the relationship of the trade unions to the national political movement.

I explained how, in our struggle to gain official recognition for our unions, which succeeded with the report of the Windham board of inquiry in 1955, we had built up our unions on an industrial basis rather than on the structure of a craft or a general union. In this respect we rejected the British, and adopted the Canadian approach.

We could not, however, adopt the Canadian system of recognition by law when the union had enrolled a fixed percentage of members of the industry. The reason is that in Kenya, as elsewhere in Africa, union membership fluctuates with the seasons of the year, since workers move back to their land during harvesting and planting periods. The fluctuations are regular, but one cannot expect a regular dues-paying membership until there is stability in the labor force.

The Carpenter Committee Report of 1953 had said there would never be stability until there was offered sufficient salary to keep a man and his family in the place of work: the committee calculated ten pounds a month to be sufficient salary and recommended that Kenya should reach that minimum by 1958. For stability, too, the committee said, a worker must have a home and not just bed space. There must also be some form of social security, to replace the system by which everyone kept "one foot in the reserve" so that in old age and during unemployment and sickness a worker could go back to his land and tribe for security and protection. With lack of statistics and also government funds, it has been difficult to set up a social security system. For this reason the labor ministers throughout East Africa have now agreed to plan compulsory registration of unemployment and improve employment registration, so that statistics can be compiled for a social security scale. In the meantime, as a nucleus for the future, it is hoped to work out a plan for a skeleton contributory national provident fund scheme — with contributions from employers, employees and government. Later this can be expanded into a full scheme, covering health insurance.

We believed that while this instability and fluctuating membership lasted, it was wrong to insist on a set percentage of members before granting recognition. The 1955 board of inquiry upheld our contention that a union should be recognized as soon as it is legally set up, if there is no other union in competition.

Another point of departure from the British practice came over the question of payment of union dues. The British argued that dues must be collected by the union itself, so that members would be kept regularly in touch with the union and express their consciousness of the union by this payment. With leaders who had not much education and could not write books properly, we had problems of organization not known in Britain. We asked the Labor Department to provide standard receipt books, standard membership cards, and standard monthly report forms for branch officials; and this made it easier for officials to fill in the reports the registrar required. But we also became convinced we would have to move to the American and Canadian system of a check-off payment of union dues, with employers deducting the dues before paying wages.

The check-off system has made a good deal of progress in East Africa. It is now legislated for in Tanganyika, and many firms have accepted it in Kenya and Uganda, where the governments are encouraging its adoption. These governments believe it should, if necessary, be established by legislation, for two reasons. First, because a union which has no finances can never be efficiently administered and can never employ the kind of leadership it needs, and therefore becomes a liability to both sides of the industry. Secondly, the leaders of a union which has no regular or adequate funds will always be subject to bribery by employers or other forces. The union will have to look for money outside the country, and this may lead to serious problems of international involvement, and leaders being bought off by this or that group in the international or even Pan-African scene. This experiment and departure from the traditional British thinking has, we believe, been very much justified.

Most of the labor legislation in former British colonies is modeled on the British laws, and we are finding we have to experiment with our own forms. We have, for instance, decided to repeal the Essential Services Ordinance, which required that before there was a strike in any essential service, twenty-one days' notice had to be given, and gave the

Labor Minister power to extend that period. What happened
in practice was that a breakdown and a strike occurred, and
you had to decide whether to apply the ordinance in full
and take to prison everyone who was defying it. In many
cases you find you cannot prosecute all involved, so you
have to shut your eyes — and the ordinance does not work.
We decided to replace it with the more practical condition
that government requires certain notice but does not insist
on compulsory arbitration. The matter of compulsory arbitration remains a very much debated issue in East Africa.

In the sphere of labor relations the biggest question which
the government of a newly independent state, a new country in a hurry for development, has to face is how far
such rights as the right to strike can remain recognized and
how far voluntary negotiation can be relied upon. Some
African countries have taken their decision on this. They
do not allow the right to strike, or restrict it so much it is
hardly there.

One has to recognize that these countries are in a hurry to
translate independence into something meaningful in the
economic sense; politically, too, it is desirable that as soon
as possible after independence there must be economic reconstruction and economic independence. The trade unions,
having played their part in the nationalist movement to
achieve political independence, are then again expected to
play their part, together with the party in power, to help
consolidate that independence and economic reconstruction.
If the trade unions appear to become an unnecessary obstacle in the way of the new governments in this stage of
development, they will stand accused of being foreign
agents or imperialist agents, or of being just negative. There
is the temptation for the new government to introduce
laws to ensure that its programs are not obstructed by either

trade unions or any other group or person. The biggest challenge for the trade union movement is to create the atmosphere in which its various rights can continue to be recognized but in which at the same time people feel they are participating fully in the cause of nation-building.

After I became Minister for Labor in April 1962, I began putting into practice the idea that instead of compulsory legislation we should work out a voluntary system — an Industrial Relations Charter — which would include all the obligations we think a trade union ought to accept in the new circumstances. This is an experiment which, I think, has been tried nowhere else in Africa. We had a wave of strikes in May, and some of my colleagues were tempted to introduce new legislation. But we decided to try something else first, and called a conference of the Kenya Federation of Labor, the Federation of Kenya Employers, and government officials. We studied the reasons behind the wave of strikes and the problems involved. We tried to discover where relations had broken down and also why certain attitudes had persisted in industry. Then we decided on two committees, one to deal with the question of demarcation — to try to eliminate interunion arguments — and the other to deal with recognition and all the issues relating to negotiating machinery. The committees consisted of employer and trade union representatives with a government chairman, and from the work of these committees we got the draft of the Charter, which was signed in October 1962.

The Charter was worked out to cover six main areas of industrial relations. First, to define recognition, so that we eliminate all unnecessary disputes over this issue. Second, to agree on a check-off system for the payment of union dues, so that legislation is avoided. Third, to provide machinery to deal with disputes. Fourth, to deal with the question of demarcation, both to eliminate interunion quarrels and to ensure that for each union there is an opposite number in the employers' camp with whom to negotiate all the time. Fifth, to set out a recognition agreement which lays down all the steps in union-employer relations from the time of recognition and which also defines the status of any agreements signed in an industry. And sixth, to provide against breakdowns in these agreements. Legislation is needed only if agreements break down, and we have planned for a permanent industrial court to which both parties may refer disputes. Arbitration tribunals and boards of inquiry are provided for in the legislation.

Each side — the trade unions and the employers — must guarantee that its affiliates will comply with the Charter, because otherwise the government must act. The trade unions, too, need to realize that industrial relations in our new countries must conform to the pace at which our people want to move. If unions do not realize this, they are bound to be victimized by the stronger forces already in the field. There is also the question of compliance with International Labor Organization conventions. In the past we have respected them and fought for them, and condemned South Africa and other countries for not complying with them. But the situation may change, and we may have to choose between compliance which entails risking a breakdown in our development and ignoring a convention so that we may develop. The stronger urge would be to develop regardless of ILO conventions, and to hope that one day it will be possible to establish a position of stability where one can begin again to respect these conventions. ILO conventions were formulated at a time when Africa was not on the labor scene, and problems of underdeveloped countries, in terms of newly independent states, had never really been considered. Consequently, some of the conventions may be out-of-date in our context and not reflect our problems at all. Some of my friends argue, therefore, that if we overlook some of the conventions we are not acting immorally but rather stressing that these conventions must be re-examined to reflect the problems of the new countries.

The employers in a country like Kenya, who during the colonial period identified themselves with the colonial power, have as much of a challenge to adapt themselves to the new circumstances as anybody else — perhaps even more. For instance, in May 1962 the Kenya Coffee Growers Association refused to recognize a union because it intended to organize the sisal workers as well as the coffee workers. As Minister, I advised them that they were wrong and that the right to freedom of association entitled the union to organize as it liked, but that suitable machinery could be created to ensure that each section was properly represented under the recognition given. This was rejected by the employers, but a board of inquiry appointed by government endorsed my original advice. Meantime an unnecessary strike had taken place. The lesson they have to learn is that if their beliefs are to be respected in our new countries, they will need to show a response to government and nationalistic requirements. If their stand appears to be negative and unnecessarily obstructive, then it is inevitable that, with this sense of urgency in our new countries, they will be overridden and completely set aside. If they show they are cooperative and become partners in the urgent need for development, then they will survive.

It is the same situation which faces the trade unions in the time of nationalist struggle for independence: if the trade unions appear to stand in the way of the nationalist movement, they will always suffer.

In fact, during the Emergency, the Kenya trade union movement found itself the main spokesman for the Africans, both politically and in the industrial field. Most of us in the trade unions felt that the movement must identify itself with the nationalist cause. If it fails to do this, it runs the risk of being accused of becoming an imperialist agency. A number of trade unionists who were not sensitive to this fact and concentrated only on industrial relations suffered this fate. Nor do I think this identification is in conflict with the main functions of a trade union movement. In the early days of our development, we had no voice in the legislature and therefore could not translate our policies into the necessary legislation. The only way we could translate our feelings was by associating with the nationalist movement, hoping that when it came to power it would adopt these policies and ideas.

The question which has to be constantly reconsidered is where one draws the line between identification with the nationalist movement and subordination to its political designs. The nationalist political parties must expect the unions to join with them at various points during the struggle, since the workers have as much interest in the struggle for independence as anyone else. Sometimes they expect the trade unions to call a strike as additional pressure. It is here that decisions have to be carefully taken, when strike action may be used for general political purposes as against industrial purposes. My own distinction has always been based on the view that the individual unions should act on an industrial basis, leaving the center — the trade union federation — as the only body which should act politically. In this way you may avoid some of the complications which may arise: it gives you also a better opportunity to negotiate with the nationalist movement on a firmer footing, with no risk of one union being played off against another, or a union being split over supporting this or that political faction. There is always a case for effective consultative machinery between the unions and the party. I expect that after independence the government will expect trade unions to play a full part in the task of nation-building and even to make sacrifices in the process.

During the Emergency the KFL felt its main task was to survive. If we had precipitated a situation in which it could have been proscribed, there would have been no voice at all left in the country. Our job was to fight for the African people, but to do it in such a manner that we were always able to survive. As it was, I think we would have been proscribed but for the fact that we had international support from the ICFTU. This is what created the deep attachment to the ICFTU, because our survival at that time depended on the Kenya government's fear that the international labor movement might come in and exert international pressure if we were proscribed. It is nearly a miracle that we came out of the Emergency with any unions at all, but the KFL enjoyed a quick growth all along. We began in 1953 with seven unions, and by 1963 we have twenty-eight. Growth has been swiftest in the years since 1958, when the Emergency ended, but during the Emergency the unions gathered a great deal of strength and influence in terms of recognition won from the employers and the government.

Trade union development started in Kenya earlier than in any other part of East Africa, and the unusual part we played during the Emergency and the help from the ICFTU helped us to advance faster than the other areas. We therefore were able to play an important role in the establishment of trade unions in both Uganda and Tanganyika. In 1955, just after Jim Bury left East Africa, I visited Dar es

Salaam to look round for the ICFTU and see what trade union development had taken place in Tanganyika. It was then I first met Rashidi Kawawa, who became Prime Minister in 1962. At that time he was secretary of the Civil Servants Association. It was the only union which was then national in character — dock workers in Tanga had no connection with those in Dar es Salaam, and the same parochialism was true of the other unions. Almost all had tried to build from the bottom upwards, and each one was trying to form a little union, in some cases merely a group of workers in one factory or shop struggling to create a union.

Almost immediately Kawawa and the other leaders agreed that the answer was to get all these unions together to form the Tanganyika Federation of Labor, and to use the TFL as the agency through which to build other and bigger unions. With Mr. Mpangala and Michael Kamaliza, who is now Minister of Labor, Kawawa got a group of trade unionists to form a committee which later founded the TFL. Having no problem of an Emergency, they moved rapidly and in many cases caught up with us. But I also remember meeting skeptical people from the Tanganyika Labor Department who said there were too many migrant workers, especially on the plantations, where men came from Rwanda and Burundi on six-month contracts, for anyone to set up any real trade unions. It is interesting today to look back and note that the first to organize a strong national union was the plantation industry, despite the attitudes of colonial civil servants who had this traditional British approach. The KFL was able to give the Tanganyikans guidance in those early days, and so did the ICFTU, with which the TFL later affiliated.

I also visited Uganda in 1955, and found the same conditions as in Tanganyika. There was the complication that some plantation employers were Africans, who resented the introduction of trade unions. They did not object to the

workers who were employed by Europeans and Asians being organized, but they did not want organization extended
to their employees. I was further told that the Baganda were
quite satisfied and did not look on themselves as workers,
and so there would be no possibility of organizing a trade
union in Uganda. To some extent these warnings were correct, for in many Uganda unions the leadership had to come
from Kenya workers resident in Uganda. Ugandans merely
took interest when the unions began to show results, and
when leaders were being sent overseas for training and
conferences. Jim Bury had done important work in training
union leaders, organizing evening and weekend schools, and
getting the ICFTU to help us send men overseas. But the
right type of people came forward late in the Uganda trade
union movement, and even today they have not shown the
keen interest that is needed. This may explain why Uganda
has the weakest trade union movement of all East Africa.
There are nearly forty trade unions registered, but only
about twenty are well constituted and lively organizations.

The British concept that a trade union should develop
from the bottom and that experience should be gained by a
man as he moves up the ladder is impossible to adopt in
Africa. The whole emphasis has to be given from the top.
The members expect the top leaders to think out the problems and devise the answers. The KFL — and the TFL later
— had the task of helping develop trade unions, rather than
the unions coming together and helping develop the KFL
and TFL. The Federation had the task of getting assistance
to weak unions, finding leaders to spread into weaker unions,
and often, on behalf of most of the unions, of negotiating.

Many times we thought about forming a regional federation of labor, but mostly in the context of the unions which
are East African in character. From the early days we peti-
tioned the different East African Labor Commissioners at

their annual meeting to plan new laws which would allow the
railway, post office and dock workers to organize on an
East African basis. After the TFL and the Uganda TUC
were formed, we met several times on a regional basis, and
I went to the island of Pemba to discuss the possibility of
federation there. That visit led to the formation of the Zanzibar and Pemba Federation of Labor. In 1959 through the
ICFTU we set up a regional trade union group throughout
East and Central Africa, of which I became chairman. We
did this because we thought it necessary to coordinate our
efforts, and also necessary to support each other in our
struggle against governments which were hostile to trade
unionism. Until 1955 the Kenya government was fighting
against the building of a trade union movement, and only in
that year did it declare it was its policy to help build the
movement. In both Tanganyika and Uganda we had to get
better legislation enacted to allow the trade unions to function. In Southern Rhodesia the laws have been completely
opposed to the kind of effective unions we have had in mind.
Originally they had racial unions, where the Africans had
virtually no rights at all and only one union of any strength
— the Railway Union based on Bulawayo. We gave advice
and used pressure on the Southern Rhodesian government
through the ILO and the British government. Under pressure of this sort, the Southern Rhodesian government de-
vised legislation which allowed nonracial unions. But this
law made sure that the only unions which would survive
would be the old European unions, which Africans would
have to join without having a full say in their decisions,
because the voting under the Industrial Conciliation Amendment Act has a heavy bias towards the skilled worker. This
nullified most of the good effects the new law could have
had, and the struggle for better trade union legislation in
Southern Rhodesia continues even today.

A final area of departure from traditional British thinking should be mentioned. More and more of the African trade unions are beginning to adopt the Scandinavian and Israeli pattern, extending from a wage interest to an economic interest. In traditional British thinking, a trade union movement is formed only to fight for better conditions for its members — higher wages, better housing, social security and the like. In the new thinking in Africa, the trade union movement should itself be involved in an economic interest, running its own cooperatives and even running large companies and banks.

When I visited Israel for the first time in January 1962, the KFL instructed me to look round and see how far we should adapt our own thinking to the Israeli pattern. As a result, a joint enterprise was decided upon between the Histadrut of Israel and the KFL. The initial scheme is one of consumer cooperatives, followed by a construction company, the sponsoring of a fishermen's cooperative on Lake Victoria and the encouragement of cooperatives among peasant farmers. Similar development has begun in Tanganyika.

The launching of such projects will establish the trade union movement as a main partner in the whole effort toward economic development, and make it possible for trade unionists to acquire a broader outlook and become more associated with the actual problems of economic development than they would be if they merely had a wage interest in the industrial world. It also places the trade unions in a position of greater influence with the parties in power: it is much more difficult to suppress a trade union movement with extensive economic interests than a trade union which is only an organization of workers formed for the sake of fighting for higher wages. Where a government is able to take on the task of implementing wage decisions and increasing wages, it could easily kill the trade union movement completely. But when a worker, in addition to a wage interest, knows that his trade union is also a profit-making agency for himself and a source of security for his family, the association is much deeper. Sometimes, as in Sweden and even in Israel, the trade unions become so powerful they can run the country; they certainly influence the political parties much more than the British TUC is able to do.

This development is logical in a country like ours which claims to be a workers' country and have a workers' government. It is the opposite of workers' participation by nationalization. It is workers' participation in the country's economy by constructive and deliberate investment policies rather than by government act of nationalization.

We are starting in the consumer cooperative field because nobody has suffered more than the African worker from being cheated when he goes to the present shops. The African has never had a real increase in wages, because every time there has been a wage increase there has also been an increase in the prices charged by shopkeepers. By creating his own consumer cooperatives he should eliminate this problem. This will also lead to the development of a better and more experienced section of African businessmen. Africans who have run their little shops for years have shown no results because they were untrained in business and were swindled by some wholesalers. These petty traders could become members of the cooperative and begin to gain some benefit, and they may even become part of the management of the cooperatives if they prove good enough businessmen. The cooperatives will also undertake wholesale trade and eliminate the middleman who exists today, so that goods will in the long run, we hope, become cheaper.

The construction company will consist of a workers'

building society which will not only help to put up houses — and better housing is one of the most urgent needs all over Africa — but also employ many of the workers. It can help, as well, to negotiate contractor finance, and moves in this direction are already being thought out. Also, it is hoped that the KFL in association with the government will sponsor cooperatives among peasant farmers and fishermen. With cotton growers, the cooperative should eventually extend to owning ginning factories and even undertaking the manufacture of textiles. In Kenya's Coast Province all the cashew nuts are at present sent overseas for processing and then brought back to be sold: clearly the processing should be done here and the KFL could help the peasants to set up a processing cooperative.

As a parallel to this development, it is intended to begin workers' credit cooperatives. These would perhaps later lead to the establishment of a workers' bank, but from the start it would give workers the opportunity to save and to borrow. At present there is a chronic problem in urban areas where there are workers who have to borrow money from illegal moneylenders at the rate of five shillings per pound — 25 percent — per month. In Tanganyika the government has started a cooperative bank which is financed by a commercial bank at the start. There is no reason why credit cooperatives cannot combine both forms of investment, seeking contributions from these banks as well as from the workers.

In the final chapter we will discuss trade unionism in a Pan-African context, but this short account should serve to show how trade unions leaders in Kenya, having built up a vigorous movement, are resolved to use this vigor to broaden their interests and make themselves indispensable partners in the development of a prosperous new state.

ELEVEN

Looking Outward

Patriotism [wrote the Earl of Sandwich] is a wider form of the love of parents for their children, and children for their parents. At the heart of patriotism is gratitude and protectiveness. It is the greatest force a political leader can hope to harness. It has no essential connection with aggressiveness or militarism. It is not the same as nationalism — a state of mind emanating more from hatred of foreigners than from love of compatriots.

YOU don't have to read far to see that the Earl of Sand-wich, who as Lord Hinchingbrooke was a very conservative British MP, is a little confused. He accuses nationalists of being filled with hatred for foreigners; yet he is the president of the Anti-Common Market League, and in the article I have just quoted went on to summarize his feelings about the European Economic Community:

There is nothing wrong about patriotism. It is natural and healthy. What a man feels about his country is real and identifiable. But what can a man feel about a *group* of nations? A committee of countries? Human nature does not permit the extension of this basic emotion to a series of initials such as EEC.

African leaders can never accept the Earl's definition of nationalism, and many of us are busily engaged in proving that human nature is capable of extending feelings of pa-

triotism over the whole continent. Since he says that patriotism is love, let me quote to him Saint-Exupéry: "Love does
not consist in gazing at each other, but in looking outward
in the same direction."

In planning for Pan-African unity, in building up regional
organizations which are a first layer of bricks in that structure, we in Africa are looking outward.

Unity throughout Africa is as much needed as unity was
needed within each territory in the struggle for independence. All independent African states want not only to establish their own independence but also to see the whole
continent free. When the independent African states met
for the first time in Accra in 1958 — there were then only
eight of them — they laid down the observance of April 15
each year as Africa Freedom Day.

They also pledged themselves to cooperate in presenting
an African personality, and they accepted as part of their
duty the liberation of all Africa. President Nkrumah put
it in these words: "The independence of Ghana is meaningless unless it is accompanied by the total liberation of
Africa." Many an African head of state (the latest, perhaps,
being Dr. Banda when he was sworn in as first Prime
Minister of Nyasaland) has since repeated this pledge.

As states north of the Zambezi River look forward to their
independence, they are aware of the struggle which must
still continue in Southern Rhodesia, South-West Africa, the
Protectorates, South Africa, Mozambique and Angola and in
the pocket states held by Spain and Portugal along the west
coast. All independent African states accept this collective
responsibility for the liberation of these parts of the continent. No African independent state can feel completely free
and respected as a nation while there are parts of Africa in

which there are minority governments or colonial powers owning large chunks of land and slaves under a ruthless administration. The most important moves in undertaking this responsibility were the calling of the two Accra conferences in 1958 — the Conference of Independent African States and the All-African Peoples Conference — and the setting up in the same year of the Pan-African Freedom Movement of East and Central Africa. And in 1963, as a major result of the Addis Ababa Heads of States Conference, has come the establishment of a nine-nation Liberation Coordinating Committee based in Dar es Salaam.

The idea of PAFMECA was born during a conversation between Julius Nyerere and myself when he came to my two-room house in Ziwani location of Nairobi. I mention the size of my house because it sheds some light on Nyerere's character. It had no bathroom and not even a sink with running water: all we could do was draw water from a tap outside, and bathe from a basin. But although he was by then the leader of a strong political party, TANU, his simplicity and humility and apparent identification with the "small man" were such that I never sensed any reaction from him at any time that these simple conditions were "not quite the thing." Through the years he has remained a very close friend and has had a strong impact upon my views. He has always been the same — charming, ready to discuss our various problems, understanding and invariably confident. He has also a profound and analytical mind. Most people meeting him for the first time are deceived into thinking him superficial in thought and weak and flexible in action. Many people who made this mistake in the days before Tanganyika's independence suddenly realized he was in fact strong-willed and, once resolved to do something,

determined to carry it out regardless of the consequences.
Anyway, we were sitting in my house discussing unity
and Pan-Africanism, and we agreed it would be good,
ahead of the All-African Peoples Conference, to bring together the nationalist movements throughout Eastern and
Central Africa. We were both at that point facing a rough
period in the independence struggle in our countries; he had
recently been charged with criminal libel against a district
commissioner, and we in Kenya were finding all efforts to
unite the district political associations in Kenya blocked by
the government. So we planned PAFMECA, to coordinate
the struggle in all these countries and harmonize policies
most effectively.

Twenty-one delegates met at Mwanza, a quiet town on
the Tanganyika shore of Lake Victoria, in September 1958.
Mwanza was chosen because it would have been impossible
to hold such a meeting either in Kenya or Uganda in those
days, and yet this lakeside town was conveniently close to all
three countries. Even in Tanganyika freedom of association
was then restricted. TANU had just won the first general
elections handsomely, but the party was nevertheless banned
in that area of Mwanza — Sukumaland — after the British
had imposed a Sukuma federal council (mainly of chiefs)
and agitation had begun against their rule. However, the
crowd which gathered untiringly round the Ladha Meghji
Library for three days showed the excitement and support
there was for our plan. There was only one delegate from
Uganda — E. M. K. Mulira — and one from Nyasaland —
Kanyama Chiume — and the rest in equal numbers from
Tanganyika, Zanzibar and Kenya, but we felt confident that
much would grow from these small beginnings.

In those three days we wrote the PAFMECA constitu-

tion and the PAFMECA Freedom Charter, as well as debating eleven broad subjects. We set out five aims in our
constitution. We would foster Pan-Africanism, to rid the
area of imperialism, white supremacy, economic exploitation and social degradation. We would coordinate nationalist
programs to hasten the independence of the area. We would
help in every way to establish united nationalist movements
in each territory. This object we saw as being particularly
important, as without unity we were sure we would be
victims of the settlers' tactics of dividing and confusing
nationalists, in order to delay independence or even to
establish a South African type of government. We would
also establish a joint freedom fund. And finally, we pledged
ourselves to champion nonviolent methods in the independence struggle.

In our Freedom Charter we declared:

Freedom is our birthright; self-government our heritage, as sons
and daughters of the free men and women who inherited Africa
for the Africans. It is therefore not only just but imperative that
we restore our birthright for ourselves and our children and our
children's children. . . . We declare that democracy must prevail throughout Africa, from Senegal to Zanzibar and from Cape
to Cairo; that colonialism, the so-called trusteeship, and so-called
partnership, apartheid, multiracialism and white settlerism are
enemies of freedom, and can be eradicated only by African nationalism, virile and unrelenting; that the right of self-determination is God-given and no man or nation is chosen by God to
determine the destiny of others; that poverty, ignorance, ill-
health and other human miseries cannot be satisfactorily eradicated under imperialism, but only under self-government and
international cooperation on the basis of equality and mutual
benefaction. . . .

Lest anyone conclude from that phrase "Africa for the
Africans" that we had a racialistic approach, let me quote

the resolution the Mwanza conference passed on "the problems of non-Africans."

. . . and whereas no country in the world is entirely homogeneous, racially or culturally; and whereas in genuinely democratic countries it has been found that the surest way of safeguarding the rights of any group is the protection of individual rights, the Conference wants it to be publicly known that:
  (a) we are dedicated to the precepts and practice of democracy;
  (b) under the democracy which we seek for our motherland, there will be no discrimination, victimization, or any form of segregation based purely on race or color or religion;
  (c) those of foreign origin residing in Africa, by accepting the rules of Governments of the Majority, by being naturalized African citizens will enjoy the full rights and protection of a citizen;
  (d) the safeguards and protection of citizens' rights and human liberties will be buttressed by uncompromising adherence to the Rule of Law; the maintenance of the absolute independence of the Judiciary; the exercise of the right to vote or stand for any office; the constant observance of the declaration of the Universal Human Rights and the United Nations Charter.

The All-African Peoples Conference emphasized the same ideals PAFMECA had, and it succeeded in establishing the African community, by drawing together political leaders, trade unionists, farmers' leaders and many other groups — in some cases people who had never heard of each other, in many cases people who had only heard of each other. But PAFMECA countries had a different kind of struggle from the one faced by West African countries, for our problem was made greater by the European settlers. In West Africa, independence had been conceded long ago by Britain, although the British had delayed the date of freedom for years by arguing "You are not ready." With us in East and Central Africa, the main question was whether independence would be handed to the Africans or to the white minorities.

There was much discussion at the All-African Peoples Conference in Accra on the question of unity, and the method of achieving Pan-African unity became a burning issue. The committee which discussed the question in detail felt the best method was to establish closer unity within five defined regions: in these regions the nationalist movements would work together to become independent and then cooperate in a plan for economic integration and political federation. When these regions had been established, the whole of the continent could come together to form the United States of Africa. Thus PAFMECA's plan fell very much into line with what was later decided in Accra.

From the Mwanza meeting onward, PAFMECA leaders attempted as their first task to bring unity in Zanzibar, Uganda and later in Kenya. Although we cannot claim to have succeeded in establishing single parties in each of these territories, we did bring closely together for realistic discussions the various leaders in the PAFMECA countries. By doing so we minimized the degree of hostility and conflict which would otherwise have existed, say, in Zanzibar. A mission led by Francis Khamisi of Mombasa (PAFMECA's first chairman) help to narrow the gap between the Zanzibar National Party and the Afro-Shirazi Party; and Nyerere and I went to Uganda on a similar mission in 1958, when parties in that country were badly split. In mid-1962 the PAFMECA secretary-general, Mbiyu Koinange, came extremely close to providing the solution over the timing of elections and self-government in Zanzibar, which would have brought the two parties together. And finally, at the end of that year, PAFMECA's days of discussion with Harry Nkumbula in Dar es Salaam and Nairobi convinced him that he should take his African National Congress into coalition government with Kenneth Kaunda's party as Northern Rhodesia's first African majority government, so spelling the end of Welensky's Federation.

Cooperation has flowed between the member organizations. When seven African elected members (including myself) faced charges of libel in Kenya, TANU and the Afro-Shirazis contributed to the legal fees. Later, funds from PAFMECA were sent to help Joshua Nkomo in the Southern Rhodesian struggle, and Kenneth Kaunda's party received help during the 1962 elections. During the Nyasaland Emergency, PAFMECA did much to publicize Dr. Banda's case and to give support to Kanyama Chiume's efforts overseas. Perhaps more important still, PAFMECA alone of Pan-African organizations has succeeded in functioning with regular meetings (in fact, it has held more meetings than originally envisaged in its constitution); and it has functioned without any lasting conflicts among its members. One reason for this success is a realistic attitude among PAFMECA countries, which recognize that the leaders in a particular country know best what is good for that country, so that there has never been a PAFMECA attempt to impose decisions on a country against the wishes of that country's leaders. Another reason is the acceptance by PAFMECA that there will be differences between the members on how to solve certain problems — for instance, racial integration and constitutional development. Again, we have agreed that "the men on the spot know best," and the kind of constitution most likely to work is one which brings harmony to the differing viewpoints in a particular country.

In this way, PAFMECA has found it possible to endorse a republican constitution in Tanganyika and a federalist constitution (complete with four kings) in Uganda, while at the same time supporting hopes for an East African Federation and condemning the Central African Federation.

This broadmindedness and realistic flexibility on PAFMECA's part has made it a more valuable organ than any other Pan-African organization. And proof of this has come with a great extension of membership from the four countries represented at Mwanza: in three years it has accepted the membership of thirteen nationalist movements reaching into the Congo and Mozambique. And at the February 1962 meeting in Addis Ababa, it was greatly enlarged, drawing to itself Ethiopia and Somalia at one end and South African, South-West African and Basutoland movements at the other. As a result, it was renamed PAFMECSA, incorporating Southern Africa as well. Leaders of eighteen countries came to the Addis meeting.

Following the Addis conference came the highly successful special conference in Leopoldville. With the successful Heads of States Conference at Addis, the need for PAFMECSA is doubtful. Whatever is decided, even if it is wound up, it has served a most significant purpose in East and Central Africa. It has helped to coordinate nationalist effort and strategy in the struggle for Uhuru, as well as in the struggle against the Central African Federation. It has also helped to keep alive and promote the idea of an East African Federation.

Every East African leader is pledged to the support of a federation for East Africa, and Julius Nyerere in 1960 went to the point of saying that he would accept a delay in the date of Tanganyika's independence if this would help the establishment of federation. (His argument then was that all

three countries should become independent and federate on
the same day, as the two parts of Somalia did.) Support has
grown rapidly, so rapidly that it is a shock to reread the
minutes of the first PAFMECA conference, where it was
agreed that the question of federation was "irrelevant at this
time." The two Kenya parties, though disagreeing on many
other subjects, both want federation. A few years ago the
word could not be used in Uganda, because it spread a fear
of white settler domination throughout East Africa. Yet the
fears melted quickly enough for a large crowd on the out-
skirts of Mengo, capital of the Buganda Kingdom, to cheer
unanimously a resolution for federation when Milton Obote,
with Kenyatta, Odinga and myself, addressed them on the
eve of Uganda's independence in October 1962. In June
1963 the Prime Ministers of Kenya and Uganda and the
President of Tanganyika met in Nairobi and signed a formal
declaration to form a federation within 1963. A working
party was set up to draft the constitution. The Nairobi
meeting was followed by a further meeting in Kampala of
the three leaders, and there the Uganda rulers and the public expressed full support for federation.

In his booklet *Africa: What Lies Ahead*, Dunduzu Chisiza placed great importance on building up a "regional
consciousness" among the people in towns and villages before attempting to unite in any federation. A great deal has
been done in East Africa to pave the way in this form.
President Nyerere has popularized the idea to the point
where people speak of "Freedom with federation." In
Kenya crowds at political rallies sing songs which look
forward to federation, such as:

Tulimtuma Nyerere [or Obote, or Kenyatta, depending
   on the verse],
Tulimtuma kwa Uhuru.

Tulimtuma Nyerere —
Kenya, Uganda, Unguja, Tanganyika,
Sisi twasaidiana.

(We have sent Nyerere,
We have sent him to get us freedom.
We have sent Nyerere —
Kenya, Uganda, Zanzibar, Tanganyika,
We are helping one another.)

And we have all been hosts to the leaders from other countries, and Nyerere, Kawawa, Obote and other political leaders from these states have spoken on our public platforms and have helped to popularize federation.

Following the Nairobi declaration in June everyone spoke not of a confederation but of a strong federation. The plan which Nyerere pressed in 1960 was for the three territories to make practical plans during the stage of internal self-government, and then all go simultaneously to independence and federation. He argued that if we set a common date for independence, the pressures on Britain would be irresistible and the establishment of federation would be simpler in the molten period before the countries had set in their separate molds; he dismissed the idea that we should each "set our houses in order first" and pointed out how much help each could give the others in this process if we were federated first. For various reasons, principally the long dispute with Britain over Kenyatta's release, and the difficulties of getting Buganda to participate in national politics, his plan was never given a chance of success. But it can now be said that independence for Kenya has been accelerated because of the pressures for federation within 1963; everyone wants federation to come immediately after Kenya's independence. The longer we put off its implemen-

tation, the more difficult it could be to achieve real political
federation rather than just economic integration, which exists
to a great extent already under the East African Common
Services Organization.

I have always advocated close political federation among
the twenty-five million people of East Africa; but it must
be a federation which can accommodate some of the local
problems or peculiarities in each of our territories. In fact
the Nairobi declaration stipulated that this would be so. It
would, however, be foolish, for instance, for the traditional
rulers in Uganda to think they are strong enough to prevent
federation — or for that matter the regionalists in Kenya. In
fact their future clearly lies in cooperation and identification
with the new forces for unity. The idea is to reserve a number of subjects for the federal authority, while reserving
other powers for the states and having also a concurrent list.
Being a member of the working party, I cannot disclose our
conclusions, but subjects such as economic planning, Central
Bank, defense, citizenship, external borrowing, technical and
research institutions could all become federal functions. This
could be done while leaving important powers for the states,
and from these foundations a strong political federation
could be built.

We would give a large welcome to Ethiopia, Somalia,
Nyasaland and the Rhodesias, and so on, if they agree to
enter an Eastern African Federation. As long ago as the first
All-African Peoples Conference a resolution emphasized that
Ethiopia and Somalia should form part of an East African
region, and the 1962 PAFMECA resolution took this further when all the six countries involved agreed "to work re-
lentlessly" to form such a federation. At the end of the conference, the Emperor of Ethiopia said: "The problem of

establishing such a federation would not be very difficult, even though Ethiopia is a constitutional monarchy."

Having investigated the probable economic effects of federation with Somalia and Ethiopia, some people state it would mean an advantage to Somalia and, to some extent, to Ethiopia but of no direct economic advantage to Kenya. But political factors outweigh these economic ones. The problems of the boundary disputes between Somalia and Ethiopia over the Haud and Ogaden, and between Somalia and Kenya over the Northern Frontier District, would disappear in such a federation. Perhaps federation is the *only* solution to some of these boundary problems. I have been several times to Ethiopia since my first visit in October 1958. When I first met the Emperor, I had the impression that he was deeply concerned with his country's economic development and educational advance. He had done everything to build up a strong army and air force, and was very proud of them. I flew with him over to the military academy at Harar to see some army exercises, and he also arranged that I should see the air force in training. He was very conscious of military power. This was a result of the Italian invasion, I suppose. I did not discuss with him the merging of his powerful army into an East African high command; but when there comes to be an East African Federation, we would expect that every member of it would agree on a common defense policy. This will be fundamental if a federation is to be sustained. Nobody can say at present how soon federation with Somalia and Ethiopia can be achieved, but all are agreed that federation between Uganda, Kenya, Zanzibar and Tanganyika is easiest because of the history and background the four share. In fact it is thought that once the East African Federation is established, an EACSO type of organization should be established to cover Ethiopia, Somalia, Nyasaland,

Rhodesia, Ruanda, Burundi, Congo, and so on, as a first step towards a yet larger federation.

These efforts to form a Federation of Eastern Africa must not be misunderstood. They are not in conflict with the spirit of Addis Ababa. They promote in practical terms the goal of an eventual African government. This must always be the aim, not to be clouded by any regional commitments.

At the southern end of PAFMECSA, we support in every way the efforts of Nyasaland and Northern Rhodesia to break up the Central African Federation and decide their own futures as independent states. Now that the Federation is completely broken up, I would have thought the two states should come together and use a new association to help the rest of independent Africa give aid to the Southern Rhodesian nationalists. Once Northern Rhodesia and Nyasaland work together as independent states, it will be much easier to assist the ZAPU leaders in Southern Rhodesia to liberate their country. Once Southern Rhodesia is independent, the three Central African states together will form one of the biggest weapons the African states will have in tackling the problem of South Africa. I have heard the view expressed that Malawi people want (at any rate, for a few years) to stand completely on their own feet, without even any association with an independent Northern Rhodesia or Zambia; the reason being that this would disprove Welensky and British officials, who have said for years that they could not stand by themselves. This attitude must be avoided: we cannot become victims of this sort of propaganda and try to argue with such people on their own terms. It pays Welensky to create this psychology because he is thereby weakening the unity of the African nationalist leaders themselves in time to come. Nyasaland has in fact defied Welensky and brought his downfall.

The All-African Peoples Conference fitted itself with a workable framework. But it has not functioned as satisfactorily as was hoped. The main reason for this failure has been the conflict or misunderstanding about what were the organizational rights of the political parties and trade unions forming the AAPC and the rights of the various African governments. Many of us felt the AAPC should incorporate only government parties in independent states and all parties in dependent territories, if it was to succeed in establishing complete Pan-African unity. We also felt that its secretariat should be set up and run independently of the country in which it was situated. The moment you ignored governing parties in any country and invited only the opposition or parties in exile, there was created an immediate threat to African unity, for this produced conflict between the AAPC and those governments. Sometimes the AAPC Steering Committee could not get necessary funds to operate, and its life depended too much on the generosity of one or two countries; this situation later created resentment, even lack of interest, among other governments. Nevertheless, through its series of conferences and the way it has brought nationalist leaders together, it has performed an important function.

The question now is whether the AAPC is still necessary in the form in which it was originally fashioned. I have begun to think it is losing both its influence and its purpose, as more and more African states become independent. We are now moving to the stage where the place of the AAPC will be taken by meetings of the independent African states. This is as it should be, because the two should not exist side by side, especially when there are only pockets of colonialism left in Africa. It will be the independent African states which determine future action over Angola, Mozam-

bique, South Africa, South-West Africa and Southern Rhodesia. This is in fact what was decided at the Addis Ababa
Conference through the African Unity Charter and establishment of the Liberation Coordinating Committee.

Before the Addis Ababa Conference we faced the problem
that the African states did not seem to be pulling along together. When the first eight states met in Accra in April 1958,
they were able to agree on common policy and the means of
making it effective through an alliance with Asian and Latin
American states at the United Nations. However, as more
African countries became independent, distinct differences
began to appear between them. The first broad division
came between the states of the French Community on the
one hand and the English-speaking states with Guinea on
the other. (Guinea, having walked out of the French Community overnight after voting "No" in de Gaulle's refer-
endum, established close relations with Ghana.) Criticism
of the French-speaking states was based on suspicion that
they were victims of neocolonialism and that they were not
genuinely independent but too subservient to France. In
particular, three incidents fed this suspicion. First, their
apparent failure to condemn France's atom bomb explosions
in the Sahara made other Africans think they were far too
complacent about this French aggression on African soil.
Second, they took no positive measures to help the Algerians,
and some people thought they had a soft spot for France
in that struggle. Third, their voting record at the United
Nations showed several occasions when some of them sided
with France against their Afro-Asian colleagues on international matters — in fact, some did take France's side on a
majority of votes when there was this conflict. Despite all
this, many of us felt we had a duty to try to understand
their problems rather than castigate them and throw them

further into the laps of France and the West. The other
African states should have tried to cultivate friendship with
them rather than attempt to develop opposition leadership
to the established governments by encouraging exiled leaders or minority groups. This line of action only helped to
increase hostility between the governments of these French-
speaking states and other African governments.

Then again there was Liberia, which some African states
thought was too much dominated by foreign investment.
When I stayed with President Tubman in Monrovia, I
came to know a man who was very different from what
many people think. I found a man who had very fully
understood the modern tempo of Africa, which is perhaps
remarkable after having been President for twenty years.
He had realized what changes were going to come and
had begun a program to secure these changes. He had,
for instance, given legal recognition to the Congress of
Industrial Organizations of Liberia, after his country had
never known trade unions before. He also spoke of the
dangers of foreign investment having too dominating an
influence over his country's economic program. At the
same time, he frankly aired his differences with some of
the other African independent states. He told me he had
argued with one African leader that the best approach to
African unity was to foster economic ties before political
union. He believed that when other nations had their own
internal problems, you could not move too fast and you
should not ignore the sovereignty of any African nation,
however small and weak it may be. His views were most
clearly set out in the Sanniquellie Declaration of July 1959,
after the meeting which he took the initiative in calling with
Nkrumah and Sekou Touré: in this the three leaders stated
six principles for the achievement of the Community of

Independent African States, and agreed that each state should "maintain its own national identity and constitutional structure" while cooperating through economic, cultural and research councils. I found his views very stimulating.

As well as being chosen chairman of the first AAPC at Accra, I was also cochairman with Kojo Botsio during that conference of the committee which discussed what steps could be taken to achieve a United States of Africa. There was much enthusiasm about the prospect, and many of us were excited to think it could perhaps be achieved within a short time. But we were not blind to the problems and the obstacles in the way.

One obstacle was the poor state of communications between the different African states. It was much easier to reach West Africa from our part of the continent by way of Rome, Paris or London than by a direct route. Some steps have since been taken, but flying from east to west still involves spending a night in Addis Ababa (if you fly by Ethiopian Airlines) or in Leopoldville (if you fly by Air Congo), and it is still easier and quicker to reach London or Paris than Accra or Lagos. Another obstacle in communications is the barrier of language. At AAPC meetings, despite simultaneous translation of formal speeches, the French-speaking and English-speaking delegates always seemed to separate for conversation. The conference virtually split into English-speaking groups who arrived, discussed matters together and left, and French-speaking groups who did the same. As well, each group had inherited from the British or French different approaches to problems, even different mannerisms. English-speaking delegates, for instance, always thought that once a committee had reached a decision after long discussion, the whole conference should simply ratify the committee's decision at the report stage rather than reopen discussion on the subject. On the other hand, our French-speaking friends felt the important discussions should be on the floor of the conference. Again, they emphasized the importance of a rapporteur at a conference, while we emphasized the importance of a chairman. One night at Accra we had a long committee meeting, and most of the members were dozing because it was about 4 A.M. when suddenly everyone was wakened by a terrific noise from one of the delegates from Nigeria. He was objecting to something a lady delegate from Senegal was saying in French. It took about ten minutes to quiet everyone and get a translation of her speech. She had apparently gone off the subject of a United States of Africa, and was complaining that the conference was not giving enough prominence to the question of women and demanding that it should call on all independent African states to make polygamy illegal. The Nigerian delegate was objecting to this most strongly on the grounds that her suggestion was anti-African and quite inconsistent with African culture. These barriers of language and thought have produced some amusing incidents, but these incidents have brought home to us the need for improved physical as well as linguistic communications throughout Africa.

This is certainly not to say we should turn our backs on African languages. Many Pan-African conferences have passed resolutions saying we should develop four African languages for general use, and usually Xhosa (from Southern Africa), Swahili (from East Africa), Hausa (from Northern Nigeria) and Arabic are cited. I think we must take as much time as we can to develop some African languages as useful media of communication. Tanganyika has introduced Swahili as an official language, with English, in the National Assembly; and some PAFMECSA meetings have been conducted in Swahili. But much remains to be done to make Swahili an effective language throughout East Africa, for different forms are spoken in different parts and the literature needs standardizing. Our problem is time; can we afford the time to develop these languages to the point where they can be used effectively? India tried, and failed, to develop one language of its own to replace English. The new nations are always rushing so fast that they cannot really stop long enough to tolerate such obstacles in their path. Most of our institutions continue to teach foreign languages, and French and English have been made the working languages which Africans need to understand if they are to get jobs in high office. There is also the question of our international relations. The first task we need to tackle in the field of language is to make the teaching of both English and French compulsory in schools all over Africa. Ghana, Guinea and now other countries like Nyasaland have done this, and in a short time this measure should eliminate the problem of communication between the former French and the former British territories. After that, we can move in the direction of developing African languages. In the meantime, we must review a recent process of eliminating vernacular languages from school syllabi in Kenya. Swahili must be restored to the curriculum in Kenya by an independent government.

A further obstacle we have faced in communicating between states has been the separate development of our countries, both economically and socially. During the colonial period each country was developed in relation to the metropolitan country — whether France, Britain or Belgium — and not in relation to its neighbors. You would find a dividing line coming, for instance, between Uganda and the Congo. This is a large barrier to surmount, and yet we must work for the day when African interdependence is greater than the interdependence of various African states with the United States or Britain or the Soviet Union. Only then will areas of mineral resources fully mature into industrial areas, supported by Africa's food-producing areas, and Africa's economic development be for Africa's primary benefit. Finally, there are differences of tribal culture to be recognized and harmonized. In some areas, traditional rulers play a prominent role, and elsewhere elders are important; in other parts there are no such authorities except the figures the colonial powers imposed, who will fade away. There are differences of religion, with Islam having great influence in Northern Nigeria and along the coast of East Africa as well as in the Arab north. These are questions which have often been referred to when talking about developing Pan-Africanism and bringing about a United States of Africa.

At the first AAPC meeting at Accra, we decided it was not useful to emphasize only the differences. The colonial powers had spent much of their time doing this, to show it was impossible to bring unity in Africa. We spent our time more positively, examining the problems of achieving unity rather than surveying the differences. We ended by being sure that the problems we face in achieving unity are less than the areas in which unity is already assured. For example, a desire for political independence and economic reconstruction, as well as the battle against poverty and ignorance and disease, is shared by all of us. We share a neutralist approach to international politics, we share in the fight against colonialism and neocolonialism. We look upon the Sahara Desert as a link between the northern and southern parts of Africa and not as a barrier.

We have never thought we could achieve a United States of Africa overnight. We have to assess realistically the practical questions already mentioned and plan how best we

can gradually remove each one of them. In a speech to the
Hebrew University of Jerusalem in January 1962, I said:

Unity seems to me to be a thing for which we will all have to
work, perhaps even harder than during our nationalist struggle.
It has got to be cultivated and it has got to be based on the principle of recognizing the sovereignty of each of our various independent African states in its entirety. Unity will not come if any
one independent African state looks down on other independent
states and thinks that no sovereignty matters except its own.
Unity will not come if any one African leader is merely working
for his own personal ambitions at the top of that African unity.
Nor will unity come until the Africans learn to respect each
other's feelings, fears and wishes and general interests. And I
think this is a process that is being clearly understood now, because in the last few years we have begun ourselves to see some
of the problems. . . .
    But in the end it is only the African who can bring unity in
Africa, and it is only the African himself who can resolve these
misunderstandings, these areas of suspicion and mistrust, and create the general goodwill and atmosphere in which African unity
is not only possible but practical and realistic. I have never lost
hope that there will be African unity, merely because we have
failed perhaps in the last two years.

    It was fortunate that immediately after the first AAPC
meeting in Accra, the UN Economic Commission for Africa
was set up in Addis Ababa. At the founding meeting of the
ECA in December 1958 we discussed the problem of
regional economic planning and the way in which much
money could be saved (or better used) by joint planning
between neighbors. The ECA is able to help such moves
throughout the five regions of Africa we demarcated at
Accra. But there have been moments when certain African
countries saw a danger that the regions might, in the process
of building up their own unities, go off in different directions

and make it more difficult to come together later. For instance, John Tettegah, who came as an observer to the PAFMECSA conference in Addis Ababa, quoted President Nkrumah at a press conference as saying that "so long as we remain balkanized, regionally or territorially, we shall be at the mercy of colonialism"; and John Tettegah went on to put it as:

Our President's view is that local associations, regional common-wealth's and territorial groupings will be just another form of balkanization, unless they are conceived within the framework of a larger union based on the model of the United States of America or the USSR.

Kenneth Kaunda, as the 1962 chairman of PAFMECSA, assured everyone that PAFMECSA was working always in the framework of Pan-Africanism, and at the close the main resolution stated that PAFMECSA:

(1) Affirms that the struggle for the total liberation of Africa launched by PAFMECSA constitutes an integral part of the con-tinental African struggle waged by the Independent States and the various peoples' organizations of Africa.

(2) Pledges its full support to the All-African Peoples Con-ference.

I do not believe anyone opposes the PAFMECSA de-velopment, but they rightly express concern that people may become so concentrated on their own region that they forget this is merely one step in the direction of Pan-African unity. I think this warning had to be made from time to time. To guard against the danger of regions moving off in different directions, it was important to hold conferences of all African independent states and devise an overall ap-proach to problems which would at the same time be flexible and practical enough to include all African states. Nevertheless, I do not believe regional development is in any way in conflict with the Pan-African ideal; on the contrary, it will speed up the process of moving toward Pan-African unity, as long as the regions develop and maintain the spirit and resolutions for African unity adopted at the Heads of State Conference in Addis Ababa. The preamble to the resolution on establishing an East African federation made this point at the Addis Ababa PAFMECSA Conference of 1962:

The PAFMECSA.
Being irrevocably committed to the ideology of Pan-Africanism, Seeking to establish a federation of the component Independent States of PAFMECSA as a first real and logical step toward the full realization of the total African political unity and as the best method of speeding up the liberation of Africa. . . .

Much of what I have said already on the subject of African unity and on PAFMECSA or regional unity must now be viewed in the context of the May 1963 Conference of Heads of States at Addis Ababa. The success of this conference brought together into unity not only the French- and English-speaking African states but also removed the original and dangerous development of "blocs" in Africa, such as Casablanca and Monrovia. It gave the lie to the overseas press which tried to present our initial teething problems as inevitable and permanent obstacles to African unity. The conference introduced a soberness and realism which some people had begun to think could not be found in Africa. Important for the still dependent territories, the conference established a committee and fund to help coordinate and assist in their struggle. The conference resolutions and decisions raise doubts whether PAFMECSA should continue at all. In fact, many people feel that it has served its purpose and should be wound up in order not to dilute the spirit of Addis Ababa. The conference did not rule against regional federation, and in fact in the spirit of the conference any such federation must be conceived of as part of the practical steps in African unity, eventually leading to continental government. The Nairobi declaration by Jomo Kenyatta, Julius Nyerere and Milton Obote emphasized this when it said:

We the leaders of the people and the governments of East Africa pledge ourselves to the political federation of East Africa. Our meeting today is motivated by the spirit of Pan-Africanism and not by mere selfish regional interests. We are nationalists and reject tribalism, racialism and inward-looking policies. We hope that our action will help to accelerate the efforts already being made by our brothers throughout the continent to achieve African unity.

This is our day of action in the cause of ideals that we believe in and the unity and freedom for which we have suffered and sacrificed so much.

Several times in this book I have referred to "the African personality" without perhaps giving a satisfactory indication of what is meant by this phrase so frequently used at Pan-African conferences. It is difficult to define in one sentence what the African personality is, but that does not mean it is any the less real. The phrase represents all the feelings and aspirations the African people have, and especially their resolve to create an African "image," as opposed to the image of Africa created by the colonial powers. We are trying to make the world look at Africa as a purely African continent without the old prefixes British, French, Belgian or Portuguese. These prefixes recall only the past arrangements, by which the world spoke to Africa through these colonial powers, interpreted Africa through these powers, and also expected Africa to be spoken for by these powers. Another aspect of the resolve to develop the African personality is the desire to show the world that Africa has her own culture, her own social structures and her own mannerisms. The colonial powers denied this, and judged that you were only good enough if in your behavior you reflected a civilized man in the eyes of the French or the British. The Dominion Party in Southern Rhodesia not many years ago solemnly suggested setting up a board of whites to judge by a dozen "civilization tests" whether an African was fit to qualify for a vote, and the assimilado or evolué systems have the same origin of insults and arrogance. What the new African personality is meant to convey is that you can be as good as anyone, even though you are essentially the product of an African culture.

There are, even at first glance, some very clear attributes of the African character which differentiate Africans from, say, Europeans or Americans. Patience is one of them: if the African were not patient, he could never have passed through all he has done without losing his head. Generosity is another, as I have explained at some length in another chapter while discussing African socialism. Again, a sense of humor has lasted and saved him through all the years of the slave trade and through colonialism. I am not suggesting other peoples do not possess these attributes at all; I am simply saying Africans possess these qualities outstandingly, and they form an important part of the African personality. Again, the identification of educated Africans with their own people, rather than being diverted into foreign matters such as the nuclear arms race and the space race, is an aspect of this personality. The university graduate, educated often outside his continent, comes back to identify himself with his people, to dress as they dress, eat as they eat and speak their language, so that he does not forget his tribal background. When he is seen in Washington or Moscow or London, he wishes to be distinguished as an African, not as a product of some foreign institution.

Perhaps Dunduzu Chisiza has written more movingly than anyone else on the African personality (he calls it "the African outlook"). It is impossible in a single paragraph or two to summarize the points he made in seven pages of vivid description in the paper he gave to the Nyasaland Economic Symposium in August 1962, a few weeks before his tragic death. But in it he claims Africans will set an example to the world in human relations, leaving spiritualism to the East and letting science and technology remain the hobbyhorses of the West. He invites foreign missionaries to come to Africa "not so much to teach love to the indigenous people but to see living examples of selfless love manifested in the African way of life." He explains how Africans do not talk possessively, and the African society is one "where, if you found seven men and one woman amongst them, you would never know — unless told — whose wife the lady is." He tells how Africans are horrified at both gloom and individualism, and how large a part of life is taken up in communal activities — fishing, hunting, canoeing, herding, dancing, beer-drinking, all undertaken in *parties*, and the beer drunk "from the same pot and from the same drinking stick (holy communion at its best!)," he wrote. He mentions generosity to strangers, particularly whites who repaid it with only ridicule and contempt, and adds:

God knows our kindness does not stem from a feeling of inferiority. God knows we are not kind because we are fools, but because He had it that we should be kindness drunk and not pride drunk.

All these characteristics Dunduzu saw culminating in the African love of music, dance and rhythm, a "relishable obsession," he calls it:

We have war dances, victory dances, stag dances, remedial dances, marriage dances, dances for women only, mixed dances, dances for the initiated only, dances for the youth — but all indulged in with ecstatic abandon. We nod our heads, rock our necks, tilt our heads and pause. We shake our shoulders, throw them back and forth, bounce breasts and halt to intone our thanks to Him who ordained that we be alive. We rhythmically hefty shake our rear ends, our tummies duck and peer, our legs quick march, slow march, tap dribble, quiver and tremble while our feet perform feats. "Dance!" What a world of emotions that word calls forth in us!

Sometimes these points, although not the love of music and dancing, are difficult to explain to American Negroes. We must not forget that they are today to a great extent as much Americans as the white Americans. Most of them have lost touch with whatever was African in their background. Only during the last few years, when more and more African states have become independent and taken honored places at the United Nations, has the American Negro begun gradually to take pride in his African heritage. There were exceptions, of course, like Dr. Du Bois, but the majority of Negroes used to be ashamed or indifferent to their association with anything African. This is perhaps not surprising, since the only knowledge the American Negro had of Africa was the garishness of sensational novels and Hollywood films. Today he sees Africans as respected statesmen, scientists, professional men. He sees flags of Africa flying high, and men everywhere standing when the national anthems of African states are sung. But his new strength of pride in Africa is not entirely a culture. It is a pride in the context of modern values, and does not include the native values of the African in his tribal and cultural setting. At heart, the Negro is still an American; and it is difficult for the African heritage and the American heritage to merge in him like two streams feeding a river, because he has for so long been cut off from the African culture.

In speaking of Pan-Africanism, one refers to the whole continent, and often the question is asked: "What about the Arabs in North Africa? Do you think of them as Africans? Do they consider themselves Africans?" I cannot answer the last question for them, but can only say that from my experience at Pan-African conferences and observing their interest in Pan-African matters, I have come to believe that the great majority of Arabs in North Africa look on themselves as African. From our side, there has been increasing recognition and acceptance of the Arabs as Africans. President Nasser, President Ben Bella, and President Bourguiba demonstrated fully at Addis Ababa their complete commitment to Pan-Africanism.

As well as wanting to identify themselves with Africa, the Arabs have a loyalty to Pan-Arabism and a desire to create a common outlook both in international affairs and in development within the Arab states. This can set a problem of loyalties, but these need not conflict. They have other problems of their own — feudalism, outdated monarchies, the need for radical land reforms — and they have the tie of the Mohammedan religion, which links them together but does not join them to many Africans. Both Arabs and Africans need to remember these points when trying to secure greater identity with each other. So long as Asian and African states are moving in the direction of unity and friendship, these conflicts of loyalty will be minimized.

But if there is hostility between Asia and Africa, there is bound to be a reflection of this conflict between the Arabs of North Africa and the Africans south of the Sahara. Again, the effort of regional development in the North should not be regarded negatively but as a step toward the goal of African unity.

Zanzibar and Pemba Islands, with a population of three hundred thousand of whom about forty-five thousand are Arab and the rest are Africans, are a particularly interesting area in this respect. As a result of the death roll during the July 1961 elections many people have predicted a dark future. Nearly everybody on the islands is Muslim, and some people have feared that Zanzibar might choose to become part of the Arab League rather than of an East African Federation. I believe the likelihood of that's happening, if it was ever strong, is fading. The Arabs, who as the principal landowners have been influential beyond their numbers, seem to accept that the future of the islands lies with East Africa and they must come to a democratic accommodation with the majority of their compatriots. But Zanzibar will certainly be one of the biggest racial experiments in East Africa.

The question of Israel is often mentioned in discussions of relationships between African and Arab states. Some of my Arab friends have, for example, criticized me for going to Israel on my honeymoon and suggested it was an unfriendly act toward the Arab states. And Arab states have frowned on Uganda and Tanganyika for signing trade agreements with Israel and accepting Israeli help with social and economic development projects. "Why did you not turn to Arab countries for help, rather than to Israel?" they ask. My answer is simply this: it would be morally wrong and in conflict with KANU policies if Kenya were to make enemies on the basis of other people's judgments. We wish to be friends with every nation or, if this proves impossible, to judge every nation on the merits of our (not someone else's) dealing with them. On the same subject of relationships, Nyerere said the day before his country became independent: "We do not want our friends to choose our enemies for us." We also think we can play a more useful part in trying to remove difficulties and misunderstandings between nations which are our friends, rather than in intensifying hatreds which existed before we came to nationhood. We hope that both Israel and the Arab states will give us an opportunity of helping them resolve this problem. If the Arab states offer us training facilities for our students and trade for our farmers and industries, we will gladly accept. But we will carry on similar relations with Israel. Neither of them should ask us or expect us to hate the other. Our sovereignty means freedom to decide our foreign relations. We cannot of course be indifferent to any problems facing a fellow African nation. We should be prepared to help find a solution.

I know it is argued that the assistance Israel is able to give is not her own but indirect assistance from the United States and other Western countries. Israel is highly dependent on investment from outside and receives a great deal of investment and technical aid from the West. But our actions should not be influenced by such an argument, for we receive direct aid from the United States already, and I expect we will receive the same from the Soviet Union soon, provided always that in each case the terms are acceptable. Some Arab countries receive aid from the Soviet Union now, and we will not refuse to accept aid from them on this account. In turn, we in East Africa hope to be able to help other states within Africa, and we trust they will not refuse aid from us simply because we may have received aid from Israel or the United States or the Soviet Union, in order to develop the facilities which we are able to make available to them later on. All countries today either coexist or are interdependent, relying on each other's generosity, assistance, or cooperation.

I cannot leave a chapter about Pan-Africanism without making clear my views about what must be done in Southern Africa. I believe the whole future there is extremely gloomy: I cannot see the Nationalist Party in South Africa changing its attitude from apartheid. She has been forced out of the Commonwealth and remains impervious to the appeals of the United Nations. South Africa's expulsion from the Commonwealth seemed only to harden the Nationalist attitudes. The effects of the Sharpeville massacre and other riots on world opinion have worn off, and something unforeseeable must happen if South Africa is to move in the right direction without an explosion. While I hesitate to say it, I cannot see anything but physical violence bringing about the necessary changes. The trade boycott has not been effective, because it has been ignored or half-heartedly applied in the countries whose trade with South Africa matters most, such as Britain and the United States and even some of the Eastern countries.

The independent African states must do more about their responsibilities in South Africa than they have done until now. They must rely less on the United Nations, for the UN will not act over South Africa unless there is action within Africa itself — either when South Africa goes to war with some African nations or when there is revolution raging in South Africa itself. The independent states' decision at Addis Ababa to help train and finance freedom fighters in South Africa is most heartening. I cannot see any other alternative. The African states must press on now and there must be no compromise with the Eastern or Western powers who pay lip service only to the South African struggle. The sale of arms to South Africa and the help she gets in trade are a betrayal of her people and must be stopped. The assistance to be given to Angola and Mozambique is all welcome. One hopes that more states will now recognize Angola's government in exile and break off diplomatic relations with Portugal.

There are those who will point to the expansion of the South African army to sixty thousand men, the equipping of their air force with Buccaneers and so on, and will ridicule the idea of independent African states invading South Africa. There were nine African states who together sent fifteen thousand troops to the Congo, and there are besides the large and experienced forces of Algeria. But this comes down not to a calculation of numbers of soldiers, but of the spirit of millions of Africans who are determined to be free. Those whose countries already have independence will not feel truly free until democracy has advanced all the way to Cape Town.

TWELVE

Africa and the World

JOHN Foster Dulles used to maintain that neutrality was immoral. Despite his sermons, many parts of Asia and independent Africa have remained neutral in the ideological struggle between East and West. We have preferred to call our neutrality "positive nonalignment," to show that it is not a negative attitude — like the attitude of that percentage of people in every opinion poll who are always recorded as "Don't know." Neutralism in African states' foreign policy simply means that they will not take sides permanently and automatically with either the United States or the Soviet Union. If an American resolution is presented to the United Nations, no African nation should be considered an automatic supporter, nor can a Russian resolution expect to find unthinking backing from Africa. We intend to decide every international issue on its merits.

African states also insist they are as much concerned in nuclear politics and the whole question of disarmament as are the nuclear powers. The view has been held too long that newly independent African and Asian states have no right to take part in discussions on disarmament and world peace. Yet the powers meeting at Geneva to discuss disarmament think not so much about world peace as about tactical

maneuvers: they are mainly concerned that any moves toward disarmament should not leave them weaker than the
other side. They are also so committed to the idea that world
peace can be maintained only through nuclear "deterrents"
that they have little room to look at disarmament from a
dispassionate and noninvolved viewpoint. The new African
states, with their tradition of positive neutrality, can inject
into these discussions fresh and objective views.

There are already several examples of occasions when
Asian and African states have successfully influenced the
United Nations in the interests of world peace. After the
Afro-Asian influence grew at the United Nations, we began
to see a more positive reaction from the United States
against French policies in Algeria; before then, the American government had been more concerned with its NATO
alliance with France. Again, there was little interest in the
appalling situation of Angola and Mozambique until independent African states were seen in numbers at the General
Assembly. Then, in January 1962, the forty-five Afro-Asian
nations sponsored a resolution by which the Assembly said
it "deeply deprecates the repressive measures and armed
action against the people of Angola as the denial to them of
human rights and fundamental freedom." Only Spain and
South Africa voted against the resolution; only France, then
deep in her Algerian troubles, abstained. Later, in December 1962, the General Assembly adopted by 57 votes to
14 with 18 abstentions a resolution calling for immediate
independence for Mozambique and Angola and for an
arms embargo and sanctions against Portugal. The United
States did not go so far against her NATO ally as to vote
for an arms embargo against Portugal, but its UN delegate
Jonathan Bingham said piously that the United States would

ensure that no American equipment sent to Portugal would be used in Angola and Mozambique.

Other aspects of African neutralism are rejection of military alliances with either East or West and refusal to have military bases on African soil. This policy is followed not only so that African states can protect Africa from embroilment in an East-West conflict — if they had one side's bases on their soil, they would be an immediate target — but also so that they are free to censure the foreign and military policies of any nation when they deserve censure. The British, whose War Department always seems to be working on plans which politics have made outdated by several years, have built at the cost of £5.5 million a base at Kahawa, outside Nairobi. In November 1961 I moved in Legislative Council that Britain cease all further development on Kahawa and other camps such as at Gilgil, and should take steps to remove naval, air force and army bases. KANU was in opposition then, and government supporters could produce in reply only the argument that British troops brought into Kenya ten million pounds a year in spending money, and that therefore their withdrawal would be disastrous to the country's economy. How can such people call themselves nationalists if they are prepared to sell their country's independence for the pocket money of foreign soldiers? The position is quite clear: the Africans of Kenya will not allow these bases to remain for any length of time after our independence, and there is no question of negotiating a military pact with Britain. It is good to see that with Kenya's independence Britain has agreed to remove her bases with no ifs or buts.

This military noninvolvement enables African states to become a useful instrument for world peace. Just as the

neutralist Swedes have done a constructive job on the bor-
ders of Israel and Egypt, so nine African states were able
to provide a military-police force in the Congo and minimize
the political and military conflicts between East and West
there. Some people in each power bloc may argue that neutralism produces a military vacuum, into which the great
powers tend to rush. I would have thought that the Congo
proved the reverse: its general policy of nonalignment
helped to check an incendiary situation which could have
flared up into outright East-West conflict.

Economically, neutralism allows African states to determine for themselves what is their best program without being committed to any foreign nation and so having to accept its directions. They are able to trade with East and
West alike and so create for themselves an economy which
is not based on the circumstances in another particular area.
In the period of economic reconstruction, we can avoid the
hangovers of colonial days, when we were forced to pursue Western economic theories and build a structure of the
West's design. It is difficult to isolate economics completely
from politics, and the African states receiving EEC Development Fund money find the package tied with French bows
and strings. But if we do not practice positive neutralism,
we will in these early years of independence find ourselves
drawn deeper and deeper into the political network of other
nations and never have room to develop our own institutions
and economic systems.

Africa is aware that despite sympathy expressed in regard
to our position of underdevelopment, all the developed countries are not prepared to give us a probationary period.
They compete with us on every market without reservation.
As we start to develop our own political institutions, it is
possible that this move is interpreted as a shift away from

the West to the East. For we start our independence from the point of having inherited certain Western institutions, and any changes we make in these forms or any later departures from the British or French system may seem like a turning to the other camp. This is not the case at all. As we consolidate our independence, we are concerned to develop institutions which reflect our own background and culture and which are understood by our own people. As new nations, we claim the right to devise such systems as we think fit without having them interpreted politically in terms of leaning Eastward or Westward. There was a great deal of misinterpretation in the West when President Nyerere announced the coming of a one-party system in Tanganyika. So many people studying events in Africa from the outside tend to assess its leaders and statesmen and systems only by an East-West yardstick. "This man is pro-East . . . this idea is a Communist one," they will say. They are too blinded by their ideological conflict to give us credit for trying to find our own way, for being guided by what we think is most suitable for Africa.

Take the example of Sekou Touré. He is a most impressive man. I met him first in Conakry in 1960, when his country was going through an extremely difficult period: he was changing the currency; he had trade difficulties after France had cut off all helpful connections so abruptly; and the world was saying Guinea would either become a Soviet satellite or just lose herself in bankruptcy. I was immediately struck by his dynamism and his confidence: he was quite certain he had done the right thing in saying "No" to de Gaulle's terms of subordination. But he needed as well to win support from other territories, and the broad-mindedness he had developed as General Secretary of UGTAN (Union Générale des Travailleurs d'Afrique Noire) helped him greatly at this time. The West should have realized from the history of UGTAN, which he formed in protest against certain ideas of the World Federation of Trade Unions, that Sekou Touré was nobody's puppet. Yet after Guinea's desertion by France, the West for a long time refused his requests for assistance (presumably because they feared the French reaction); and when Yugoslavia and other socialist states came to his help, he was immediately classified as a pro-Eastern leader. Later, when the Russian ambassador in Conakry was expelled and Sekou Touré emphasized Guinea's neutralism, the West became jubilant in their misinterpretation that here was a trend toward its camp. Western leaders refused to believe that Sekou Touré could simply act in the general interests of Guinea, regardless of what East or West thought. They had never seen him, as I did on that visit, address a huge crowd while he explained about a conspiracy against Guinea which had just been uncovered and in which the French had been implicated. He is a tremendous orator, and I could see he had his audience entirely with him. He has great organizing ability and possesses a strong hold on his party machine. But above all, I could see in the faces of the crowd and of his lieutenants, who came later to the presidential palace, the obvious loyalty to their leader. It sprang from their conviction that Sekou Touré's actions were based on being pro-Africa, simple and solely.

In the same haze of misinterpretation, some of us, including myself, have been often described as "moderate" and "pro-West." Because I have helped many students go to the United States, and because I have many American friends, people in the West interpret this as hope for the success of American foreign policy in Kenya and think we will run to the United States for help against the East. They do not seem to realize that like any other African leader I want to establish friendly relations with the East when Kenya is independent and hope to take from the East ideas about institutions and assistance for our development. I have no cause so far to hate the East. In June 1962, as Acting Minister for Education, I made a motion in Legislative Council to permit Kenya students to go openly to Eastern countries and to set up a nonpolitical committee to coordinate all organizations dealing with overseas scholarships. Until that time, the students who went to Moscow and Eastern Europe had had to leave by an "underground route"; but we had now reached the political stage where we could decide for ourselves about where to send our students. Some of my American friends have interpreted this action as a political move away from them towards the East. I have never regarded it as a political move in any direction; it was simply a move in the direction of serving our own interests.

Perhaps I have been called pro-West because I have not yet visited the Eastern countries. Such a conclusion is of course very superficial. My inability to visit them was entirely due to prevailing circumstances in Kenya at the time. It had nothing to do with ideological questions. In fact I do not believe that in Africa we can agree to be led by the nose and told not to visit this or that country for fear of being infected with their policies or ideologies. We are capable of making our own decisions.

Closely bound up with these misinterpretations of African neutralism are attitudes to American aid. The United States government has disbursed since 1946 some £33.5 billion ($97.6 billion) to foreign nations, and the total American aid to Africa from 1946 to 1960 was about £280 million ($822 million). The scale of this aid has risen sharply, so that in 1959-1960 the year's figure was nearly £100 million alone. Ethiopia, Libya, Morocco and Tunisia were the main recipients in the early years, but Nigeria was later offered £89 million to back its six-year development plan and Tanganyika was promised an Uhuru present of £10 million (of which agreements covering £6.2 million were signed during the following eighteen months). Private American industry has a capital investment of about £285 million in Africa. While we are very impressed by the great size of these figures, are grateful for the help in developing our countries which these figures summarize, we still need to look closely at the motives behind the giving of this aid.

I believe that in the past the Americans gave aid in expectation of friendship and even of political support. But increasingly they are becoming aware that such a process brings them in return resentment rather than friendship. The change in American attitudes over aid has come because the number of independent states has grown and the voice of the colonial powers, finding an echo in the United States, has become weaker. Like everyone else, the Americans have now had to come to grips with the real Africa, meeting and negotiating with African leaders rather than doing their business through the British and French. The Kennedy administration has shown a more liberal attitude, as well; but most of this liberalization has been forced by the realities of the new Africa. Moving away from the Dulles view of the immorality of neutralists, American leaders are beginning to fear that if they try to force any nation to commit itself to the West, it may well turn to the East in resentment; rather than risk provoking such a reaction, they are prepared to play along with the desire of African nations to be left out of the East-West conflict. The neutralist stand taken by the African states has produced this healthier situation; and the experience the Americans gained over the financing of the Aswan Dam, when Egypt decided to go ahead regardless of Western conspiracy and blackmail, taught both them and the British a lesson. I wrote in an article in *Current History* in December 1956 that:

In the field of foreign policy America's position in the eyes of Africans is rather disappointingly hazy. She has not lived up to their expectations, and internally the segregation problems have affected American prestige and moral standing. Her people are however still regarded with friendship and expectancy, although it has become generally recognized that there exists a great deficiency of informed opinion on Africa."

Six years or more later, there has been considerable improvement in all the areas I referred to in the paragraph just quoted. Most of this improvement has been due to the new forces released by the growing number of independent African states, and to some extent due to the greater education about Africa throughout the world.

But America's standing in Africa must remain affected by the Negro problem at home. In this, recent developments have not altered the situation. The Kennedy administration appears too cautious, for this is an issue where no compromise is possible to explain. Negro freedom is part of our freedom struggle to give dignity to the colored man wherever he may be.

We are witnessing today in the United States the unfolding of a colossal freedom struggle on the part of the oppressed Negro people whose status in many ways is very similar to that of colonial peoples throughout the world. This people has committed itself to struggle for freedom against the oppressive rule of the white man. Here, too, American actions will speak louder than words. Swift steps to emancipate the Negro from bondage, to guarantee his equal rights and the dignity of a human being, will speak volumes concerning American intentions as a great power with a forward-looking posture. A policy of democracy and justice toward its own black subjects will have an instantaneous impact throughout the colonial world, and nowhere more than in Africa.

And Negroes must beware of the problem of liberating themselves from inferiority complexes and of receiving flattery by the whites. This could weaken their own struggle, for in the end Negro freedom and equality will be won by the Negro himself.

African neutralism faced a test when the India-China dispute became an armed clash in 1962. It was particularly a test in Kenya, which has a population of over 200,000 Asians, nearly all originating from India. The warfare in the Himalayas precipitated a new quarrel between KANU and KADU. The KANU view was that we should not exploit the India-China dispute, and we should not draw that conflict into local politics in the hopes of winning the votes of the Kenya Indian community on the score of our sympathy. We also resisted the argument of some people that this was a war between communism and democracy. We replied that there would be no hope of peace if such an attitude were adopted, for we would logically have to say there could be no settlement until either communism or democracy was wiped out. Instead, we acknowledge there are communist states and states which are democratic, but add that the world is so small that both must find ways to live together.

We did not think that "Commonwealth ties" should bind us to take India's side automatically. Such an attitude would lead you into proclaiming, "My Commonwealth, right or wrong!" If a Commonwealth country is wrong, I think our duty to the Commonwealth requires that we say so clearly and set about finding a formula to end disputes. India has not gained support because she is a Commonwealth country, or because she is a democracy, but because she has been attacked and there was proof that Chinese troops were encamped on Indian territory. We must not engage in ideological warmongery but must find a formula by which the two most populous nations in the world can agree on a just solution and live in peace. India desires such an end, and I believe China wants to live in peace also. We agree that India cannot think of accepting peace at the expense of her territorial rights, any more than we would surrender our sovereignty for the sake of peace. But we must, in the India-China case and other international incidents, separate the ideological factors from the basic rights and wrongs. India has shown the moral courage to do that: while she was being attacked by Chinese troops, she justified her claim to neutralist status by voting for China's entry into the United Nations at the General Assembly session. Her neutralist stand on that occasion is similar to the one KANU has taken in looking at the India-China clash in the Kenyan context.

I have already indicated that I do not consider "Commonwealth ties" to be very rigid thongs. The Commonwealth has been a unique structure in the world. It has evolved with remarkable smoothness and has accommodated itself to drastic changes both in the personality of the nations which compose it and in the ex-colonies which have joined it. India turned into a republic, Ghana developed a socialist economy and sought stronger ties of trade with the East and created her own institutions. Yet the Commonwealth is so elastic and flexible that these changes have been accepted without conflict.

Some pessimists suggest these are not genuine accommodations, it is simply that the "old dominions" have given a
certain amount of ground and the old Commonwealth ties
are under such strain that a few more of these necessary "accommodations" may break the Commonwealth altogether. I think such people are far too gloomy. At one
time, it was felt that the expulsion of South Africa would
break up the Commonwealth, or that it would disinte-
grate when many nonwhite nations came to Commonwealth
status and the old — but now outnumbered — dominions
would retreat to their corners of the world. But neither
event had any shattering impact on the Commonwealth.
The negotiations over British entry into the European
Common Market provided the stiffest test. Had Britain succeeded in her application, and economic ties between Britain and the rest of the Commonwealth been weakened as a
result, then the Commonwealth would have been modified
considerably; but I hesitate to say it would have broken entirely. Historical and social ties would have continued, ties
of emotion and of language would have endured, Britain for
her part would have striven to preserve as much as she
could. It would not have been like a shipwreck, with nothing to show where it had been. One thing we have pledged
is that if Britain grants independence to the white minority
in Southern Rhodesia we would withdraw from the Commonwealth. We would also do so if it became an obstacle in
the way of African unity.

There are other tests ahead which we can see already: the
"white Australia" policy, for example. This policy must
change, and Australians are beginning to realize there is no
longer hope for such a policy. There was a time when no
nonwhite immigrants were allowed in Australia, but today
thousands of colored students — particularly from Malaya

— have been welcomed there. There were days when Australia was so far "down under" away from the world that she felt she was a world unto her own self. But today she is growing swiftly closer to her neighbors and the rest of the world. Canada, also, has known its racial problems: although we never had any unpleasantness in our students' airlift dealings with the immigration authorities, for other non-white immigrants there were humiliating conditions attached at times. In January 1962 Canada dropped many discriminatory aspects of her immigration laws, and one hopes Australia may follow the example of Canada. It would certainly remove a likely cause of antagonism between Commonwealth countries.

Enthusiasts for the Commonwealth have suggested several innovations which they believe would strengthen the structure. In his book *The Commonwealth Challenge*, Derek Ingram, the assistant editor of the London *Daily Mail*, mentions many possible innovations and presents a strong case for several. The idea of a Commonwealth parliament is hardly practicable, since the neutralist states would not want to be too closely associated with certain of Britain's military or political liaisons. But a Commonwealth information service, set up to spread understanding between the nations, could serve an important purpose. The conference of Commonwealth Prime Ministers, which has always traditionally taken place in London with the British Prime Minister as chairman, could well rotate around the different countries. So could its chairmanship, and perhaps the best arrangement would be if the premier of the host country were automatically chairman. Other enthusiasts (and the novelist Nevil Shute was among them) have suggested that the Queen should move her residence around the Commonwealth countries. I doubt whether this is a sensible idea: the

Queen, after all, means much more to the British people than she means to members of the Commonwealth in distant countries. If she came to live in Nairobi for a month or so, the people of Kenya would simply look on her visit as some temporary festivity; they would still owe greater allegiance to their own Prime Minister than to the Queen. Nor would she be revered, during such a visit, as a great historical symbol by, say, the National Assembly of Kenya, as she is by the British House of Commons. The day may indeed eventually come when the position of head of the Commonwealth may itself rotate, rather than that the Queen be asked to move house all the time. With more and more republican countries comprising the Commonwealth, there may be a move toward making the Queen simply one of several who hold the position in rotation. Does that thought shock the royalists? It would be a test of their adaptability, certainly; but they, like myself, take pride in the many ways the Commonwealth has reshaped itself to fit the times of change.

One of the important issues in Africa is the development of the trade union movement. The most controversy centers around the question of how free of government control trade unions should be. There is also the inflammatory subject of international affiliations. I have many times been involved in discussions of both these questions, and I have sometimes been criticized by some of my trade union colleagues and also some African political leaders for the stand I have taken. Let me explain my views. The issue of whether or not African trade unions should retain affiliation with international bodies — such as the ICFTU (International Confederation of Free Trade Unions), the IFCTU (the International Federation of Christian Trade Unions) and the

WFTU (the World Federation of Trade Unions) — has often been brought up in the context of the policy of neutralism. But let me start with the general subject of trade union development.

We have to decide at the earliest stage whether there is going to be trade union freedom or not, and whether or not the Conventions of the International Labor Organization are worth upholding in our new states.

During the struggle against colonialism we have fought for the freedom of the trade unions. In many cases the colonial powers made it impossible for workers to safeguard their rights on their own account. In our struggle we always appealed to the ILO Conventions and to friendly nations to help us uphold trade union freedom. At the same time we have condemned Portugal and South Africa for not allowing workers the freedom to organize and negotiate through collective bargaining. Should we, then, when we are independent, begin to compromise on these issues — or continue to fight for the principles we have upheld in the past? Before answering that question, we need to decide whether the processes of collective bargaining would be in conflict with our efforts, as an independent African state, to consolidate that independence and reconstruct the economy.

I stated my views on these most important questions during a conference of the International Federation of Petroleum Workers in Kampala in June 1962, two months after becoming Minister for Labor. I said:

"I do not believe in excessive intervention by the state. As a trade unionist, I still cherish the ideal of freedom of action for the trade union movement. I sincerely believe in the intrinsic superiority of free and voluntary collective bargaining as a method of regulating the conditions of people's working lives.

"Our government is committed to the concept of allowing management and labor freedom the widest possible scope to regulate their mutual relations as they see fit — in effect, the concept which is sometimes labeled as 'self-government in industry.' "

While we continue to condemn Portugal and South Africa for repressing these freedoms, we must also question the rightness of any African state's resorting to the same measures. If a government either denies trade unions their existence or tries to subjugate them to government policies without consultation or seeking cooperation, then we must condemn such a government, no matter whether it is led by whites or Africans. It is possible for trade unions to fulfill two purposes in Africa: they can defend the rights and promote the interests of the workers, and at the same time cooperate with government in economic reconstruction. It may seem a more difficult task to do this than it was to identify the trade unions with the nationalist movement during the colonial period, but there is no essential conflict between unions and government.

The trade union movement in Africa cannot afford to be a blueprint of its counterpart in Europe, the United States or the Soviet Union. The European trade union movement is a product of social frictions in Europe and is part of European history. The African trade union movement must also be part of the history of Africa, by reflecting the struggles and achievements here. It must respond to the challenges of independence, the efforts to create an African personality and an African socialist system. Responding involves certain sacrifices, or self-discipline, and certain alterations of the movement's structure. But if certain limitations are imposed, these need not encroach fundamentally on the freedom of association or the freedom to organize.

For example, I believe it is right for government to give some guidance on the question of association, because lack of guidance may lead to a disruption in the government's economic efforts. Ghana, Guinea and Tanganyika have given varying degrees of guidance of this sort, such as the acceptance of the principle that the trade union movement should have only one central organization in the country, and that all trade unions should affiliate to it. This means that any differences among trade unionists must be resolved within the movement itself rather than by creating splinter groups or by organizing opposition political parties or by siding with an opposition party — which would simply be using the workers as a political weapon against the government. This guidance also eliminates the possibility of splinter groups or national centers of trade unions being formed at the instigation and with the money of foreign powers. This is one example of the changes I believe are necessary. But if there is proper consultation between government and trade unions, these changes can be made without anyone's trampling upon the legitimate freedom of the trade union movement to organize.

Then there is the question of the right to strike in terms of free and voluntary collective bargaining. I believe unions should be free to try to achieve the best conditions possible for their members. There is, however, the question of how far a new country can afford to have this freedom used (I should rather say, abused) by industrial workers to disrupt economic progress and frighten off investment by senseless strikes. It seems inevitable that if unions misuse their power and freedom, the right to strike must be curtailed by legislation. Whether or not such a right will survive depends just as much on the unions as it does on the party in power. The unions should remember that unless there is economic

growth their efforts will be in vain. They should also remember that most of our new governments are working-
class governments with officials genuinely interested in the
workers' and peasants' conditions. There should be no real
conflict between the two and plenty of room for cooperation, consultation and joint effort. Restraint on their part
is necessary not only to help economic growth but also for
the unions to survive the impatience and geniune determination of our new nations to move ahead in this world of cut-
throat competition.

Now let us look at the question of international affiliations. It is a question which I think has been overstressed,
both by the world press and by those African leaders who
have campaigned for disaffiliation. In his book *Pan-
Africanism*, Colin Legum writes that attempts to establish
a single All-African Trade Union Federation (AATUF)
"have produced perhaps the angriest of all divisions in the
Pan-African front." It is true there were angry scenes, as
when thirteen delegations walked out of the Casablanca
conference in May 1961, and there have been harsh words
spoken, as when the *Ghana Times* called me "an imperialist
stooge, under the thumb of America." But I have never
believed the question of international affiliations is the most
serious problem facing Africa. Most of our problems can be
resolved regardless of what happens about affiliation.

In those African countries where the independence
struggle is still raging, the nationalists obviously need to
have as many friends and contacts as possible. Some of these
friends are found in the international trade union centers,
to which various trade unions are affiliated. The ICFTU,
to whom some one and a half million African workers are
connected through their unions, gave great help to Algerian
workers during their country's struggle; during the emer-

gencies in Nyasaland and Kenya we again had much help
from the ICFTU. When the nationalist movement was
completely muzzled in Kenya, the only organ through
which we could appeal to the world was ICFTU — I gave
examples of its help in a preceding chapter. This is something which those who have experienced such assistance
cannot ignore lightly now. For there are still countries fighting for independence, and friendships were made in those
hard days which you do not flippantly discard.

Apart from these factors of past help and friendship, it is
an ever-present truth that no African state is going to exist
in isolation from the rest of the world. This is not what
neutralism means. African states are members of the Commonwealth. Some African leaders are members of the Privy
Council of the Queen of England. These are both African
connections with Britain, and Britain is in the Western bloc,
yet who would say these leaders or countries are compro-
mising their neutralist principles? If there are agencies which
operate in the interests of a power bloc or an ideology and
seek to nullify our policy of neutrality, then the African
trade union movement would be best advised to keep clear of
such involvements. The question is whether the ICFTU has
tried to commit us to the West. It has taken Africa's side
against the French in Algeria, against the French atomic
tests in the Sahara, against the British in Kenya, Nyasaland
and the Rhodesias, and against South Africa. Nevertheless,
the problem in the international labor movement is that the
two bodies — the ICFTU and the WFTU — have become
involved in ideological battles which at the moment have
little meaning in Africa and which are identifiable with
Eastern and Western ideology.

The question before those of us who wish to see a Pan-
African trade union movement does not rotate around

affiliation, but rather around whether we can lay down what every African country must do before we can move toward Pan-African unity. It must be recognized that African independence and neutrality do not imply an isolationist policy or tendency. The attempt to harmonize various interests in Africa as the basis for unity means that at times we have got to be prepared to accommodate people who may not be able to move all the way toward a given stand. Above all, it means recognizing strictly that each country is sovereign and all institutions will of necessity reflect first their country's interests and policies. In effect, each country must in principle be free to determine its own policies without interference or coercion by another African state. African unity is so important and so broad that this principle should not create immediate conflict.

Many writers — and several trade unionists — have suggested that it has been argument over the affiliation issue which has made it impossible for us to create a united All-African Trade Union Federation. This is a wrong diagnosis. The problem met here was the same problem which we encountered in establishing the conferences of independent African states. We had to accommodate diverse interests, and work gradually to the point where these interests were harmonized and a genuine African interest created. Trade unionists reflected these same divisions, and when they found themselves at odds on general points of self-interest, both those who were for continuing affiliation and those whose wished to end it decided to make affiliation the issue on which they met each other head on.

My line of approach has been that regardless of affiliation, our first effort should be to create an All-African Trade Union Federation. It should be developed into an organization to which every African trade unionist could look for advice and assistance. This would be done by spreading regional headquarters throughout Africa, and by these centers' working hard to eliminate all suspicion that the AATUF was going to be used by any outside group — the ICFTU, the WFTU or any independent African state — for its own purposes. If we had worked more for unity along these lines, and refrained from emphasizing disunity by virtue or our different affiliations, we would by today have succeeded in creating effectively the All-African Trade Union Federation.

At the Casablanca Conference of May 1961, there was much area of agreement, but later publicity and statements overlooked all this and concentrated on promoting disunity. There was agreement on a charter and principles of a trade union organization for Africa. But one group was determined to make disaffiliation the big issue. Some of us thought we should have worked on a constitution and created a proper secretariat. We felt that if we had worked on the task of winning the confidence of all the African trade union centers, we would have created this AATUF without difficulty. There was a weakness in the organization of the conference in that the steering committee was restricted to a few countries, and invitations were issued to splinter and unrepresentative groups. Concentration on the disaffiliation issue sent the conference down the wrong track. Even today some unions which had accepted disaffiliation have not carried out this policy, including some of those which led the campaign for disaffiliation.

One fundamental mistake which can be made by trade unionists in Africa is the failure to recognize the difficulties of colleagues in other parts of Africa who have constantly to bear in mind the best tactical moves to achieve political objectives in the struggle for independence. In the heat of strong feelings those trade unions which did not accept the ten-month ultimatum to disaffiliate were threatened by one African trade union leader, who said: "We shall isolate them, break them, enter their countries and form AATUF unions there. It's as simple as that — total war."

I think it is wrong for any one independent African state to begin to operate throughout Africa in an attempt to create dissension within the national trade union centers of other countries. These trade unions are playing a large part in carrying out their government's policies, and a deliberate move by another state to cause splits between the workers will only succeed in disrupting the economic program of that government. This is a point which some independent African states have not fully realized: that a declaration of "total war" in trade union affairs means disruption of political relationships between the countries concerned.

Some people have argued that it was a mistake to have formed the African Trade Union Confederation of forty-one labor organizations at Dakar in January 1962. It was a mistake, they say, because it set up another camp for trade unionists to rally round and thereby increased disruption among Africans. It would seem, however, that the formation of ATUC was essentially an act of mutual protection in the face of this "declaration of war": of the forty-one delegations, twenty-three were affiliates of the ICFTU and twelve of the IFCTU (the "croyants," or Christian unions in French-speaking Africa). It did not seem to have aggressive intent. It was the manifestation of lack of unity and of the fact that AATUF had not so far united the whole of Africa.

I think it is still possible to bring AATUF and ATUC together, and for us to go back and start again from the point where we went wrong. If we begin to emphasize unity for the future rather than concentrating on present points of disunity, and if we agree that Africa is trying to find her feet and that we must each recognize the sensitivities and problems and political-economic realities each country has to face, we can still work out a basis for an All-African Trade Union Federation. Such a federation would itself be free of any international affiliation. I still believe it would be useful to try again. It would add much to the efforts now being made throughout Africa for unity. The independent states' recent conference at Addis Ababa gives new hope for trade union unity without compromise on basic issues. No African trade union should be committed to the ICFTU, WFTU or IFCTU at the expense of any of our basic pledges. There seems to be no real conflict so far, and in any case the first step is for us to create the Organization for Pan-African Unity in the spirit of Addis Ababa.

I finish writing this book on an appropriate date. Not only is it the eve of the day when the date for Kenya's last general elections before independence will be announced, a moment when we stand on the threshold of a wide-open future which we will determine in full for ourselves — and, I hope, along the lines I have sketched in this book. It is also the sixth anniversary of Ghana's independence, the event which gave so much encouragement to nationalists in African countries farther south. Many of us have felt inspired by the way Kwame Nkrumah led his campaign for Ghana's independence, his resolution and organizing ability. When I first met him in Accra in 1958 and heard him speak, I was captivated by his obvious dedication. I wrote an article on my return to Kenya describing his dedication and saying he would take Ghana a long way and would never compromise when he knew what was right. I said he had the interests of all Africa at heart. More inspiring today is the creation of the Organization for Pan-African Unity, at the Addis Ababa Conference in May. It is proof of Africa's determination to give meaning to the aspirations of our people in asserting our independence and personality, and in securing the total liberation of Africa. The agreement at Addis Ababa gives hope to the dependent countries.

Africa, in these last five years, has been cutting new trails. Anyone who has hacked his way through a forest undergrowth knows that you cannot go far without some scratches and even some blood on your legs. Too many journalists and sensational writers have concentrated on these scratches and, getting this scene totally out of perspective, have interpreted Africa as a continent of violence and bloodshed. Being patient and unusually good-humored people, we are amused that this should be the view of white men who have started two world wars and burned up thousands of civilians with atomic bombs, and even now crouch in terror lest their opponents in East or West may loose their huge nuclear armories in their direction. Is this what they call freedom? We in Africa are confident that despite momentary falterings in the undergrowth, which I have frankly described, we are heading in the right direction along our new trail. Our road is a classless socialism, based on Ujamaa, the extended family. Our goal is to share the blessings of a richly endowed continent among all its inhabitants; to make a reality of the brotherhood of "the extended family" in a United States of Africa; and to spread this feeling of kinship further through our international policy of positive neutralism to the conclusion of friendship with all nations. We are happy in the conviction that before many more years have passed we will be showing the rest of the world what freedom really means.

What could be more satisfying for me personally and for Kenya than the knowledge that at last we too shall celebrate next Christmas as FREEMEN? And, what is more, we may by then have established an East African Federation, thereby making our initial contribution to Pan-African unity. It is a good ending to our story of the national struggle and a most hopeful beginning of our future as an independent state.

Nairobi, Kenya
March 7, 1963

Kenya's Industrial Relations Charter Signed in Nairobi on October 15, 1962

Kenya's Industrial Relations Charter Signed in Nairobi on October 15, 1962

The Industrial Charter was signed in October 1962, six months after I had become Minister for Labor. In those early months there had been several strikes which, it was apparent to me, could have been avoided if Kenya had possessed a recognized procedure for trying to settle differences before they became disputes and then grew into strikes. I could see that if strikes occurred with this frequency much longer, there would be mounting pressure to limit the freedom of trade unions; and this I, as both a democrat and a trade union leader, was reluctant to do. However, far-reaching action was necessary if Kenya's economy was not to suffer greatly at a crucial stage of development. So, through subcommittees of employers, trade unionists and government officials, we analyzed the most common causes of grievance — nonrecognition of a union, imprecise demarcation of jobs, inadequate machinery for consultation, and so on — and agreed on a code of conduct which both employers and union leaders would do their utmost to follow, in order to minimize the number of disputes and avoid the need for restrictive legislation.

In the hope that the points we agreed upon in Kenya will be helpful toward framing a similar industrial relations charter in other countries, or simply in guiding the conduct of labor relations in particular instances, I am reprinting here our Charter in full.

The Government of Kenya, the Federation of Kenya Employers and the Kenya Federation of Labor:

1. Considering that at their Conference held in Nairobi on Tuesday, the 3rd, and Thursday, the 5th July, 1962, convened by and under the Chairmanship of the Minister of Labor, The Hon. T. J. Mboya, Member of Legislative Council, agreed to endeavor to prepare an Industrial Relations Charter;

2. Realizing that it is in the national interest for the Government, Management and Workers to recognize that consultation and cooperation on a basis of mutual understanding render an essential contribution to the efficiency and productivity of an undertaking and that progress can only be made on a foundation of good terms and conditions of employment which include security of service and income, also the improvement of Workers' conditions of service;

3. Desiring to make the greatest possible contribution to the success and prosperity of Kenya;

agree upon the following Charter of Industrial Relations.

1. *Agreed Responsibilities of Management and Unions*
   - (*i*) that the existing machinery for settlement of disputes should be utilized as quickly as possible;
   - (*ii*) that both sides undertake to settle any or all industrial disputes at the appropriate level and according to the procedure laid down hereafter;
   - (*iii*) that affirming their faith in democratic principles, they agree to settle all future differences, disputes and grievances by mutual negotiation, conciliation and voluntary arbitration or strikes or lockouts as a last resort;
   - (*iv*) that there should be no strike or lockout without notice;
   - (*v*) that neither party will have recourse to intimidation or victimization or conduct contrary to the spirit of this Charter;
   - (*vi*) that they undertake to promote maximum cooperation in the interests of good industrial relations between

their representatives at all levels and abide by the spirit of agreements mutually entered into;

(*vii*) that they undertake to observe strictly the grievance procedure outlined in the Recognition Agreement which will ensure a speedy and full investigation leading to settlement;

(*viii*) that they will educate the Management Personnel and Employees regarding their obligations to each other for the purpose of good industrial relations;

(*ix*) that they respect each other's right to freedom of association;

(*x*) that they will deal promptly with all correspondence that arises between them.

2. *Management Agree*

(*i*) to recognize the Union appropriate to its particular industry and to accord reasonable facilities for the normal functioning of the Union in the undertaking;

(*ii*) to discourage such practices as (a) interference with the rights of employees to enroll or continue as Union members, (b) discrimination, restraint or coercion against any employee because of recognized activity of trade unions, (c) victimization of any employee and abuse of authority in any form, (d) abusive or intemperate language; and (e) generally to respect the provision of the I.L.O. Convention No. 98;

(*iii*) to take action for (a) settlement of grievances and (b) implementation of settlements, awards, decisions and orders, as speedily as possible;

(*iv*) in cases of misconduct to distinguish between misdemeanors justifying immediate dismissal and those where discharge must be preceded by a warning, reprimand, suspension or some other form of disciplinary action and to arrange that all such disciplinary action should be subject to appeal;

(*v*) that every employee has the right to approach Management on personal problems and agree always to make accredited representatives available to listen to the day-to-day problems of employees;

(*vi*) to impress upon their staffs the contents of this Charter and to take appropriate action where Management inquiries reveal that the spirit or contents of this Charter have been contravened and to give full publicity on their Notice Boards to this Charter;

(*vii*) to discourage any breach of the peace or civil commotion by Employers or their Agents.

3. *Union(s) Agree*

(*i*) not to engage in any activities which are contrary to the spirit of this Charter;

(*ii*) to discourage any breach of the peace or civil commotion by Union members;

(*iii*) that their members will not engage or cause other employees to engage in any Union activity during working hours, unless as provided for by law or by agreement;

(*iv*) to discourage such practices as (a) negligence of duty, (b) careless operation, (c) damage to property, (d) interference with or disturbance to normal work, (e) insubordination, (f) abusive or intemperate language; and generally to respect the provisions of I.L.O. Convention No. 98;

(*v*) to take action to implement awards, agreements, settlements and decisions as speedily as possible;

(*vi*) that where strike or lockout action occurs essential services (the cessation of which would cause injury to humans or animals) shall be maintained, but the employees concerned shall not be called upon to perform any other duties than the maintenance of the service concerned;

(*vii*) to display in conspicuous places in the Union offices the provisions of this Code and to impress upon their officers and members the contents of this Charter and to take appropriate action where Union inquiries reveal that the spirit or contents of this Charter have been contravened.

RECOGNITION

It is agreed that the Model Recognition Agreement as Appendix "A" * is hereby accepted as a guide to parties in all future agreements and that the following principals should apply:

(i) that provision by the Registrar of Trade Unions to F.K.E. or to the employer of a certificate that the Union is properly registered and exists effectively to represent the particular employees should decide the question of recognition and negotiations should then commence based on the Model Recognition Agreement and for the eventual setting up of Joint Machinery as may be appropriate to the particular Industry or undertaking;

(ii) that minor breaches of agreements by either party shall not give justification for withdrawing recognition but shall be processed as "disputes";

(iii) that these principles be brought to the notice of parties who are not affiliated to F.K.E. or K.F.L.

JOINT K.F.L./F.K.E. DISPUTES COMMISSIONS

Machinery exists at industrial level as provided for in the Recognition Agreement for dealing with disputes that may arise from time to time, firstly through the local or district negotiating committee or through the Joint Industrial Councils. That machinery is not intended to be superseded in any way by the procedure of the Joint Disputes Commissions, and it is agreed that both sides will wherever possible endeavor to settle disputes, using the machinery provided in the negotiated agreements.

The specific object of the Joint Disputes Commissions is to prevent disputes involving loss of time and money to all concerned, and to deal immediately and effectively with disagreements, in order to prevent any unnecessary stoppage of work. The use of the Commissions is entirely voluntary and is not intended to prevent parties who so wish utilizing the processes provided under the terms of the Trade Disputes (Arbitration and Inquiry) Ordinance.

It is agreed that, on receipt of recommendations from a Joint Disputes Commission, both parties to the dispute should indicate acceptance or rejection of the Commission's recommendations on the matters referred to it, within a period of seven days from

* The Model Recognition Agreement is subject to many variations, and Appendix "A" is therefore not included.

the date of receipt of the Commission's report or such longer period as the Commission shall decide.

REDUNDANCY

In the event of redundancy, the following principles will apply:

(i) the Union concerned shall be informed of the reasons for and the extent of intended redundancy;

(ii) the principle should be adopted of "Last in, first out" in the particular category of employees affected subject to all other factors such as skill, relative merit, ability and reliability being equal;

(iii) the redundant employee will be entitled to the appropriate period of notice or pay in lieu. The principle of severance pay is agreed but the form and amount of such pay shall be subject to joint negotiation.

EMPLOYMENT POLICY

The provisions of the I.L.O. Convention adopted June, 1962, Article 14, shall apply as follows:

1. It shall be an aim of policy to abolish all discrimination among workers on grounds of race, color, sex, belief, tribal association or trade union affiliation in respect of:

   (a) labor legislation and agreements which shall afford equitable economic treatment to all those lawfully resident or working in the country;

   (b) admission to public or private employment;

   (c) conditions of engagement and promotion;

   (d) opportunities for vocational training;

   (e) conditions of work;

   (f) health, safety and welfare measures;

   (g) discipline;

   (h) participation in the negotiation of collective agreements;

   (i) wages rates, which shall be fixed according to the principal of equal pay for work of equal value in the same operation and undertaking.

2. All practicable measures shall be taken to abolish, by raising the rates applicable to the lower-paid workers, any existing differences in wages rates due to discrimination by reason

of race, color, sex, belief, tribal association or trade union affiliation.

3. Workers from one country engaged for employment in another country may be granted, in addition to their wages, benefits in cash or in kind to meet any reasonable personal or family expenses resulting from employment away from their homes. This is to apply in cases of special skills not available locally.

4. The foregoing provisions of this Article shall be without prejudice to such measures as the competent authority may think it necessary or desirable to take for the safeguarding of motherhood and for ensuring the health, safety and welfare of women workers.

STRIKES AND LOCKOUTS

It is agreed that in future the Federation of Kenya Employers on the one hand, and the Kenya Federation of Labor on the other hand, shall discourage and seek to bring to an end any strike or lockout which may arise from or be caused by any question, difference or dispute, contention, grievance or complaint with respect to work, wages or any other matter, unless and until the following steps have been taken and these shall have failed to settle such question of difference, etc.,

(i) the matter in dispute shall first of all be considered by the appropriate machinery as set out in the Recognition agreement;

(ii) failing settlement at Joint Industrial Council, such dispute shall be reported forthwith by the parties concerned therein to their respective National Officials and be immediately jointly dealt with by them either by invoking Joint Disputes Commission procedures or by reference to the Chief Labor Officer.

INTIMIDATION

It is hereby agreed that employees and management shall enjoy adequate protection against any acts of interference by each other or each other's agents or members. Such protection shall apply more particularly in respect of such acts as:

(*a*) will make the employment of an individual employee sub-ject to the condition that he shall or shall not join a union;

(*b*) the dismissal of an employee by reason of union member-ship or acts of participation in union activities outside working hours or with the consent of the employer within working hours;

(*c*) the drawing up, issuing or publication of discriminatory lists or any action which will prevent a supervisor or shop steward from carrying out his normal functions.

JOINT CONSULTATION

Management and employees recognize that consultation and cooperation on the basis of mutual confidence render an essen-tial contribution to the efficiency and productivity of an under-taking and also contribute to the social and economic well-being of all.

It is therefore agreed that:

(*i*) full support will be given by both parties to the constitu-tion and the regulations of the National Joint Consulta-tive Council and to all other freely negotiated joint ma-chinery set up under the Recognition Agreement in the various industries throughout Kenya;

(*ii*) encouragement shall be given to voluntary agreements between the parties;

(*iii*) management shall take appropriate measures to facilitate the proper functioning of joint machinery by making available facilities for meetings and, in appropriate cases, the staff essential thereto. It shall also allow representa-tives of the employees the necessary time within reason to attend such meetings without loss of pay;

(*iv*) it is clearly understood, however, that the employees' representatives, not being full-time paid officials of the union, are first and foremost employees of industry and as such their first and prime responsibility is to carry out the duties assigned to them as employees of their em-ployer Company during working hours;

(*v*) (*a*) that means should be readily available whereby any question which may arise, affecting all employees or any category of employees, covered by the Agreement can be fully and promptly considered with a view to a satisfactory settlement;

(b) that the recognized procedure covering negotiations and discussions between both parties should be so far as is practicable fully known and understood by the employees and by all members of Management;

(c) that an essential factor in successful negotiations and discussions is the clear statement or report of the issues involved and of the resulting decision after mutual agreement between the parties.

PRESS STATEMENTS

That during negotiations the Kenya Federation of Labor and the Federation of Kenya Employers agree to recommend to their affiliates that statements to the press and the Kenya Corporation should be jointly made although the right of either party to communicate individually is accepted.

The Federations will also recommend that letters be not normally copied to the press or to the Ministry of Labor.

CONCLUSION

Both the Federation of Kenya Employers and the Kenya Federation of Labor agree to observe and abide by this Charter of Industrial Relations.

SIGNED:

SIR COLIN CAMPBELL
for and on behalf of the Federation of Kenya Employers

P. F. KIBISU
for and on behalf of the Kenya Federation of Labor

T. J. MBOYA
Minister for Labor

Index

Index

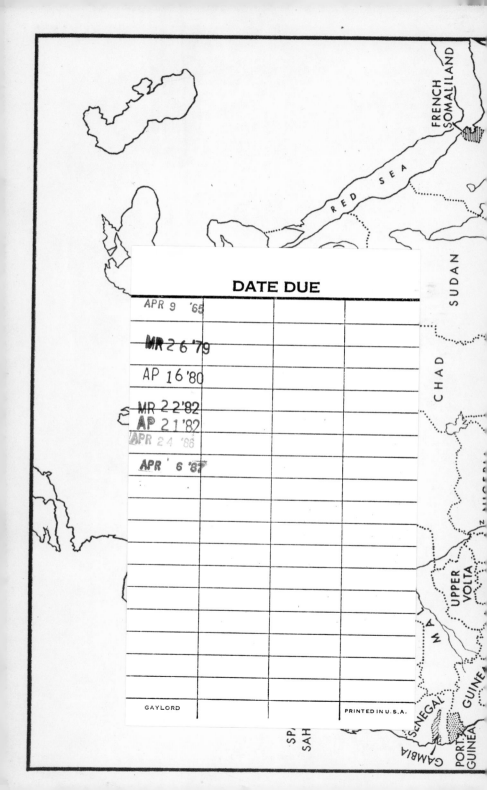

DATE DUE

APR 9 '65			
MR 2 6 '79			
AP 16 '80			
MR 2 2 '82			
AP 21 '82			
APR 24 '86			
APR 6 '82			
GAYLORD			PRINTED IN U.S.A.